*f*P

CONFIDENTIALITY
and PRIVACY
in SOCIAL WORK

*A Guide to the Law for
Practitioners and Students*

DONALD T. DICKSON, J.D., PH.D.

The Free Press
New York   London   Toronto   Sydney   Singapore

THIS BOOK IS DEDICATED TO THE MANY STUDENTS IN MY LAW CLASSES

AT THE RUTGERS SCHOOL OF SOCIAL WORK WHO THROUGH THEIR EXPERIENCES

AND INSIGHTS HAVE STIMULATED ME IN MY WORK.

_____

*f*P

THE FREE PRESS
A Division of Simon & Schuster Inc.
1230 Avenue of the Americas
New York, NY 10020

THE FREE PRESS and colophon are trademarks
of Simon & Schuster Inc.

Manufactured in the United States of America

10 9 8 7 6 5 4 3 2 1

Library of Congress Cataloging-in-Publication Data

Dickson, Donald T.
    Confidentiality and privacy in social work : a guide to the
law for practitioners and students / Donald T. Dickson.
        p.   cm.
    Includes bibliographical references (p.   ) and index.
    1. Social workers—Legal status, laws, etc.—United States.
    2. Confidential communications—Social case work—United
    States. 3. Social workers—Professional ethics—United
    States.   I. Title.
    KF3721.D49   1998
    344.73'0313—dc21   97-34912
                                                      CIP

ISBN 0-684-82657-7

Contents

CONTENTS

Preface

In 1978, *Confidentiality for Social Workers* (Free Press) was published, written by the late Suanna Wilson. The book surveyed the legal landscape at the time, including the then-recent California court decision holding that therapists had a legal duty to protect another when harm was threatened, mandatory reporting requirements for child abuse in some states, the federal Privacy Act of 1974 protecting the privacy of some federal records, and references to the ten states that provided privilege protections for communications to social workers.

In the ensuing two decades, many significant changes have occurred. Privilege has been extended to licensed psychotherapists in all states and to licensed social workers in most states. Mandatory child abuse reporting laws now apply to social workers in all states, and a number of states now include reporting requirements for elder abuse, domestic violence, institutional abuse, and abuse of persons with disabilities. The growth of computerized databases—in their infancy in the 1970s—has had significant repercussions for privacy of client and worker records. The recent explosive growth of managed care health systems has made serious inroads upon privacy and confidentiality. New techniques for data collection, storage, retrieval, and transmission have been developed. The Internet and e-mail, unforeseen in the 1970s, now allow for the transmission of records, files, and data, including voice and visual images, almost instantaneously around the world. New scientific techniques, such as DNA testing, mean that more information about an individual may now be gathered and stored. AIDS, apparently nonexistent in the 1970s, is a significant factor in privacy law. And, as medical means are developed to restrict its transmission or prolong the life of infected individuals, laws that once almost toally protected the confidentiality of an individual's HIV/AIDS condition are now being modified to allow for more extensive release of that information. Privacy in the workplace continues to undergo change. Drug testing is commonplace in the private sector and increasing in the public sector. Where worker surveillance once consisted of direct observation by eye or ear, now surveillance is commonly accomplished by means of video cameras, tape recorders, monitoring of telephone conversations and computer key strokes, reading of electronic mail, and accessing of computer files. All have consequences for privacy and confidentiality.

Confidentiality and privacy remain cornerstones of social work practice. Yet while social workers might like to assure their patients or clients that whatever is disclosed will remain secret, and patients or clients may want that assurance before freely disclosing highly personal information, the reality is that assurances may not be possible. Sound social work practice often necessitates supervision, consultation, and peer review of cases, making total secrecy impossible. Careful documentation in case records, often necessary for decision making, consultation, record review, and protection from possible future litigation, results in a written record, which at a later time can become partially or totally accessible.

Significant legal protections for confidential communications and personal privacy have developed in recent years in both the state and federal legal systems, and yet at the same time the number of limitations to these protections has expanded. The resulting patterns appear at times inconsistent and irrational, especially to the non-lawyer. Nonetheless, the social worker must operate within these legal mandates and constraints and, where appropriate, explain them to patients and clients. Why certain information is confidential and private, why other information is not, and why even confidential and private information may be never totally confidential or private are issues which professionals and clients must struggle with frequently. This book is an attempt to present the realities to the social work professional and student, including the patterns, complexities, and seeming inconsistencies. To accomplish this end, choices had to be made between what is necessary or more important and what is not necessary or less important. Where possible, references to topics not addressed have been supplied.

The book is divided into two parts. Part I consists of introductory materials and basic concepts. Chapter 1 presents an overview of confidentiality and privacy for social workers and an introduction to law, legal systems, and legal material helpful in understanding succeeding chapters. Chapter 2 discusses the law of confidential communications in detail. Included here are the many different meanings a promise of confidentiality may entail, necessitating a clear explanation of what such a promise means. Confidential and privileged communications are addressed, differences across states are noted, and a recent U.S. Supreme Court decision upholding social worker privilege in federal courts is discussed. Limitations to privilege are addressed and the elements of waiver are examined. Chapter 3 addresses broader privacy law, examining decisional privacy, personal privacy, and informational privacy. The final chapter of Part I discusses the social worker's ethical responsibilities, tracing their development from several general confidentiality provisions in the 1960 NASW Code of Ethics to the extensive and inclusive provisions found in the recently adopted 1996 Code.

Part II addresses specific issues in law and practice. Chapter 5 surveys workplace privacy. Here the discussion focuses on workplace searches and surveillance, monitoring of employees on and off the job, public and private sector drug testing, sexual harassment, and confidentiality in employee assistance programs. The focus of Chapter 6 is records and record keeping. Access to specific types of records, the use of dual record keeping, releases, subpoenas, and record retention and destruction are covered. The federal Privacy Act of 1974 is examined in some detail, regarding both its strengths and shortcomings. Finally health records, records in managed care organizations, and DNA data banks are examined.

Chapter 7 turns to the problematic subject of the social worker's duty to protect an individual from harm, tracing the development of that duty from the well-known *Tarasoff* decision in California to the current trend toward professional immunity from liability when the duty is discharged. Chapter 8 focuses on minors and privacy, looking at minors' decision-making, personal, and informational privacy. Privacy in schools is examined in detail, including privacy of the person, privacy of educational records, and the difficulties surrounding privacy of a minor's communications to a professional. Chapter 9 turns to privacy and AIDS, a rapidly developing and rapidly changing topic. Finally, in Chapter 10, a range of topics not covered elsewhere is presented: confidentiality with specific types of records, such as those of federally funded substance abuse programs, child protective service records and adoption records, and confidentiality when dealing with several individuals or groups.

As always when dealing with the law, the social work practitioner or student must be aware of variations among the states and look for recent changes in the law. Finally, differences may exist between law on the books and its implementation in practice or procedure, and social workers must be alert to these differences for the protection of themselves as well as of their patients and clients.

Acknowledgments

Many individuals have helped with this book. Much is owed to Dean Mary Davidson of the Rutgers University School of Social Work for her indefatigable support and assistance throughout. Provost Roger Dennis, formerly Dean of the Rutgers University–Camden School of Law, has provided significant aid by enabling me to conduct extensive legal research through that school. Betty McCoy, my secretary, has been an able assistant and cheerleader. Philip Rappaport, my editor at The Free Press, has been helpful, tolerant, persistent, and encouraging. Who could ask for more? Professor Ray Albert and Professor Madeleine Stoner have provided extensive and helpful comments. Particular thanks are owed to Robert Cohen, Esq., former general counsel for the National Association of Social Workers, who has given unselfishly of his time, making numerous insightful comments and suggestions. Elizabeth Holmes has provided thorough and competent copy editing. The book is far better because of the assistance of all of these individuals.

Rutgers University has provided a sabbatical leave, releasing me of teaching duties and allowing time to complete the manuscript. Reed Elsevier's *LEXIS,* an online legal retrieval system, has been an invaluable resource. Several libraries have been particularly useful in this project and should be acknowledged for providing access to their extensive collections: Rutgers University Libraries, Princeton University's Firestone Library, the University of California at Berkeley Libraries, the New Jersey State Library, and the California State Library. On the home front, son David Dickson and other family members and friends have been supportive and remained tolerant and forgiving for the instrusions of such a project.

In addition, thanks are owed to the National Association of Social Workers for supplying their recently adopted Code of Ethics, which forms the basis of one chapter. Arthur Manyoky remains an outstanding photographer. Finally, a great debt is owed to those many students—to whom the book is dedicated—who have often challenged me, intrigued me, and brought forward issues, questions, and problems from their work and field experience. Many are reflected here. This text has been greatly enhanced by the contributions of all of the above-named, as well as nameless individuals; errors or omissions remain mine alone.

PART ONE

BASIC PRINCIPLES
for the PROFESSIONAL

Part I presents an overview of basic principles of confidentiality and privacy law. This material forms an important base for the following chapters in Part II. Stressed in Chapter 1 is the importance of confidentiality in social work practice—social work patients and clients rely on promises of confidentiality when they reveal sometimes very personal information about themselves or others, information often necessary for diagnosis and treatment. The social worker's legal and ethical obligations to maintain a confidence are discussed, and it is emphasized that confidentiality is not absolute but subject to important limitations. In a section tracing changes in the law over the past two decades, one of these limitations, the duty to warn about intended harm, is identified, to be addressed in detail in a later chapter. Also stressed in this section is the importance for social workers to know the existing law and to keep abreast of legal changes in this rapidly evolving area. Some common violations of confidentiality in social worker practice are reviewed, violations that can be committed by professionals as well as novices and students. Here the purpose is not to discuss all possibilities, but to alert the reader that this area calls for constant vigilance.

The chapter then turns to a discussion of the basis of privacy law and its various forms. The constitutional basis for privacy—a right to privacy—is not found in the actual words of the United States Constitution but in judicial interpretations of certain phrases that have been read to include an intent to protect privacy. Thus, outside of some clear protections against illegal searches and seizures—only one form of privacy—other types of privacy (privacy in making personal decisions and privacy of information) are implicit, not explicit in the constitution. The remainder of Chapter 1 discusses basic legal principles, outlines the American legal system, describes the types of law with which the text deals, and includes an important section on the use of legal citations. This material is basic for recognizing the type of law, the jurisdiction, and, for a court decision, what level of court has decided the case. The reader is urged to read this section carefully.

Chapter 2 moves to the topic of confidential communications. Here the focus is on two types of social work patient and client communications, those that are confidential and those that are privileged. The distinction is an important one since only privileged communications are so protected that they cannot—with certain exceptions—be required to be disclosed in a court of law. Given their importance and the differences between these two types of communications, there are strong ethical and practice reasons to make clear to a patient or client what confidentiality actually means and what limitations exist. In particular, the law of privileged communications is one that can cause confusion among professionals. It is a very limited part of confidentiality law, applying to certain professions and perhaps certain agency settings depending on the jurisdiction—that is, state—where the social worker is practicing. Some major differences among states are addressed, and the reader is referred to the Appendix for references to the privilege statutes and rules for social workers in forty-five states where they exist, and for psychotherapist privilege laws in all fifty states. In brief, only certain communications to certain professionals by certain individuals in certain settings are privileged, and this is a major part of the discussion. A recent United States Supreme Court decision holding that social worker privilege exists in cases brought in federal courts is discussed and analyzed. Then the discussion turns to limitations on privilege. This includes the obligation of the social work professional to break privilege when there have been disclosures leading to a suspicion of child abuse, and others such as the obligation to breach a confidential communication to protect another from harm. This particularly important exception is reserved for detailed treatment in a later chapter. Finally, the elements of a knowing waiver of privilege are detailed, along with conditions that may sometimes operate to nullify privilege, such as the presence of a third party.

Chapter 3 continues the theme of basic principles, here in the broader area of privacy. Privacy law is a large, at times unwieldy topic. In a constitutional sense it encompasses three distinct types of privacy, each of which protects the individual from action by agents of the government—national, state, or local: decisional privacy, personal privacy, and informational privacy. Each is discussed in some detail, for not only is each of consequence for social workers and their patients and clients, but together they set the stage for later, more specific privacy material. Within decisional privacy, privacy in abortion, contraception, sexual conduct, and the right to die are addressed. Personal privacy includes governmental searches, surveillance, and monitoring. Here the law pertaining to personal and property searches is addressed, for it is basic to later discussions of student searches in public schools, drug and DNA testing, and electronic surveillance and monitoring in the workplace. The third and probably least developed area of constitutionally protected privacy is informational privacy, the right of the individual to prevent the state from disclosing personal information about himself or herself. This discussion forms the basis for a later examination of records, computerized databases, and managed care.

The final chapter in Part I examines the social worker's ethical responsibilities in the areas of confidentiality and privacy. The development of the National Association of Social Workers (NASW) codes of ethical standards in confidentiality and privacy is traced from several general provisions in the 1960 code to the 1996 NASW Code of Ethics, which contains twenty-two separate provisions in the area, clearly emphasizing the importance of confidentiality and privacy for social workers today.

CHAPTER ONE

CONFIDENTIALITY *and* PRIVACY *in* SOCIAL WORK: *An* OVERVIEW

Confidentiality and privacy are critical elements in effective social work practice. Clients and patients[1] rely on professionals to keep their communications private and limit access to personal information in their records. Personal information may be disclosed only because of this reliance. Fear that a confidence will be not be kept may affect what is told to the professional, thereby limiting a diagnosis or a treatment plan. This is true for most aspects of social work, but it particularly significant for those in clinical practice. In a decision upholding privilege protections for licensed clinical social workers and psychotherapists in federal courts, the Supreme Court recently said: "Effective psychotherapy . . . depends upon an atmosphere of confidence and trust in which the patient is willing to make a frank and complete disclosure of facts, emotions, memories, and fears. Because of the sensitive nature of the problems for which individuals consult psychotherapists, disclosure of confidential communications made during counseling sessions may cause embarrassment or disgrace. For this reason, the mere

possibility of disclosure may impede development of the confidential relationship necessary for successful treatment" [*Jaffee v. Redmond*, 135
L.Ed.2d 337, 345 (1996)].

Professional codes of ethics also recognize the importance of confidentiality. The recently adopted National Association of Social Workers
(NASW) Code of Ethics has no fewer than eighteen separate provisions
relating to social worker and patient or client confidentiality, and seven
others relating to privacy and records.[2] (The growing recognition of the
importance of these issues is also reflected in the American Psychological Association's code of ethics, which contains ten provisions relating to
confidentiality [American Psychological Association, 1992]. Devoting a
significant portion of ethics codes to these issues signals both their importance in ethical practice and the complexities they present for the professional.

This chapter first discusses some of the complexities of the law in this
area, and then details some of the many changes that have occurred over
two decades since Suanna Wilson published her important text, *Confidentiality in Social Work*. Then the importance of confidentiality and privacy
for social work practice is addressed, followed by a discussion of breaches
of confidentiality that can be committed by both experienced and inexperi-
enced social workers. An introduction to the law and the legal foundations
of confidentiality and privacy follows. Though this information is familiar
to many, these sections provide an important background for the entire text,
since they discuss the types of law and the always perplexing interplay of
federal and state legal systems. Concluding the chapter is a section on finding and using legal materials, including the use of legal citations. The reader
is urged to review this material carefully, since it provides a background to
understanding discussions of law in the following chapters.

The Complexities of
Confidentiality and Privacy Law

While privacy and confidentiality often apply to the social worker's practice,
one cannot assume that confidentiality laws will protect all communications
and all records, or protect them in the same way. The legal privacy of com-

munications and records may vary with the individuals involved, the setting where the communication takes place, where the record is maintained, and the content of the communication or record. For example, privileged communications—those made to certain professionals and protected by statute—may not be disclosed even in a court of law, while the same communication made to someone who is not covered by statutory privilege is not protected and may be subject to disclosure. Patient information maintained in federally funded substance abuse programs is protected to a far greater extent than many records maintained in other agencies, even if the content is the same. While much of the information shared by a patient or client with a social worker about one's past life or future plans may be protected by confidentiality, communications that would lead the worker to suspect abuse of a child or that the patient or client intends imminent, serious physical violence to another would not be protected. In sum, different types of information—or even the same information communicated or recorded in different settings—have different types of privacy protections, ranging from near-total protection to no protection at all.

THE CHANGING LEGAL LANDSCAPE

In the past two decades, confidentiality and privacy laws have undergone dramatic changes. For example, in 1978 Suanna Wilson noted: "Thus, social workers are now fighting for the right of privileged communication, in an effort to avoid forced disclosures of confidential information" [Wilson, 1978:98].

In her book she listed ten states that then had statutory privilege for social workers. By 1997 all fifty states had enacted statutes extending privilege to licensed psychotherapists, and forty-five had extended privilege to social workers. In 1975 Congress enacted federal evidence rule 501, which often has been interpreted to bar privilege for social workers, psychotherapists, and psychologists in federal courts [Knapp and VandeCreek, 1987:39–42]. In 1996, the U.S. Supreme Court held in *Jaffee v. Redmond* there was privilege for psychotherapists and social workers in cases brought in federal courts (see page 41). In 1974 Congress enacted the Federal Privacy Act, 5 U.S.C. §552a, which among other provisions made an unauthorized release of an individual's personal records maintained by the government a federal offense. That act has been amended and broadened by the Computer Matching and Privacy Protection Act of 1988, which, among other provisions, forbids the government from matching and thereby linking an individual's records across computerized data sets.

In 1976 the California Supreme Court handed down its well-known *Tarasoff* decision, *Tarasoff v. Regents of University of California,* 551 P.2d. 334, holding that a therapist incurs a duty to breach a confidential relationship and reveal information necessary to protect an identifiable third party where a determination is made that a patient or client presents a serious danger to that person. Since then, courts in a number of states have adopted *Tarasoff,* some have extended it, and others have questioned it. Some states, including California, have legislated the decision in statute form, and California and other states have enacted statutes limiting civil liability of social workers and therapists who breach confidentiality and follow certain steps in protecting third parties.

Other changes are equally striking. In 1977 some states had enacted mandatory reporting laws for child abuse, superseding privilege and confidentiality laws, but many had not. By 1997 all states had enacted mandatory reporting laws which take precedence over statutory privilege or confidentiality. The confidentiality of an individual's HIV or AIDS status— a disease not recognized and perhaps not in existence in the United States in the 1970s—is now afforded significant legal protection, sometimes with equally significant exceptions. Also, communications with sexual assault victim counselors are now protected in a number of states.

At the same time, in some areas where confidentiality was assumed twenty years ago, it is now being questioned and modified. Access to adoption records by adult adoptees, previously possible only with a court order issued for good cause, is now allowed under various conditions in an increasing number of states. Child protective service records, once scrupulously protected by statute as well as agency policy, may be reviewed by a court or others for some purposes, and some states have enacted statutes to allow for the expunction of unsubstantiated reports. Where juvenile court records were once confidential, there are movements both to limit that confidentiality and to allow for record expunction.

In the area of privacy law, a number of court decisions in the past twenty years have broadened privacy protections for adults, minors, and families in some areas. Since *Roe v. Wade,* 410 U.S. 113 (1973), and *Planned Parenthood of Central Missouri v. Danforth,* 428 U.S. 52 (1976), the Supreme Court has further elaborated on the privacy rights of women and minors, and on the role of parents and courts in abortion decisions. Along with privacy in making decisions, a number of judicial opinions have addressed privacy of information and privacy in respect to searches of the person, including blood, urine, and DNA.

The workplace is another area where laws of privacy and confidentiality are evolving. Where once surveillance in the workplace might consist of a supervisor watching workers from a doorway, surveillance mechanisms now might include video cameras, tape recorders, telephone call monitoring systems, reading e-mail, measuring computer key strokes, and instant copying of computer screens, output, and files. Here assaults on privacy may have exceeded legal protections. Other workplace privacy issues include psychological testing and mandatory drug testing of workers, now commonplace in the private sector. Sexual harassment has been only recently recognized at law. Here, too, there are significant ramifications for privacy both in the protection of workers from harassment and in limitations imposed on employee speech and behavior both on and off the job.

Looking to the future, it is probable that vast technological changes will continue. If so, the compilation of information about patients and clients—and workers—as well as its storage, retention, retrieval, and transmission, will only increase in magnitude, presenting even more challenges for confidentiality and privacy law, and for social workers, their patients, and clients. Centralization of health care, welfare, and other social services could compound the problems. Some health care specialists are calling for a unique identifier of every recipient receiving health care which could link medical and treatment records to welfare, social security, social service, and other records, with a concomitant loss of privacy [Minor, 1995]. It is interesting to note in this context that greater privacy protections are provided for the videos one rents or the books checked out, questions asked, and searches conducted at public libraries.[3]

THE IMPORTANCE OF CONFIDENTIALITY AND PRIVACY IN SOCIAL WORK

There are sound practice, ethical, and legal reasons for social workers to be knowledgeable about the law in this area and to keep abreast of changes.

In terms of social work practice, the social worker needs to know when information is protected by confidentiality and privacy laws, under what conditions, and to what extent—and when it is not. Put in another way, it is vital to know in what areas a free flow of communication and information is possible, and in what areas there are legal limitations. A promise of confidentiality that cannot be kept may destroy a relationship with a patient or client and with other patients or clients as well. Similarly, a wrongful disclosure of confidential information may subject both the social worker and the agency to a lawsuit for a breach of contract or on some other basis. Moreover, the client needs to know the boundaries of confidentiality. Informing a client that a worker or agency may not be able to keep private some information may or may not have impact on what is disclosed, but the client can make an informed choice about what to say. This is particularly true in working with couples, groups, and minors, where confidentiality is weaker, privacy harder to maintain.

Similar issues arise when dealing with client files and records. In many situations, the client has a legal right to access his or her own records—or parents have a right to access their minor child's records. But the client needs to know agency policies and legal rules governing access. In this way, recorded information can be explained and interpreted, clarified or corrected. At the same time, the case file may contain information harmful to a client or information given in confidence by others. Here, too, a knowledge of the law is crucial for the worker to decide what can or must be disclosed and what should not or cannot.

Social work supervisors need to be aware of the legal context of their employees' practice, since they are consulted first and must give advice. They need to be able to tell workers when information must be disclosed or need not be revealed, when access to records is permitted and when it is not, and how to respond to requests for information from individuals outside the agency. Similarly, social work administrators need to know the legal boundaries of privacy and confidentiality to develop sound policies for their agencies, employees, and clients.

Social workers have a number of ethical obligations in relation to confidentiality and privacy. One of the broadest is to "keep current with emerging knowledge relevant to social work" [National Association of Social Workers, 1996: standard 4.01(b)]. It is important to note in this context that privacy law is changing rapidly, as is demonstrated by the laws regarding HIV/AIDS and the emerging privacy concerns in relation to the electronic compilation, storage, and transmission of records and files.

In addition, social workers have an ethical requirement to protect client confidentiality where legally possible, and when disclosure is required, to inform the client, where possible, that confidential information will have to be released. Also, social workers have an ethical responsibility to inform clients about the limits of confidentiality in their particular situation. (See generally Chapter 4.)

Finally, breaches of confidentiality and privacy may put an agency or worker at risk of fines, loss of funding, criminal penalties, or civil actions. Violations of confidentiality of educational records could result in a loss of federal funding. Violations of confidentiality in substance abuse programs can result in a fine of $500 to $5,000 for each offense. Violations of the Privacy Act of 1974 can result in significant penalties. In addition, there are a number of legal grounds for holding individuals and agencies financially liable—including compensatory and punitive damages and reasonable attorney's fees—for breaches of confidentiality or invasions of privacy. Malpractice actions, though infrequent in social work, are growing. Most breaches of confidentiality and privacy go unnoticed, and many of those litigated are unsuccessful since it is hard to prove that there was actual harm, or, if there was harm, that the breach of confidentiality was the cause. Yet even an unsuccessful lawsuit has costs—in terms of money, time, and effort, and at times unfavorable publicity. And, even if there was no injury accompanying the breach of confidentiality, it could still result in sanctions imposed by a professional association or a state regulatory body.

In situations such as a failure to take steps to protect a client or another person from harm, causal links are clearer and damage awards can be substantial. In many states, a failure to report suspected child abuse is a criminal violation and could result in civil liability as well. Failure to deal with sexual harassment complaints can result in substantial damage awards.

In short, confidentiality and privacy law is inextricably tied to social work practice and social work ethics, and the existence of significant legal liabilities makes it imperative that social workers and administrators have knowledge of the law. In this, they need not act as lawyers or give clients legal advice; rather, they need to know the legal limits of their practice, when a potential legal problem arises, when to consult another, and when to get legal advice.

VIOLATIONS OF CONFIDENTIALITY AND PRIVACY

Most violations of confidentiality and privacy are probably unintentional, and unfortunately probably occur with some frequency. Those committing these violations may be unskilled personnel, students, or professionals. There are myriad ways for such violations to occur at the office, at school, traveling to and from work, or during leisure away from the office. Unless great care is exercised it is as easy for the experienced professional to commit a breach as one with less training.

At work, a professional may need to discuss a case or situation with fellow workers or supervisors, and this is a reasonable expectation. Steps can be taken to limit the identifying information, and to discuss or consult on a need-to-know basis. Referrals may be needed and case records may need to be shared with other agencies or professionals, and this too is appropriate, as long as the legal requisites—which may involve a patient's or client's informed consent—are observed.

However, discussing an interesting case with those who have no need to know the information presents the potential for a violation of confidentiality, particularly if the case or individuals are in any way identifiable. An appropriate discussion taking place in an inappropriate location, such as a restaurant, lunchroom, elevator, or wherever it may be overheard, presents confidentiality problems. Even discussing a case in an appropriate location, such as a private office, may be problematic if a door is open or another party—a fellow worker, visitor, or repairperson—enters the room. Similarly, confidential discussions by telephone may be overheard by another already within or entering an office.

It is interesting to note that the current NASW Code of Ethics has an ethical standard related to these issues: "Social workers should not discuss confidential information in any setting unless privacy can be assured. Social workers should not discuss confidential information in public or semipublic areas (such as hallways, waiting rooms, elevators, and restaurants)" [NASW, 1996: standard 1.07(i)].

A frequent workplace privacy problem is leaving records where others may see them, either at a workstation or in a private office. An open door to a records room, where clients' names are clearly visible on individual record books, presents a confidentiality problem. Similarly, a half-completed letter in a typewriter or a computer screen left on while the worker is away from the workstation is a problematic situation.

Telephone calls requesting information may be a problem. When a fellow professional—doctor, psychiatrist, or another social worker or psychotherapist, or one describing himself as such—calls and requires information immediately, the tendency is to comply. When a lawyer calls, the tendency for compliance seems greater still, especially if a subpoena is threatened.

All of these threats to confidentiality—where any one of them constitutes a breach of professional ethics and may be legally actionable—suggest the need for caution in dealing with confidential material, and perhaps as important the need for periodic, effective training to keep these issues salient.

The temptation to bring the interesting aspects of one's work home or to leisure activities is strong. Discussing unique, interesting cases or those that are timely or relate to matters currently in the news is a real temptation that must be resisted. With the electronic revolution taking place and the demarcation between home and office disappearing, there is a great potential for breaches of confidentiality. One does not necessarily think of the home as an office setting where confidentiality and privacy of patient and client information must be protected. It is easy to leave records about and computer screens visible, and to conduct conversations that can be easily overheard by family, friends, or visitors.

The Legal Foundations of Confidentiality and Privacy

The legal foundations of privacy and confidentiality are sometimes explicit and sometimes implicit in federal and state constitutional law, statutes, and regulations. The existence of an individual or family "right of privacy" is often taken for granted; however, privacy as a legal right remains tenuous and variable, and is still developing.

The United States Constitution—a source of much of the law of privacy—has no specific provision addressing privacy, and in fact does not contain the word "privacy." The court decisions that have developed and elaborated a constitutional right to privacy have done so by finding this right implicit in other constitutional provisions, for example those guaranteeing freedom from unreasonable searches, a right not to incriminate oneself, a right of free speech, free exercise of religion and free assembly, and perhaps most important, protection from deprivations of life, liberty, or property without due process of law.

Thus court decisions that have held that a woman has a privacy right to make a decision with her physician to have an abortion in the first twelve weeks of pregnancy, without interference by the state, have found such a right implicit in the U.S. Constitution. The Fourteenth Amendment prohibitions of deprivation of life, liberty, and property without due process have been the basis for court decisions in this century invalidating laws which prevented interracial marriage, the sterilization of inmates who committed felonies, and various intrusions and limitations on family decision making, among others.

Some state constitutions do explicitly include a right of privacy for their citizens—for example, the California constitution—while in other states a right of privacy has been found implicit in the state constitution.[4]

Various federal and state statutes also protect privacy and confidentiality of social work patients and clients. These are more specific, applying to particular programs, clients, or professionals. For example, protections are extended to child welfare records, mental hospital records, developmentally disabled citizens, and specific professionals such as social workers, psychotherapists, school counselors, and marriage counselors, among others.

However, this complex set of laws that govern privacy and confidentiality forms a pattern of variation and inconsistency. While any one law may be logical and explicable, taken as whole they are difficult to explain and their inconsistencies hard to justify. Over time, these laws have developed and expanded in response to a variety of situations, problems, pressures, and technological advances. The result is that some areas of law are more developed than others, and some individuals, problems, or programs are extended more legal protection.

Later in the text, the laws governing privileged communications and limitations on that privilege will be discussed. Although there is greater uniformity in extending privilege to various professionals than before, it remains that communications to a licensed social worker or therapist will be protected differently from state to state, and within a state different standards of privilege may apply to social workers, psychotherapists, psychologists, marriage counselors, and family therapists. In many states, a psychotherapist has greater privilege protections, but in some others, a social worker or a marriage counselor has a greater degree of protection. It makes sense that certain communications should not be protected, for example, those which indicate future harm to oneself or to a third person. This is the law in many states, but it is less clear in others. In some, the duty to breach confidentiality to protect another will hinge on the identifiability of that person; in others, this is not the case. In some states, there is a legal duty to protect a third person from harm, but not the same duty to protect a patient or client from self-harm. In all states there is now a requirement to report suspected abuse of a child, but in many states this does not apply to abuse of an elderly person or a spouse. And in some states privilege does not apply to communications that may be relevant to a child custody proceeding; in others it does.

Similarly, different protections apply to different records. Information in adoption records, school records, protective services records, juvenile court records, and substance abuse records, among others, is protected to a far greater degree than information in many other records. Information about a person's HIV status is protected more than other medical information. Parents generally have access to their child's medical records, including those pertaining to surgical procedures, but may not have the same degree of access to records pertaining to their child's drug or alcohol abuse, sexually transmitted diseases, or birth control or abortion history.

Many of these distinctions are defensible, many are based on sound policy decisions. Others are harder to rationalize and more difficult to explain, yet remain the law. For the social worker, then, an awareness of these laws and their differences is key to effective practice.

Introduction to Law and Legal Systems

If law is complex and can present difficulties, anomalies, and ambiguities for lawyers and judges trained in the law, for the nonlawyer—even the professional or the student—it is often bewildering. Although there has been a dramatic move away from the arcane language of the past and the reliance on Latin terminology, the language of law, many legal concepts, and the overall complexity of the law are daunting. Lawyers at times do speak a different language and may approach a problem very differently than a social worker, employing a different logic. This text is not the place to deal with these broader issues. However, one part of the difficulty in understanding the law—and a major part—stems from the complex legal system in which we operate. In this section the legal system will be addressed, and the next will deal with a related topic, how to find and use legal materials.

THE AMERICAN LEGAL SYSTEM

Much of the complexity of the American legal system stems from the fact that it is an amalgam of different types of law, coming from different sources at different times. For example, much of the English common law present in the thirteen original colonies continued in those states after the American Revolution. Similarly, French and Spanish civil law particularly influence the laws of Louisiana and Puerto Rico. Another complicating factor is that there are different types of law coming from different sources, the legislative, judicial, and executive branches of government. And finally, there are in reality two, or possibly fifty-one, legal systems operating somewhat independently of each other. This is the principle of federalism, where federal and state authority are at times overlapping and at times independent of each other.

Types of Law. The American legal system consists of four basic types of law: constitutional law, statutory law, judicial decisions, and administrative law. Each type of law is distinct; each has a different source. Constitutional law is broadest, overarching the others. The federal constitution is the source of the three branches of federal government and specifies the powers and duties of those branches. The three other types of law have their sources in the three branches of government: statutory law, enacted by the legislative branch; judicial law, consisting of decisions made by the courts; and administrative law, those rules and regulations promulgated by the executive branch.

Constitutional Law. The federal government and every state have a constitution. The federal constitution contains the enabling laws for establishing the government and legal system, and provides for basic rights of the people. The amendments to the U.S. Constitution establish basic rights of all citizens, such as the rights to free speech and assembly, protections against search and seizure, and the Fifth and Fourteenth Amendment provisions prohibiting deprivations by the federal and state governments of life, liberty, and property without due process of law. Both amendments are sources of the individual's right of privacy in decision making and personal information.

Statutory Law. Statutory law or legislation is what many people think of as "the law." These are laws enacted by the federal Congress and state legislative bodies. These laws, for example, are a primary basis for protecting the confidentiality of communications to social workers, extending privilege to them, and protecting the privacy of student educational records and an individual's HIV-positive medical status. At the same time, legislation is the source of mandatory reporting of child abuse, institutional abuse, and in some states elder abuse, which may result in breaches of the confidential relationship between professional and patient or client.

Judicial Decisions. The role of the judge is to apply existing law to a set of facts brought before the court and to decide on this basis which party should prevail. However, by interpreting laws or by filling gaps in the existing law, judges may make law as well. For example, in the well-known *Tarasoff* decision (see Chapter 7), the California Supreme Court held that therapists had the affirmative duty to breach confidentiality and protect identifiable victims of their clients if they should have reasonably known that their client intended harm. In this, although the court drew upon existing statutory exceptions to confidential communications, the decision was primarily new law, addressing an area not covered by the statutes.

Administrative Rules and Regulations. This area comprises a large, complex, and very detailed body of law. All told, it includes both federal and state administrative codes, state agency policies and procedures, and local government regulations. These laws are usually promulgated by the executive branch of government, as in the case of the Code of Federal Regulations. Often the legislative branch will delegate broad rule-making powers to the executive branch, which will draft and adopt rules and regulations designed to implement legislation or to manage agencies and institutions. For example, by statute patient records in federally funded substance abuse programs are protected from unauthorized disclosure by stringent confidentiality requirements. But what is federal funding, what is a program, who is a patient, what are records, and what constitutes a disclosure—all crucial questions—are found not in the statute but in the accompanying definitions in the administrative regulations.

THE ROLE OF THE JUDGE

In interpreting the law, harmonizing differences among laws, filling gaps within laws, adapting the law to current societal norms, and applying the law to a dispute and a set of facts, the judge or judges are crucial.

> Courts hear an array of disputes, and resolve them by referring
> to rules gleaned from prior cases. The disputing parties end up in

court because they cannot (or will not) resort to force, because they cannot reach a mutually acceptable compromise, because they feel entitled to their "day in court," or some combination of all of these. Motivation notwithstanding, they seek a court-imposed solution. In so doing, the parties may agree more or less with the judicial remedy, but their ultimate satisfaction with the outcome will depend upon whether they feel they are treated fairly. And in our legal system, fairness is conveyed when similar disputes receive similar treatment.

This method of dispute resolution produces "case law": a system where the rules applied in a dispute today were not only gleaned from earlier disputes between A and B but may also become relevant to future conflicts between C and D. Case law development embodies the doctrine of precedent, which expresses the notion that similar cases should be handled similarly, regardless of the specific parties involved. [Albert, 1986:11]

Justice Stewart Pollack, a New Jersey Supreme Court judge, drew comparisons between the work of a judge and an artist, arguing that there are many similarities both in their work and in how it is a reflection of their time:

Stated most simply, judging consists of analyzing the facts of a case, selecting a dispositive rule of law, and applying that rule to the facts. The process, however, is more complex, requiring myriad choices at every step. Making these choices is an art as well as a science. If law were purely scientific, judges analyzing the same facts and applying the same rules of law would reach the same result for the same reasons. Often, however, a single case will produce several opinions. The differing results and rationales reveal the obvious, but often overlooked, point that judging is not just a science.

Differences between judges can appear in activities as fundamental as describing the facts. . . . The judge's art extends also to the description of the dispositive legal principles, the selection of relevant authorities, and the holding of the case. At each stage, the judge makes choices that reflect his or her perception of the judicial role. A judge's perception of community values influences such basic choices as the existence of constitutional rights, the interpretation of a statute, or the extension of the common law. . . . Neither artists nor judges, however, can escape the time and place in which they live. . . . Thus, judicial opinions are bound to reflect the pressures of the time. No wonder as the nation grows more diverse and ideologies change that the transformation should manifest itself in judicial opinions. [Pollack, 1996:594]

Trends in areas such as abortion, contraception, sexual behavior, and sexual harassment, as well as trends toward permitting increased surveillance, widespread testing for substance abuse, and searches and monitoring in the workplace—all discussed later in the text—are examples of laws changing over time.

LEGAL SYSTEMS

The legal context of social worker practice is complicated by the coexistence of the state and national governments and the overlap of state and federal laws. This is federalism: power is shared by state and federal governments, and the states, although part of the national system, remain in many ways separate. Under the Supremacy Clause of Article VI of the U.S. Constitution, the federal constitution and federal laws are the "Supreme Law of the Land." However, the Tenth Amendment provides that "the powers not delegated to the United States by the Constitution nor prohibited by it to the states are reserved to the states respectively, or to the people." As illustrated in Table 1, the American legal system combines parallel federal (national) and state legal systems with their own constitutional, statutory, judicial, and administrative law.

TABLE 1. THE AMERICAN LEGAL SYSTEM

Federal	State
U.S. Constitution	State constitutions
Federal statutes	State statutes
Federal court decisions	State court decisions
Federal regulations	State regulations

Because each state government and its legal system are independent from the others, the result is essentially fifty-one legal systems. For social workers—students or professionals—the federal law and the law of their state are primary. However, changes in the law in other states (for example, a move to open sealed adoption records) may presage legislative changes in their own state, and court decisions in other states may be viewed favorably and adopted by judges in their own state.

While the federal system overarches the state systems and federal constitutional law takes precedence over state laws, in many areas the states remain independent of the federal government and other states. For example, each state determines if—and to what extent—confidential communications between a patient or client and a social worker should be protected by statutory privilege. Similarly, a state may choose to enact a law by which the duty to protect a third party takes precedence over any confidentiality provisions that might exist. While each state has mandatory reporting requirements for suspected child abuse, who must report, what constitutes child abuse, and the degree of certainty that abuse has occurred vary across the states.

It must be emphasized that since each state is legally independent of the others, the student or professional cannot assume that a statute, court decision, or regulation that applies in one state will be the law in another. For example, some states have adopted California's *Tarasoff* "duty to protect" formulation almost verbatim, others have limited it, and still others have broadened it. Some state legislatures have enacted laws providing for immunity from liability for professionals in "duty to protect" situations; others have not.

COURTS IN THE FEDERAL AND STATE LEGAL SYSTEMS

In the following chapters, there will be numerous references to and quotations from court decisions. A little clarification is called for. As most readers know, within federal and state court systems there are usually three levels, from the trial court, the court of original jurisdiction where the litigation began, to the highest court, often—but not always—called the supreme court. Most states and the federal system follow some variation of the simplified pattern illustrated in Table 2.

TABLE 2. FEDERAL AND STATE COURT STRUCTURE

Level	Federal System	State System
Highest	U.S. Supreme Court	State supreme court
Intermediate	U.S. courts of appeals	State appellate courts
Trial	U.S. district courts	State trial courts

Litigation begins with the court of original jurisdiction, usually at the trial court level. Many cases may never actually be heard in court, or if they do get to court are settled prior to a decision. If there is a decision, that result often may be appealed to the next level of court, the appellate level. Usually any further appeal is at the discretion of the highest court. If the highest court refuses to hear an appeal, the appellate court decision stands.

As the table shows, in the federal system, the U.S. district courts are usually the trial courts, the U.S. courts of appeals—sometimes known as circuit courts of appeal—are the intermediate appellate courts, and the highest court is the U.S. Supreme Court. The same pattern generally exists in the states although the names may vary. In the states, the trial court may be a county court, a juvenile court, a family court, a criminal court, a probate court, or any number of other courts of original jurisdiction where cases are first heard. Decisions often can be appealed to the appellate level, and at times to the highest level, frequently called the state supreme court. Usually a decision by this highest court is final, unless an appeal is allowed into the federal system.

Federal courts are organized geographically. One or more U.S. district courts are located within a state, and the geographic range of appeals—or jurisdiction—of the U.S. court of appeals will include cases from the district courts in a number of states arbitrarily grouped into one geographic region, known as a circuit. A single U.S. district court's geographic jurisdiction does not extend beyond one state's boundaries, and the geographic jurisdiction of a U.S. court of appeals includes entire states rather than parts of them. In this way, a district court's decision usually does not affect more than one state, and a circuit court's decision can be binding on some number of states in their entirety.

The legal concept of jurisdiction pertains to which cases or disputes may be heard by a specific court.[5] Federal jurisdiction, or the range of cases that can be heard in the federal system, is specified in Article III, Section 2, of the U.S. Constitution and in federal statutory law.[6] For our purposes, most federal cases will involve a federal statute, federal regulation, or a U.S. constitutional question.

In most situations either or both parties may appeal a decision by a trial court to an intermediate appellate court. Usually appeals must be based on legal, not factual, issues. That is, a party can appeal on the basis that laws or procedures were misstated, misapplied, or violated in the lower court proceeding, but generally cannot appeal solely on the factual determinations made at trial. Many appeals beyond the intermediate appellate court to the highest court are not automatic or by right but are discretionary and require permission of the higher court. In the federal system, a major avenue of appeal to the Supreme Court is by *writ of certiorari,* which essentially means that the Court has decided that it wishes to rule on the issue. Of the thousands of cases appealed to the U.S. Supreme Court each year, the Court may agree to hear less than one hundred appeals. In deciding not to hear a case, the Court need not give any reason or justification but only state that the appeal was denied.

If a case is not appealed from the U.S. court of appeals or if the U.S. Supreme Court refuses to hear the case, then the appellate decision is binding (precedent) within that circuit, and may or may not be followed in other circuits.

Appeals within state systems are similar. Either or both parties have the right to appeal most decisions to the next higher court level on the basis of legal, not factual, issues. Appeals beyond that level are often discretionary, with the highest court having the ability to choose which cases it wishes to hear.

Finding and Using Legal Materials

It may become necessary for a social work professional or student to research some of the legal issues in this text, or to update an issue where the law has changed. Given the sheer bulk of legal materials—state and federal statutes, state and federal court decisions from as many as three different court levels, and state and federal regulations—the task can be daunting. Fortunately, there is a uniform system of citation to all primary legal materials, allowing the social worker easily to identify the type of law in question and the jurisdiction—state or federal. With access to a library or a computerized database, it is not difficult to locate legal materials using the appropriate legal citation. With citations, one can quickly ascertain whether the jurisdiction is state or federal; whether the law is a statute, a court decision, or an administrative regulation; and if it is a court decision, what level court decided the case. Every published case, statute, and regulation should be accompanied by a citation that provides this information. Following is a brief overview of legal citations.[7]

FEDERAL STATUTES

Federal statutes are compiled in several sets of laws, each with its own unique citation. For example, the citation for the Americans with Disabilities Act is *Pub. L.* No. 101-336, 104 *Stat.* 328, 42 *U.S.C.* §12101 *et seq.* (where the abbreviation for *et sequentia,* "and the following," indicates there are multiple sections). Here, *Pub. L.* No. 101-336 refers to the public law number (the 336th law enacted by the 101st Congress); 104 *Stat.* 328 refers to the *Statutes at Large,* where the laws are published chronologically (both part of the *Session Laws,* a chronological compilation of laws enacted by each session of Congress); and 42 *U.S.C.* §12101 refers to the *United States Code* (or in its annotated form, the *U.S. Code Annotated*), a compilation of all federal statutory law organized by subject matter into titles— broad subject areas such as education or public health. Citations to the *U.S. Code* include the title number, the abbreviation for the *U.S. Code* (*U.S.C.,* or *U.S.C.A.* if the annotated version is used), and the specific section—often indicated by the symbol §—where the material is located. In this text, *U.S. Code* citations will used when available. In addition statutes are often given popular names, such as the Civil Rights Act of 1964, the Rehabilitation Act of 1973, or the Americans with Disabilities Act of 1991, which may or may not follow their official statutory designation. Ideally, but not always, the popular name will be accompanied by a statutory citation.

STATE STATUTES

State statutes may be organized chronologically into session laws or may be organized by subject matter. Each has its own unique citation. In some states statutes are organized separately by topic such as business and professions laws or public health laws, and a reference might be to a section of the California Business and Professions Code or the New York Public Health and Safety Code. In other states, as in Minnesota and Washington, the statutes may be organized topically but are merged into a single compilation. The statutory immunity from liability for social workers who take steps to protect an identifiable victim from foreseeable harm is found in the California Civil Code, with the citation California Civil Code §43.92. A similar statutory immunity for social workers in Minnesota is found in the Minnesota Statutes, with the citation Minn. Stat. §148.975, §148.976.

FEDERAL COURT DECISIONS

Citations to court decisions include the *case name,* followed by the *volume number* of the report where the decision is printed, the name of the *reporter series* where the decision is printed, and the *page* where the case is to be found. Often the date when the case was decided and other information about the court will be included as well. This is an easy way to tell which level of court decided the case, since a case citation is usually unique to a certain court level.

U.S. Supreme Court decisions are compiled in three collections of reports, one official and two unofficial, and a single decision may have as many as three citations. The *U.S. Reports* is the official version and is abbreviated *U.S.* The other two are the *Supreme Court Reporter,* abbreviated *S.Ct.,* and the *Supreme Court Reports, Lawyers Edition,* abbreviated *L.Ed.* (or *L.Ed.2d* for the second series). Of the three, the official citation is preferred. The multiple citations are called parallel citations. The complete U.S. Supreme Court citation for *Roe v. Wade,* the abortion decision, is *Roe v. Wade,* 410 U.S. 113, 93 S.Ct. 705, 35 L.Ed.2d 147 (1973). Note that each citation follows the pattern of *volume number* followed by *reporter name* abbreviation followed by *page number.* Another source of U.S. Supreme Court decisions is the *U.S. Law Weekly* (abbreviated *U.S.L.W.*), which prints recent Supreme Court cases and some lower court cases in a weekly updated, loose-leaf format. Still other sources are on-line computerized legal services, such as Reed Elsevier's *LEXIS,* which contains the year and *LEXIS* document number.

In this book, the official citation is used when available. However, the official *U.S. Reports* version is the last to be published and the *LEXIS* document is one of the first available. The reader will occasionally find a citation with only the *Lawyers Edition (L.Ed.)* or *LEXIS* citation. Until the *Lawyers Edition* version was published, the citation for *Jaffee v. Redmond,* the 1996 decision holding that in federal courts communications to licensed social workers are protected by privilege, was *Jaffee v. Redmond,* 1996 U.S. LEXIS 3879.

Federal court of appeals decisions are published in the *Federal Reporter,* abbreviated simply *F.* An example of a federal court of appeals citation is

Compassion in Dying v. State of Washington, 79 F.3d 790 (1996), a decision dealing with the legality of physician-assisted suicide. The citation in that case indicates that the case appears in volume 79 of the *Federal Reporter* (where 3d refers to the third series of the *Reporter*), beginning at page 790. The citation also tells the reader that the case was decided in 1996 by the federal court of appeals for the Ninth Circuit, an intermediate court in the federal system. (The decision was recently reversed by the U.S. Supreme Court; see pp. 56.)

Federal district court case decisions are published in the *Federal Supplement,* abbreviated *F.Supp.* An example of a Federal district court citation is *Doe v. Borough of Barrington,* 729 F.Supp. 376 (D.C. N.J. 1990), a decision holding that there could be liability for invasion of privacy for revealing a person's AIDS condition. That citation indicates that the decision appears in volume 729 of the *Federal Supplement,* beginning at page 376. The citation also tells the reader that the case was decided in 1990 by the federal district court of New Jersey, a trial court in the federal system.

STATE COURT DECISIONS

A similar pattern obtains for cases decided within the state courts. The case name is followed by a volume number, the name of the state reporter, the page number, and the date of the decision. Cases decided by the state's highest court often will have the initials of that state as the name of the reporter. For example, a citation of the *Tarasoff* case is *Tarasoff v. Regents of University of California,* 17 Cal.3d 425 (1976). Some state appellate decisions and occasional state trial court decisions are published, usually with their own citations.

Many state supreme and appellate court cases are also compiled in the *National Reporter System,* an unofficial collection of cases organized into *Regional Reporters.* Each *Regional Reporter* includes state court cases from a geographic region. For example, state court cases from the Southeast appear in the *Southeast Reporter,* state court cases from the West appear in the *Pacific Reporter,* and so forth. The same pattern for citation is followed. The same *Tarasoff* decision also appears in the *Pacific Reporter* as *Tarasoff v. Regents of California,* 551 P.2d 334 (1976). *Regional Reporters* include *Atlantic (A.), Southeast (S.E.), Northeast (N.E.), Northwest (N.W.), Southwest (S.W.),* and *Pacific (P.),* as well as separate compilations for New York *(N.Y.S.)* and California *(Cal. Rptr.).*

ADMINISTRATIVE LAW

Federal regulations first appear as proposed regulations in the *Federal Register,* abbreviated *Fed. Reg.* Once the regulations have been adopted, they are printed in final form in the *Federal Register* and are organized by subject matter in the *Code of Federal Regulations,* abbreviated *C.F.R.* A reference to a federal regulation would be 42 C.F.R. §2001(d), indicating Title 42 of the Code of Federal Regulations, section 2001(d).

States vary in the manner in which state regulatory law is compiled and published, but published regulations will have a similar pattern of citation.

SECONDARY LEGAL MATERIALS

Federal and state statutes, case decisions, and regulations are primary legal sources; that is, they are the law. For those trying to better understand the law or conduct legal research there are a wide range of secondary legal sources and commentaries on the law. Among these are law reviews, looseleaf services, legal treatises, and legal encyclopedias. Law reviews are legal journals published by law schools and other organizations. They contain a wide range of articles and notes on current legal topics such as confidentiality, drug testing in schools, or informing mothers of the HIV status of their newborn children. The law reviews are to be found in law school libraries, state law libraries, and other libraries with collections of legal materials, and are indexed in the *Index of Legal Periodicals.*

ON-LINE LEGAL RESEARCH

There are an increasing number of on-line legal material retrieval sources, for both primary and secondary legal materials. Some are by subscription and some are free. Two major computerized systems for retrieving legal materials are *LEXIS* and *WESTLAW.* These may be available to social workers through libraries or state government agencies. Recently a number of states, including New York and California, have begun to enter their statutes and court decisions on the Internet. Federal court decisions can be located through Web pages for Cornell, Villanova, and Washburn Universities, among others, and the federal government is in the process of providing voluminous legal materials on the Internet.[8]

CHAPTER TWO

CONFIDENTIAL *and* PRIVILEGED COMMUNICATIONS

Confidentiality is a cornerstone of social work practice. Clients assured of confidentiality may reveal information vital to their diagnosis or treatment which might otherwise remain undisclosed. In the process, very personal information, long-held secrets, potentially embarrassing or bothersome events all may be revealed. Even the process of revealing the information may have therapeutic benefits for the client. Conversely, patients and clients advised that communications may not be kept confidential may limit the information disclosed, and this could have consequences for diagnosis and treatment.[1]

While the benefits of the disclosures are generally accepted (Menninger Foundation, 1996), the legal status of the confidential communications and records is less clear. Some communications and information can remain secret, others cannot. In general, for social workers—as for most professionals—confidentiality is not an absolute but depends on where the communication takes place, its content, the recipient of the communication, and at times, the presence or absence of others when the communication was made, among other factors.

In this chapter, we will address two topics of particular importance for social workers, confidential and privileged communications. We will also address some exceptions and limitations to them—for example, situations where there is an intentional or unintentional waiver or where there is a legal duty to breach the confidential status of the communication to report suspected abuse or criminal acts. Due to its complexity and importance, the professional's legal duty to breach confidentiality and warn or protect another from harm will be reserved for Chapter 7.

Confidential and Privileged Communications

Social workers, both professionals and students, are familiar with the concept of confidentiality from their education, training, work experience, and professional code of ethics. The term has both a common, everyday meaning and more a precise legal definition. Thus, treating a conversation as "confidential" is generally understood to mean that one is not to reveal it to another unless the individual making the communication agrees that it can be disclosed.

A legal definition of "confidential" is: "Intrusted with the confidence of another or with his secret affairs or purposes; intended to be held in confidence or kept secret; done in confidence," where confidence is defined as "Trust, . . . Reliance on the discretion of another" (*Black's Law Dictionary,* 1991). Though not precise, this definition suggests the communicator's intent to keep the communication secret combined with an expectation that the recipient will abide by the intended secrecy.

Confidential communications made to certain professionals may fall within the more specific category of "privileged communications." These are legally defined as "those statements made by a certain person within a protected relationship . . . which the law protects from forced disclosure on the witness stand" (*Black's Law Dictionary,* 1991).

Privileged communications are exceptions to the general principle of complete disclosure in court proceedings.[2] Although states vary in their terminology, in the following discussion, privileged communications will be treated as a subset of the broader area of confidential communications, applying specifically to communications made within a "protected relationship," and which cannot be required to be divulged in a court of law.[3]

Confidential Communications

In general, communications made to another in confidence outside of a professional relationship (such as confiding in neighbors and friends) have little legal protection. One may have a moral obligation to keep the secrets of a friend or fellow student, but it is unlikely that a promise of confidentiality in this setting can be enforced at law.[4]

The situation changes where a special relationship exists between the parties. Where the party receiving the communication or information is functioning in a professional capacity and the person making the communication is—or reasonably believes himself or herself to be—a patient or client, there often is an expectation of confidentiality and many times an ethical and legal obligation to maintain confidentiality.

Confidentiality may be protected by state or federal statutory law, court decisions, administrative rules and regulations, or agency policy. Yet when, to what extent, and with what limitations a communication or record is confidential varies greatly among professions and across states.

PROMISES OF CONFIDENTIALITY AND PATIENTS' OR CLIENTS' EXPECTATIONS

Confidentiality may be explicit, where a promise of confidentiality is actually made, or implicit, where the patient or client assumes from the setting, context, and personnel that the information communicated will be kept in confidence. An assurance of confidentiality without further explanation could mean very different things. It might mean that no one else will ever learn of the communication. This may in fact occur, but perhaps with the exception of communications to the clergy (and this is not certain), not all confidential communications can be legally protected. It could mean that no one else will have access to the information without the patient's or client's permission, unless the information is required in a judicial proceeding or unless it falls within other legal disclosure requirements discussed below. This is possible but will depend on statutory law, case law, and perhaps agency policy. Or it could mean that except for the legal disclosure requirements, no one but fellow workers and supervisors who have a need to know or who may be consulted will have access to the information. This is legally possible but may hinge on the legal protections provided to those in the agency. It could mean that except for the legal disclosure requirements the information will not go beyond the walls of the agency, or it could mean that the information will be transmitted only to others inside and outside the agency who are also bound by confidentiality and who have a need to know the information. These others might include related organizations, researchers, external reviewers, and the like. Thus, while some degree of secrecy is inherent in a promise of confidentiality, the number of individuals and agencies having access to some or all of the information communicated may vary substantially.

INFORMING PATIENTS AND CLIENTS ABOUT CONFIDENTIALITY

Given this, a strong argument can be made that patients and clients should be informed at the outset of a professional relationship of the particular meaning of confidentiality and its limitations. There are both legal and ethical rationales for this, although such a policy is not without difficulties.

Legal Requirements. Some states require by statute that certain professionals provide clients with written information about the state's confidentiality laws. The Washington statutes, for example, require: "Persons registered or certified under this chapter shall provide clients at the commencement of any program of treatment with accurate disclosure information concerning their practice, in accordance with guidelines developed by the department, that will inform clients of the purposes of and resources available under this chapter, including the right of clients to refuse treatment, the responsibility of clients for choosing the provider and treatment modality which best suits their needs, *and the extent of confidentiality provided by this chapter*" (emphasis supplied) [Wash. Rev. Code 18.19.060].

In Massachusetts, licensed social workers in private practice or those employed by governmental agencies have a similar statutory obligation: "During the initial phase of the professional relationship, such social worker shall inform the client of such confidential communications and the limitations thereto . . . in accordance with sound professional practice" [Mass. Gen. Laws 112:135A].

To date, this type of statute is the exception, not the rule. Most states do not specifically require professionals to inform clients about confidentiality laws and the possible uses of the information that may be communicated. There are parallels, however, in other areas of the law. Under the law of informed consent, a patient or client should be adequately informed of all material risks before making a decision whether or not to undergo treatment or therapy. In those states that have accepted the reasonable patient standard, the professional has the obligation to reveal all those material risks that a reasonable patient or client would need to know to make an informed choice [Rozovsky, 1990]. Applying this logic, the limits of confidentiality and the possible consequences of, for example, mandatory reporting of suspected abuse would fall within the concept of a "material risk."

Ethical and Practice Considerations for Disclosure. Even if state law does not require a disclosure of the limitations of confidentiality, such a disclosure is consistent with professional ethics. Codes of ethics for social workers, psychologists, and related professionals state that there is a professional obligation to inform clients wherever possible of the limits of confidentiality [Dickson, 1995].

It can be argued that informing patients and clients of the legal limitations of confidentiality will impact the professional–patient/client relationship, and may inhibit the communication of important information necessary for professional diagnosis and treatment, or which could be used to protect another from harm. Conversely, it can be argued that under the basic law of informed consent, the patient or client is entitled to an adequate disclosure of all important information prior to sharing personal information, and to inform the client/patient that information must be reported only after it has been communicated is both unfair and more destructive to the professional–patient/client relationship. Limited data suggest that although most therapists subscribe to the ethical responsibility to inform clients about limits of confidentiality, in practice many do not do so. One study found that over one-half of the professionals surveyed did not tell clients about mandatory child abuse reporting until they became suspicious or actual disclosures were made [Levine, 1993:723]. Those who do provide information about the limits of confidentiality may deal in generalities and avoid specific details, such as the consequences of a child abuse report, or may not clarify the issues for those with limited understanding, such as children.[5] Here, the principle of informed consent suggests that the disclosure of information depends on the needs and capacity of the patient, not what the professional believes is necessary.[6] It is important that the client be made aware of the entire range of individuals and agencies who have or may have access to the confidential information. The tendency may be to focus on the legal limitations of confidentiality, thereby ignoring the more common ways in which the information may be disclosed such as to supervisors, fellow staff, and related agencies.

Finally, an unexpected disclosure of information believed to be confidential may impact a treatment relationship, resulting in a sense of betrayal or termination of the relationship. Levine cites data showing that about 25 percent of psychotherapy clients who are subject to a mandatory child abuse report drop out of treatment after the report is made [Levine, 1993:730].

Privileged Communications

Privileged communications are a subset of confidential matters, and are limited to certain communications made within a legally protected relationship. While a communication made to a professional may be made in confidence, it is not necessarily privileged [Wigmore, 1961:§2286]. The importance of privilege is that, generally, a privileged communication cannot be introduced in court without the consent of the person making the communication. This is usually the patient or client, who is legally the "holder of the privilege."[7] As such, privilege operates as an exception to the general principle of full disclosure in court: the obligation of "every person to give testimony upon all facts inquired of in a court of justice" [Wigmore, 1961: §527]. Privilege can be asserted by the holder of the privilege, or if incompetent or under eighteen years of age, by a representative or guardian. It can also be asserted by a professional or an agency on behalf of the holder of privilege. Unless a communication is privileged, promises by a professional to maintain its confidentiality may not be honored in judicial proceedings.[8]

THE LAW OF PRIVILEGE

Privilege laws are technical, complex, and at times confusing. Except for a few common-law privileges such as attorney-client or husband and wife, privilege for most professionals has been extended by statutes, licensure, or regulations.[9] Often these apply to a specific profession, such as social worker, psychotherapist, or marriage counselor. Privilege may be linked to licensure provisions, and as different professions emerge and become licensed, they may be extended their own privilege laws. They may be modeled on existing laws or may differ in coverage and limitations.

All of this produces great variation. Privilege laws can vary with the profession of the individual receiving the communication, the material communicated, the purpose of the communication, whether the proceeding is criminal or civil, and whether the professional is employed by the state or is in private practice, among other factors.

It must be emphasized that privilege laws are specific to a profession. Even in the same state, the same communication made to professionals who perform the same functions, such as psychotherapy or counseling, but are in different professional classifications, such as social workers, psychologists, guidance counselors, or marriage and family therapists, or are public rather than private employees, may sometimes be covered by privilege and sometimes not. Communications made to psychiatrists and psychotherapists in private practice often have more protection at law than communications made to social workers or marriage counselors.

It is interesting to note in this respect that the U.S. Supreme Court in *Jaffee v. Redmond* adopted a functional approach in holding that communications to social workers should have the same privilege protection in federal courts as communications to psychotherapists. The Court said: "We therefore agree with the Court of Appeals that 'drawing a distinction between the counseling provided by costly psychotherapists and the counseling provided by more readily accessible social workers serves no discernible public purpose'" [135 L.Ed.2d 337, 349 (1996)].

Given these many variations, it is incumbent on professionals and students alike to ascertain the laws in their state that apply to them, their agencies, and their patients or clients.

GROWTH OF PRIVILEGE

The extension of privilege to professionals has grown slowly over time. Since privilege restricts what can be revealed in court, legislatures and courts have been reluctant to grant it to new professions, and where it does exist courts have tended to interpret its boundaries narrowly. A common-law privilege for communications between attorney and client was first recognized in Elizabethan England in 1577.[10] English courts still do not recognize a privilege between other professionals and their patients and clients. In the United States, privilege was first extended by statute to communications between patient and physician in New York in 1828, and in Missouri in 1835 [Wigmore, 1961:§2380]. Later a number of states protected communications between clergy and parishioners, and this privilege is now found in most states. Privilege has gradually been extended to many professionals including physicians, psychiatrists, psychotherapists, social workers, psychologists, marriage counselors, school guidance counselors, and sexual assault victim counselors.

RATIONALE FOR PRIVILEGE

Various justifications have been advanced for determining whether or not to extend privilege to certain communications in certain settings. The most frequently cited criteria for establishing a privilege are those of Dean Wigmore in his classic treatise on evidence:

(1) The communication must originate in a *confidence* that it will not be disclosed.

(2) This element of *confidentiality must be essential* to the full and satisfactory maintenance of the relation between the parties.

(3) The *relation* must be one which in the opinion of the community ought to be sedulously *fostered*.

(4) The *injury* that would inure to the relation by the disclosure of the communication must be *greater than the benefit* thereby gained for the correct disposal of the litigation. Only if these four conditions are present should a privilege be recognized. [Wigmore, 1961: §2285][11]

These criteria can be narrowly or broadly interpreted, extending privilege to numerous situations and professional relationships or very few. Using these criteria, Wigmore himself argued for a narrow interpretation—that privilege should be extended only to a very few relationships, such as husband and wife, attorney and client, or clergyperson and parishioner. Wigmore's justification is basically utilitarian, that a relationship should be privileged only where the benefit of the protection exceeds the cost of not having information revealed in court. Other rationales have been advanced for explaining privilege, including privacy, the need to keep private certain communications such as those between spouses whatever the cost; and power, where the extension of privilege depends on the political power of the group—clergy, reporters, lawyers, and physicians have privilege, while community organizers, welfare workers, and those dealing with the homeless generally do not [Note, Developments, 1985:1472].

PRIVILEGED RELATIONSHIPS

Communications made to social workers may be privileged because of specific legal provisions granting privilege to those professionals, or they may fall within the privilege granted to other professionals which extends to the work of the social worker. A social worker with only limited professional privilege might come within the broader privilege protection of another professional. An example might be information gathered by a social worker in a mental health clinic for the purposes of diagnosis or treatment made by a physician or psychiatrist. In this situation, whether or not the information was protected by a social worker privilege, the information would normally be protected by physician-patient or psychiatrist-patient privilege. Privilege is extended to psychotherapists in all fifty states, and in some form to licensed social workers or licensed clinical social workers in forty-five states. Since social workers may perform a range of noncounseling roles—such as income maintenance, child protection, or testing—depending on the jurisdiction, only some communications or some social workers may be covered.

STATE PRIVILEGE LAWS

Every state protects some communications between patients or clients and their licensed psychologists and psychotherapists made in the course of a professional relationship from involuntary disclosure in court, and most protect some communications between patients or clients and some licensed social workers made in the course of a professional relationship. However, no state protects all such professional communications. The difficulty then is in determining where and when privilege attaches and where and when it does not. Many state privilege laws have similar forms and wording since they are based on either the Uniform Rules of Evidence or the draft Federal Rules of Evidence. However, in a number of states these rules have been modified or broadened, and in some states the number of exceptions to privilege has been significantly expanded. The following analysis includes a representative sample of these laws but is necessarily incomplete due to space limitations. (References for state privilege statutes for social workers and psychotherapists are listed by state in the Appendix.) Also, privilege laws may differ in civil and criminal proceedings. Here the focus will be on privilege laws in civil proceedings since this is the forum where social workers are most likely to appear.

Professionals with Privilege. Privilege arises out of a protected, confidential relationship between the professional and the patient or client. A few states, such as Hawaii and North Dakota, limit privileged relationships to a small number of professional groups, such as physicians, psychotherapists, and the clergy [Hawaii Rules of Evidence §504, 504.1; North Dakota Rules of Evidence §503]. In other states, privilege is extended to a far wider range of professions. For example, in Arizona privilege is extended to "certified behavioral health professionals," which includes social workers, marriage and family therapists, professional counselors, and substance abuse counselors, among others [Ariz. Rev. Stat. §32–3283].[12] In California, privilege extends to psychotherapists, defined broadly to include psychiatrists; licensed psychologists; licensed clinical social workers; school psychologists; marriage, family, and child counselors; registered and supervised psychological assistants; registered and supervised marriage, family, and child counselor interns; registered and supervised associate clinical social workers; supervised psychological interns and trainees in a supervised required practicum; and certain psychiatric nurses (Cal. Evid. Code §1010].

In Texas those "licensed or certified by the State of Texas in the diagnosis, evaluation or treatment of any mental or emotional disorder" are included among professionals with privilege [Texas Rules of Civil Evidence §510(a)(1)]. In Florida privilege is extended to "mental health counselors," in Nebraska to "mental health practitioners," in Rhode Island to "health care providers," and to "mental health professionals" in Vermont.[13] And, in some states, privileged communication status is granted to other professional groups such as licensed marriage or family therapists, school counselors, licensed substance abuse counselors, and domestic violence and sexual assault victim counselors. Any of these might include social workers, who would then have the privilege to the extent it is granted to any category.

In most states, licensed clinical social workers are granted privilege in their own right, although sometimes the coverage is limited to those in private practice. In some states privilege is extended more broadly to "licensed social workers,"[14] "certified social workers,"[15] or more generally to "social workers,"[16] with coverage depending upon the statutory definitions of those categories.[17] In some states, social workers employed by the state are specifically excluded from privilege statutes, and in some privilege for social workers is limited to noninvestigatory professional practice.[18]

Communications That Are Privileged. Depending on state law and specific legal disclosure requirements (such as child abuse), there are differences in communications covered by privilege. In this respect, the privilege granted social workers at times may be broader than that granted other professionals. In Oregon, communications to a psychotherapist are privileged if they are made "for the purposes of diagnosis or treatment of the patient's mental or emotional condition" [Ore. Rev. Stat. §40.230]. In the same state, any communications made to a clinical social worker (with the usual exceptions) are privileged: "A clinical social worker licensed by the State Board of Clinical Social Workers shall not be examined in a civil or criminal court proceeding as to any communication given the clinical social worker by a client in the course of noninvestigatory professional activity when such communication was given to enable the licensed clinical social worker to aid the client" [Ore. Rev. Stat. §40.250].

In Arizona, both communications and knowledge are protected: "In any legal action a certified behavioral health professional shall not, without the consent of his client, be examined as to any communication made by the client to him or as to any such knowledge obtained with respect to personnel dealing with the client" [Ariz. Rev. Stat. §32-3283].

In those states where a privilege for licensed psychotherapists is on the same basis as an attorney-client privilege, most communications to these professionals as well as work products are privileged, with the exception of mandatory disclosures. In some states, even the identity of the patient or client may not be divulged.[19]

In some states privilege extends beyond verbal communications to gestures and objects, opinions and advice.[20] In others, the communications are privileged, but observations, opinions, and conclusions are not.[21] A court may also distinguish between a communication for the purpose of treatment and one made for other purposes.[22] In at least four states—Maine, New Hampshire, North Carolina, and Virginia—social worker privilege is further restricted in that a court may compel the disclosure of any communication, making privilege tenuous at best.[23]

In *People v. Bridges,* 538 N.Y.S.2d. 701 (1989), a victim of sexual abuse spoke to a volunteer at a rape crisis center. The defendant charged with the abuse subpoenaed the records of those conversations, arguing that they would contain important exculpatory material such as inconstant accounts of the abuse, its time, and location. The counseling center contested the subpoena, arguing that the records were privileged. The court ruled that there was no privilege, since the volunteer was not a certified social worker: "Based on the circumstances of this case, the rape crisis volunteer was not working in conjunction with a certified social worker, nor was she a certified social worker herself, such as to bring her notes under the protection of CPLR 4508. Accordingly, Planned Parenthood's motion to quash the subpoena for the notes of the rape crisis volunteer pursuant to CPLR 4508 is denied and Planned Parenthood is directed to turn those materials over to the defense pursuant to the properly issued subpoena" [538 N.Y.S.2d 701 (1989)].[24]

Thus great care must be taken in ascertaining the exact scope of privilege. For this, social workers may need to go beyond the statutes and rules found in the Appendix of this book and consult the annotated statutes, case law, and notations to the administrative rules for their particular state jurisdiction.

There are also a number of specific types of communication excluded from privilege in some, many, or all states. These are discussed at page 44. Generally they include communications linked to the welfare of children, communications indicating future harm to self or others, communications indicating present or past abuse where it must be reported, and communications indicating the commission of crimes.

Holder of Privilege. The individual making the communications or sharing information with the professional is in legal terminology the holder of the privilege. Generally, this is the patient or client, or if that individual is incompetent, the guardian or conservator. For a minor, the holder of privilege is that person's legal representative, usually an adult parent or guardian, although in a child custody case a Maryland court required that an independent guardian *ad litem* (a special law guardian) be appointed to represent the child's interests.[25] In the case of an emancipated minor—one who has the legal decision-making power of an adult—the minor is the holder of privilege. Where an individual has been legally determined to be incompetent, the holder of privilege is the legally appointed guardian. In the case of a deceased person, states vary. Generally privilege continues even after death, and a legal representative, executor, next of kin, or heirs of the deceased can assert it.[26] While the holder of the privilege decides whether or not to assert it, the professional may assert it on behalf of the patient or client holder. Conversely, if the patient or client waives the privilege, the professional generally cannot assert it on behalf of the patient or client.

Defining Patients and Clients. Privilege attaches when a patient or client engages the services of a covered professional, forming the protected relationship. Occasionally questions arise as to whether the individual assumed to be a professional really was a professional or was acting in a professional capacity, whether there was an intent to make a confidential communication, or whether the patient or client really was a patient or client of the professional and therefore covered by the privilege. If the patient or client reasonably believes that the individual to whom she or he is communicating is a professional with privilege, in many states the communication will probably be privileged even if this was not the case.[27]

Whether there was an intent to keep the communication confidential may present difficulties. In a South Dakota case, *State v. Martin*, 274 N.W.2d 893 (1979), the defendant made an early morning call to a licensed certified psychiatric social worker with whom he had a professional relationship and told him, "I just killed somebody." The social worker told Martin that he would have to notify the police and did so. The police investigated and found the murder victim at Martin's house. One of the issues on appeal was whether the conversation between Martin and the social worker was privileged under South Dakota law. The South Dakota statute states: "No licensed certified social worker, social worker, or social work associate or his employee may disclose any information he may have acquired from persons consulting him in his professional capacity that was necessary to enable him to render services in his professional capacity to those persons" [SDCL 36-26-30]. The court held the conversation was not privileged because there was no indication that it was made in confidence or with the expectation that it would be confidential, although Martin had been a client of the social worker for six to eight months.[28]

Whether the individual was in fact a patient or client may also arise. In an Oregon case, *State v. Miller*, 709 P.2d 225 (Ore. 1985), one issue was the existence of a professional relationship which would protect the confidentiality of the communication. The defendant had called a state mental hospital, asking to speak with a doctor because he had just killed a man. He spoke with the psychiatrist on duty, a stranger, who kept him on the phone for ten or fifteen minutes while the police traced the call. During the conversation, which was similar to an intake interview, the psychiatrist ascertained the caller's name after promising him confidentiality. In addition, the defendant then proceeded to make a number of incriminating statements. At trial, the psychiatrist testified that although she had promised confidentiality, she had no intention of diagnosing or treating the defendant, but was only trying to keep him on the phone while the police arrived. The defendant attempted to suppress all statements made to the psychiatrist, under the Oregon psychotherapist-patient privilege act. On appeal to the Oregon Supreme Court one question was whether the defendant could qualify as a patient and come within the protection of the act. In the Oregon statute, a patient is "a person who consults or is examined or interviewed by a psychotherapist" [OEC 504(1)(b)].

The court found that the statements were privileged even though there was no preexisting psychotherapist-patient relationship and no intent on the part of the psychiatrist to provide psychotherapy. The court distinguished Miller's situation from a chance meeting between an individual and a psychotherapist:

> In light of the policy behind the rule and its similarity to the attorney-client privilege, we conclude that the psychotherapist-patient privilege protects communications made in an initial conference for the purpose of establishing a psychotherapist-patient relationship, even if such a relationship is never actually formed. The psychotherapist-patient privilege "necessarily includes communications made in the course of diagnostic interviews and examinations which might reasonably lead to psychotherapy." This is required to encourage patients to discuss frankly and freely their mental or emotional problems so that the professional can accurately determine whether he or she is qualified to treat them. If information revealed during the initial conference

indicates to either party that an ongoing professional relationship should not be formed, the confidences revealed in the initial consultation are protected nevertheless. . . . In order for statements made in an initial encounter to be covered by the privilege, the psychotherapist and patient must agree, or at least reasonably appear to agree, that they intend to establish a psychotherapist-patient relationship. There must be some indication from the psychotherapist that he or she is willing to embark upon such a relationship. An indication of this intent may be inferred from the circumstances. It might come from the setting alone. For example, if a prospective patient talks to a licensed psychotherapist in a professional practice setting, such as a mental health clinic or a private practice office, the patient could fairly infer that the psychotherapist has indicated a willingness to enter into a confidential relationship. The requisite willingness could also be shown by the psychotherapist's behavior, apart from the setting. . . . Where a psychotherapist has given reasonable assurances to the patient that they are embarking upon a privileged relationship, an ulterior motive or purpose on the part of the psychotherapist will not prevent the patient from claiming the privilege. [709 P.2d 225, 234 (1985)]

Privileged Communications in Federal Courts

The privileged status of communications made to clinical social workers and psychotherapists has been recognized by the U.S. Supreme Court in the recent case *Jaffee v. Redmond*, 135 L.Ed.2d 337 (1996). There the administrator of the estate of a man killed by a police officer demanded access to the notes of a licensed clinical social worker made during counseling sessions with the police officer. The notes were to be used to cross-examine the officer in an action brought in federal court for damages and wrongful death. The police officer and the therapist argued that the notes were protected by psychotherapist-patient privilege and could not be divulged. The trial judge concluded that although there was a privileged status for communications made to psychotherapists and clinical social workers in many states, there was no privilege between psychotherapist and patient in the federal court system and ordered that notes be produced. After a trial in which the notes were not produced and both therapist and patient refused to testify about their contents, the trial judge instructed the jury that there was no legal justification for not producing the notes and the jury could infer that they would be unfavorable to the defendant's case.

The resulting verdict and monetary awards for the plaintiff were appealed to the federal court of appeals for the seventh circuit. That court reversed, finding that a psychotherapist-patient privilege did exist in the federal system under the guidelines of Federal Rules of Evidence Rule 501.[29] The appellate court qualified the privilege, holding that it would not apply if the need for disclosure in a particular case outweighed the privacy interests of the patient. In this situation, the court ruled that the presence of numerous eyewitnesses to the shooting reduced the need for disclosure, which was outweighed by the police officer's privacy interests.

The case was appealed to the U.S. Supreme Court, which agreed with the appellate court, finding that confidential communications between patient and psychotherapist in the course of diagnosis or treatment were protected by a psychotherapist-patient privilege in the federal court system under Rule 501. The Court said:

> Effective psychotherapy . . . depends upon an atmosphere of confidence and trust in which the patient is willing to make a frank and complete disclosure of facts, emotions, memories, and fears. Because of the sensitive nature of the problems for which individuals consult psychotherapists, disclosure of confidential communications made during counseling sessions may cause embarrassment or disgrace. For this reason, the mere possibility of disclosure may impede development of the confidential relationship necessary for successful treatment. . . . The psychotherapist privilege serves the public interest by facilitating the provision of appropriate treatment for individuals suffering the effects of a mental or emotional problem. The mental health of our citizenry, no less than its physical health, is a public good of transcendent importance. [135 L.Ed.2d 337, 345 (1996)]

Extending the privilege to licensed social workers conducting psychotherapy, the Court said:

> All agree that a psychotherapist privilege covers confidential communications made to licensed psychiatrists and psychologists. We have no hesitation in concluding in this case that the federal privilege should also extend to confidential communications made to licensed social workers in the course of psychotherapy. The reasons for recognizing a privilege for treatment by psychiatrists and psychologists apply with equal force to treatment by a clinical social worker such as Karen Beyer. Today, social workers provide a significant amount of mental health treatment. Their clients often include the poor and those of modest means who could not afford the assistance of a psychiatrist or psychologist, but whose counseling sessions serve the same public goals. Perhaps in recognition of these circumstances, the vast majority of States explicitly extend a testimonial privilege to licensed social workers. We therefore agree with the Court of Appeals that "drawing a distinction between the counseling provided by costly psychotherapists and the counseling provided by more readily accessible social workers serves no discernible public purpose." [135 L.Ed.2d 337, 348 (1996)]

Finally, the Court disagreed with the balancing of interests test used by the appellate court:

> We part company with the Court of Appeals on a separate point. We reject the balancing component of the privilege implemented by that court and a small number of States. Making the promise of confidentiality contingent upon a trial judge's later evaluation of the relative importance of the patient's interest in privacy and the evidentiary need for disclosure would eviscerate the effectiveness of the privilege. . . . "[I]f the purpose of the privilege is to be served, the participants in the confidential conversation 'must be able to predict with some degree of certainty whether particular discussions will be protected. An uncertain privilege,

or one which purports to be certain but results in widely varying applications by the courts, is little better than no privilege at all.'" [135 L.Ed.2d 337, 349 (1996)]

Exceptions and Limitations to Privilege and Confidentiality

Privilege is rarely an absolute. There are numerous exceptions, both statutory and judge-made. A number are discussed below, but the list is not exhaustive. Moreover, in light of the judicial tendency to construe privilege statutes narrowly, many exceptions arise in specific situations where a judge makes a decision that there is a "compelling need" or a "sound public policy" which requires privilege to yield. Faced with this, social workers and other human service professionals must always consider the real possibility that a promise of confidentiality may not be able to be kept short of being in contempt of court.

LIMITATIONS ON PRIVILEGED COMMUNICATIONS: CHILD ABUSE

All states have enacted mandatory child abuse reporting laws, which for social workers supersede privilege. Many social worker privilege statutes specifically exclude child abuse from privilege protection; others have been so interpreted by the courts.[30] These laws mandate reporting to the child protective service agency when there is a reasonable belief, reasonable suspicion, suspicion, or similar standard that abuse of a child by a parent or guardian has taken place. Often coupled with the reporting law are provisions providing for civil or criminal immunity for good faith reporting and civil and criminal penalties for a failure to report.

What constitutes child abuse or neglect, the requisite degree of suspicion or belief that abuse has occurred needed to file a report, and how to deal with reports of abuse occurring months or years in the past depend on particular state statutes, regulations, protocols, and child protective service policies. The social worker, supervisor, and agency administrator will need to have a clear idea of the requirements of their state. Moreover, while a suspicion of abuse must be reported and is not protected by confidentiality or privilege, further communications by the patient or client about the abuse

may be protected and excluded from courtroom testimony. Here the rationale is that the mandatory reporting law is designed to protect children, not
to prosecute adults, and the role of the social worker or other human service
professional is to report abuse but not to function as an interrogator for the
state.[31]

LIMITATIONS ON PRIVILEGED COMMUNICATIONS: CHILD WELFARE

Limits on privilege and confidentiality are particularly common where the
information pertains directly or indirectly to the welfare of a child. Along
with child abuse exceptions many states have excluded from privilege communications that would be of use in adoption, child custody, child visita-
tion, termination of parental rights, or child welfare proceedings or that are
"in the best interests of the child."[32] Many states also exclude communications that indicate a minor has been a subject or a victim of a crime. Given
such a broad scope, it is possible that the confidential nature of many communications directly about, related to, or from a child could be challenged.
Here, good judgment, consultation, proper documentation, and legal advice
may be particularly important.

OTHER LIMITATIONS ON PRIVILEGED COMMUNICATIONS

While the number and type of exceptions vary across the states, there are
some commonalities. One is the professional's obligation to take steps to
protect an individual from harm—which is the law in many jurisdictions;
this matter is discussed in detail in Chapter 7. In addition, many states have
enacted mandatory reporting laws for institutional abuse, elder abuse, and
abuse of individuals who are disabled. While many of these jurisdictions
specifically include references to such abuse as exceptions to privilege
statutes, others do not. However, it is likely that these mandatory reporting
statutes supersede privilege provisions, much as child abuse does.

Often, court-ordered investigations, interviews, and treatment are excluded from privileged status, although some states have provided that
while the fact that the individual was attending counseling was not privileged, what transpired during the counseling sessions was. Communications
made as part of a civil commitment or mental health evaluation are generally excluded from privilege protections, as are communications that are
relevant to later claims of a breach of duty by the professional. Often
communications in which there was an intent to obtain aid in the planning

or conducting of a crime or for escaping detection will not be covered by privilege laws. Also, in some states communications about any past criminal act, or in others certain serious criminal acts, are not protected by privilege and must be divulged.[33] For the social worker, this may require a difficult judgment as to whether the criminal conduct falls within the statute as well as whether the behavior can be considered an indication of future criminal conduct or harm and is therefore reportable. In such cases, consultation with a supervisor and an agency attorney, if available, coupled with careful documentation, may be the best course of action.

WAIVER OF CONFIDENTIALITY OR PRIVILEGE

A waiver is "the intentional or voluntary relinquishment of a known right, or such conduct as warrants an inference of the relinquishment of such right" (*Black's Law Dictionary*, 1991). Waiver can be expressly stated or implied through conduct indicating this intention. A waiver of the confidential or privileged status of a communication can be made only by the holder of the privilege—the individual communicating the information, or his or her legal representative. The social worker or other human service professional cannot waive the privilege independently of the patient or client.

The waiver can be intentional or inadvertent, and written or oral. An intentional waiver occurs when the patient or client knowingly and intentionally terminates the confidential or privileged status of the communication by executing a valid waiver. At its simplest, this waiver should be based on the elements found in an informed consent: a decision made by a competent person free of coercion after there has been adequate disclosure of the consequences.

The individual executing the waiver must be legally competent and should be functionally competent. That is, a person who retains legal competence because there has been no judicial determination of incompetence may nonetheless be incapable of making many decisions and may be functionally incompetent. If the individual is functionally incompetent, a waiver decision might be legally binding, but an ethically and legally preferred course of action would be to apply for a court determination of the person's competence or the appointment of a temporary guardian for the purpose of executing the waiver. Failing this, consent by the individual and a family member might be sufficient. If the individual is a child, the waiver decision often legally resides with the parent or guardian, although with an older child, the best course is to have both parent and child concur.

In addition there should be an adequate disclosure of the consequences of the waiver for the patient or client. The individual executing a waiver should know what information will be released to whom and for what purpose. This should be disclosed to the patient or client in a careful, comprehensible manner, keeping in mind that the disclosure might include information long forgotten or information of which the patient or client is not even aware. Thus the client needs to know what information is in the case record as well as who recipients will be. Finally, the waiver should be made freely and voluntarily, without coercion.

An example of requirements for an informed waiver is found in the Connecticut statutes:

> All communications and records shall be confidential and, except as provided . . . a social worker shall not disclose any such communications and records unless the person or his authorized representative consents to such disclosure. Any consent given shall specify the individual or agency to which the communications and records are to be disclosed, the scope of the communications and records to be disclosed, the purpose of the disclosure and the expiration date of the consent. A copy of the consent form shall accompany any communications and records disclosed. The person or his authorized representative may withdraw any consent given under the provisions of this section at any time by written notice to the individual with whom or the office in which the original consent was filed. The withdrawal of consent shall not affect communications and records disclosed prior to notice of the withdrawal, except that such communications and records may not be redisclosed after the date of the notice of withdrawal. [Conn. Gen. Stat. §52-146q(c)]

In *Community Service Society v. Welfare Inspector General*, 398 N.Y.S.2d 92 (1977), a welfare recipient signed a form as part of an application for welfare stating: "I give my consent to the Department of Social Services to make such collateral contacts and visits as may be necessary to determine my eligibility for assistance." The court rejected the argument that this constituted a generalized waiver of privilege which would permit the state to access forms filled out by the recipient as part of her request for service from a social welfare agency, forms that were privileged communications with a certified social worker. The court held that there was no waiver: "To constitute a waiver there must be a clear relinquishment of a known right. The language in the alleged waiver relied upon by the Inspector General does not clearly demonstrate that the client knew or should have known she was waiving her right to assert her statutory privilege against disclosure of communications to lawyers, doctors, clergymen or social workers" [398 N.Y.S.2d 92, 95 (1977)].

While it is not necessary to have a written waiver, this is certainly preferable. If the waiver is oral, the presence of a disinterested witness coupled with contemporaneous notes could be used if the oral waiver later was challenged.

Along with an intentional, knowing waiver, a waiver may also be implied through the conduct of the individual, which may suggest the intention to waive the matter. Disclosing the confidential communication to a third party, especially if that party is not also bound by legal privilege and the disclosure was not made to further treatment, will often terminate the privilege. The rationale for this is stated by McCormick: "Obviously, the law has no reason to conceal in court what has been freely divulged on the public street, and the only question in such cases becomes the voluntariness of the revelation and the scope of the waiver" [Strong, 1992:383].

Introducing a private matter, such as the individual's mental or emotional health, into litigation—known as the patient litigant exception—will often operate to terminate the existing confidentiality or privilege, as may the patient's or client's own testimony in court about his or her treatment or condition. Also, a malpractice action by a patient or client against a social worker or therapist would terminate the patient or client privilege.

OTHER EXCEPTIONS: THE THIRD PARTY RULE

At common law, a communication made in the presence of a third party is not confidential, since the communicator could not have intended confidentiality knowing another could overhear it. Many statutes now explicitly state that the presence of others who are furthering the interest of the individual does not affect confidentiality. For example, the California statutes contain the provision:

As used in this article, "confidential communication between patient and psychotherapist" means information, including information obtained by an examination of the patient, transmitted between a patient and his psychotherapist in the course of that relationship and in confidence by a means which, so far as the patient is aware, discloses the information to no third persons other than those who are present to further the interest of the patient in the consultation, or those to whom disclosure is reasonably necessary for the transmission of the information or the accomplishment of the purpose for which the psychotherapist is consulted, and includes a diagnosis made and the advice given by the psychotherapist in the course of that relationship. [Cal. Evid. Code §1012]

Where such a statute or rule is not present, caution is advised. Without a statutory basis, a court disposed to limit the extent of privilege could rule that the presence of third parties invalidated the confidentiality of the communication. A similar problem exists in marital, couple, or group counseling. Whether privilege can attach in these settings will depend on the statutory wording and judicial interpretation. A few jurisdictions specifically include communications in group or joint therapy within privilege. (See generally Chapter 10.)

Finally, some jurisdictions have held that even if the patient or client was unaware of a third party overhearing the confidential communication, this condition would terminate privilege. This exception, the "eavesdropper rule," was rejected by the California Supreme Court in *Menendez v. Superior Court,* 834 P.2d 786 (Cal. 1992). There the Menendez brothers were unaware that the therapist's lover was hidden in the next room, secretly listening to their confidential psychotherapy sessions. The court held that this did not defeat the brothers' privilege, and they could prevent the psychotherapist from revealing the confidential communications. (In *Menendez,* however, the court held that the statutory "dangerous patient" exception did apply to several counseling sessions, and they were not privileged.)

CONFIDENTIAL COMMUNICATIONS IN SOCIAL WORK PRACTICE

In light of the foregoing discussion, social work professionals and students have both a legal and an ethical mandate to learn the law of confidential communications applicable to their location. Sometimes this is relatively easy to ascertain, such as the references to state privilege statutes in the Appendix. However, as the text demonstrates, there are other important factors, such as limitations to confidentiality because of what is disclosed or who is present, which may be found only in other statutes, regulations, case law, or agency policy. If the patient or client is executing a waiver to allow disclosure of a confidential communication, the best course is to be sure that it is made with full knowledge of what will be disclosed to whom for what purposes, and that the waiver be in a written form, signed, dated, and witnessed.

CHAPTER THREE

PRIVACY *and the* LAW

Privacy and confidentiality are related, overlapping concepts in the law. Privacy is in many ways the broader concept, at times protecting a social worker's or client's person, family, home, office, files, and records from surveillance or intrusion by a governmental authority. Privacy may have a broad constitutional basis or it may be found in more narrow statutory provisions, rules, and regulations, applicable to specific individuals, records, or agencies. The term "privacy" does not appear in the federal constitution, thus making federal constitutional protections of privacy—except in the search and seizure area—implicit rather than explicit. That is, where the courts have found a constitutional basis for a privacy protection, they have held it to be inherent within certain constitutional provisions such as Fifth and Fourteenth Amendment due process.

In contrast, some state constitutions specifically refer to a right of privacy. The California constitution, for example, states: "All people are by nature free and independent and have inalienable rights. Among these are

enjoying and defending life and liberty, acquiring, possessing, and protecting property, and pursuing and obtaining safety, happiness, and privacy"
[California Constitution, Article I, section 1].[1]

In addition, there are a wide range of statutory privacy and privacy-
related provisions in both federal and state laws, ranging from privacy protections for certain populations such as individuals with disabilities and
hospital or mental hospital patients to privacy in the workplace to privacy
in personal matters, such as an HIV test result. The privacy of and access to
an individual's records maintained by the federal government is protected in
the federal Privacy Act of 1974.

Within these various privacy protections there continues a tension between the state—broadly defined to include any federal, state, or local governmental authority—trying to access personal information or place limits
on personal decision making, and the individual's privacy rights. For social
work professionals and students, this area of law has serious implications
for their patients and clients and for themselves.

In this chapter, we will address some of these broader issues, in particular the privacy of making certain decisions, such as contraception, abortion,
sexual conduct, and termination of life support systems; the privacy of the
individual's person and property from governmental searches; and the privacy of personal information and records.

A Constitutional Right of Privacy

At least three types of privacy are afforded some form of protection from
governmental action under the U.S. Constitution. Constitutional scholar
Philip Kurland wrote: "The concept of a constitutional right of privacy still
remains largely undefined. There are at least three facets that have been partially revealed, but their form and shape remain to be fully ascertained. The
first is the right of the individual to be free in his private affairs from governmental surveillance and intrusion. The second is the right of an individual not to have his private affairs made public by the government. The third
is the right of an individual to be free in action, thought, experience, and
belief from governmental compulsion" [*Whalen v. Roe*, 429 U.S. 589, 600
n. 24 (1977)].

Thus, in privacy law there is a *decisional privacy* which has to do with the autonomy to make decisions for oneself or one's family without restriction by the state; a *personal privacy* which has to do with freedoms from governmental surveillance, eavesdropping, and intrusion; and an *informational privacy* which has to do with keeping personal information private and not disclosed by the state.

In all three areas, privacy is rarely a legal absolute. At times governmental intrusions, restrictions, or access to otherwise private information may be permissible, depending upon the purpose and underlying public policy. For example, within the constitutional protections of decisional privacy, many decisions made by parents for their children are shielded from interference by the state, such as decisions about medical treatment, education, dress, or diet. However, parental decisions to provide no medical treatment, no education, improper dress, or inadequate diet may be successfully challenged by the state [Areen, 1992]. Similarly, within the constitutional protections of personal privacy, the state may not generally withdraw blood or analyze urine of citizens without a warrant based on reasonable cause, but the Supreme Court has held it may do so to assess sobriety of drivers or drug use of railway employees, customs workers, or public school athletes.

Decisional Privacy: Personal Autonomy

The existence of a right of privacy implicit in the federal constitution was first proposed in a seminal 1890 *Harvard Law Review* article [Warren and Brandeis, 1890]. It was later succinctly summarized by Brandeis—after he became a Supreme Court justice—in *Olmstead v. United States,* 277 U.S. 438 (1928): "The makers of our Constitution undertook to secure conditions favorable to the pursuit of happiness. . . . They sought to protect Americans in their beliefs, their thoughts, their emotions, and their sensations. They conferred, as against the government, the right to be let alone— the most comprehensive of rights and the right most valued by civilized men" [277 U.S. 438, 478 (1928), dissenting opinion].

There appear to have been few early court decisions protecting the privacy of citizens from the state, but in the twentieth century the courts have held that a number of essentially personal activities are protected from governmental interference by the constitution. Complicating this is that some of these decisions did not specifically rely on a right to privacy, but instead held that under the constitution in general the state could not infringe on certain types of personal decisions, such as the choice of a foreign language to study in school, the choice of private over public education, the choice of whether or not to be sterilized, and the marriage of individuals of different races.[2] Some more recent decisions have identified the source of a right of privacy within certain constitutional provisions. However, the area remains unclear. The constitutional basis of some decisions has been the due-process-clause protection of life, liberty, or property. In others, such as the right to terminate life support systems, the Supreme Court has drawn upon a common-law right of informed consent.

CONTRACEPTION AND ABORTION

In the areas of contraception and abortion, the Supreme Court has so far held that personal decisions are protected by a constitutional privacy right. In cases beginning with a challenge to a Connecticut criminal statute forbidding the use of contraceptives and culminating in a challenge to a Texas statute criminalizing abortion, the Supreme Court has held that individuals have a constitutional privacy right to make decisions in these areas. In *Griswold v. Connecticut,* 381 U.S. 479 (1965), the Supreme Court voided a Connecticut statute making it a criminal offense to use or prescribe contraceptives. In that case, two physicians had been arrested, tried, found guilty, and fined for providing advice on preventing conception and prescribing contraceptives to married couples.

In his opinion, Justice Douglas wrote:

> The present case, then, concerns a relationship lying within the zone of privacy created by several fundamental constitutional guarantees. And it concerns a law which, in forbidding the use of contraceptives rather than regulating their manufacture or sale, seeks to achieve its goals by means having a maximum destructive impact upon that relationship. Such a law cannot stand in light of the familiar principle, so often applied by this Court, that a "governmental purpose to control or prevent activities constitutionally subject to state regulation may not be achieved by

means which sweep unnecessarily broadly and thereby invade the area of protected freedoms." Would we allow the police to search the sacred precincts of marital bedrooms for telltale signs of the use of contraceptives? The very idea is repulsive to the notions of privacy surrounding the marriage relationship. We deal with a right of privacy older than the Bill of Rights. [381 U.S. 479, 486 (1965)]

Seven years later in *Eisenstadt v. Baird*, 405 U.S. 438 (1972), the Court struck down a Massachusetts statute that, among other things, made the distribution of contraceptives and contraceptive information a criminal offense. Justice Brennan wrote: "if the right of privacy means anything, it is the right of the individual, married or single, to be free from unwarranted governmental intrusion into matters so fundamentally affecting a person as the decision whether to bear or beget a child" [405 U.S. 438, 453 (1972)].

In 1973, in *Roe v. Wade*, 410 U.S. 113 (1973), the Court was faced with a Texas statute making it a crime to procure or perform an abortion. Finding "that the right of personal privacy includes the abortion decision," the Court presented its now well-known three-trimester analysis, prohibiting state interference with the decision of a pregnant woman and her doctor for an abortion during the first stage; allowing state regulation during the second stage if reasonably related to maternal health; and permitting state regulation or proscription of third-trimester abortions when the fetus "has the capability of meaningful life outside the mother's womb" [410 U.S. 113, 163 (1973)].

The Court said:

This right of privacy, whether it be founded in the Fourteenth Amendment's concept of personal liberty and restrictions upon state action, as we feel it is, or, as the District Court determined, in the Ninth Amendment's reservation of rights to the people, is broad enough to encompass a woman's decision whether or not to terminate her pregnancy. The detriment that the State would impose upon the pregnant woman by denying this choice altogether is apparent. Specific and direct harm medically diagnosable even in early pregnancy may be involved. Maternity, or additional offspring, may force upon the woman a distressful life and future. Psychological harm may be imminent. Mental and physical health may be taxed by child care. There is also the distress, for all concerned, associated with the unwanted child, and there is the problem of bringing a child into a family already unable, psychologically and otherwise, to care for it. In other cases, as in this one, the additional difficulties and continuing stigma of unwed motherhood may be involved. [410 U.S. 113, 152 (1973)]

PRIVACY AND THE RIGHT TO DIE

More recently, courts, and especially the Supreme Court, have been more equivocal about a Fourteenth Amendment constitutional privacy right in personal decisions. One example is in right to die cases. If the beginnings of life implicate significant personal decisions and the role of the state in that decision making, so too does the termination of life. The legal context is clouded, however, in that several legal principles have been drawn upon in these decisions. In addition to a privacy right, some courts have held that common-law rights of self-determination and informed consent—generally included within the Fourteenth Amendment right to liberty—are involved. In one of the earliest decisions on termination of life support, *In re Quinlan,* 70 N.J. 10 (1976), the New Jersey Supreme Court found that Karen Quinlan, then in a persistent vegetative state, had a privacy right under both the state and federal constitutions to make a decision, if she were capable, to terminate her life support system. In her comatose state, the court held that her father could exercise her privacy right and make such a decision for her. In later decisions upholding the termination of life support systems, however, the New Jersey court has focused more upon the person's right to self-determination than on a right to privacy.[3] The U.S. Supreme Court addressed this issue in *Cruzan v. Director, Missouri Department of Health,* 497 U.S. 261 (1990). In that decision, the Court upheld a Missouri statute requiring clear and convincing evidence that a person did not wish to be maintained solely by artificial life support systems—a fairly difficult standard of proof to meet. The Court also upheld the right of Nancy Cruzan—and her parents on her behalf—to make such a decision. Rather than basing this on an individual's right to privacy, the Court relied on the common-law right of informed consent to accept or reject treatment.

In June 1997, the Supreme Court decided two cases involving challenges to state laws criminalizing assisted suicide. *Washington v. Glucksberg,* 1997 U.S. LEXIS 4039, was an appeal from a Ninth Circuit court decision invalidating a Washington statute prohibiting assisted suicide as an unconstitutional invasion of privacy. *Vacco v. Quill,* 1997 U.S. LEXIS 4038, was an appeal from a Second Circuit decision invalidating a similar New York statute on equal protection grounds. In both decisions, the Supreme Court reversed the circuit courts and upheld constitutionality of the statutes. Both were unanimous decisions in that all justices agreed the state had valid interests in promoting life and discouraging suicide, and in furthering these aims by prohibiting someone from assisting another in a suicide attempt. However, the justices differed in their views of constitutionally protected personal autonomy; four justices argued as in *Cruzan* that only a narrow range of personal decisions were protected, while several others argued that constitutional protection of individual liberty was much broader.

The Washington statute read: "Promoting a suicide attempt. (1) A person is guilty of promoting a suicide attempt when he knowingly causes or aids another person to attempt suicide. (2) Promoting a suicide is a Class C felony" [Wash. Rev. Code §9A.36.060].

Parties in the case included physicians who treat terminally ill patients and would assist them in suicide if it were legal to do so, a nonprofit organization that counsels people considering physician-assisted suicide, and terminally ill patients with cancer and AIDS who were suffering and wanted to be aided in suicide. They claimed that the statute violated their constitutional right to a physician-assisted suicide, inherent in the Fourteenth Amendment. The plaintiffs won at the trial level and before the entire circuit court. That court concluded that "the Constitution encompasses a due process liberty interest in controlling the time and manner of one's death— that there is, in short, a constitutionally-recognized 'right to die'" [*Compassion in Dying v. Washington,* 79 F.3d 790, 816 (1996)]. The circuit court held the statute unconstitutional "as applied to terminally ill competent adults who wish to hasten their deaths with medication prescribed by their physicians." During the appeal to the U.S. Supreme Court, all the terminally ill plaintiffs had died. The U.S. Supreme Court reversed. Chief Justice Rehnquist and three other justices defined the case as a challenge to the states' right to discourage suicide and a call for a broad constitutionally protected right for anyone to commit suicide:

Turning to the claim at issue here, the Court of Appeals stated that "properly analyzed, the first issue to be resolved is whether there is a liberty interest in determining the time and manner of one's death," or, in other words, "is there a right to die?" . . . As noted above, we have a tradition of carefully formulating the interest at stake in substantive-due-process cases. For example, although Cruzan is often described as a "right to die" case, we were, in fact, more precise: we assumed that the Constitution granted competent persons a "constitutionally protected right to refuse life-saving hydration and nutrition." The Washington statute at issue in this case prohibits "aiding another person to attempt suicide," and, thus, the question before us is whether the "liberty" specially protected by the Due Process Clause includes a right to commit suicide which itself includes a right to assistance in doing so. [1997 U.S. LEXIS 4039 at 35]

The Court then examined two prior decisions relied upon by those challenging the statute, *Cruzan* and *Planned Parenthood of Southeast Pennsylvania v. Casey.* "The right assumed in Cruzan . . . was not simply deduced from abstract concepts of personal autonomy. Given the common-law rule that forced medication was a battery, and the long legal tradition protecting the decision to refuse unwanted medical treatment, our assumption was entirely consistent with this Nation's history and constitutional traditions. The decision to commit suicide with the assistance of another may be just as personal and profound as the decision to refuse unwanted medical treatment, but it has never enjoyed similar legal protection. Indeed, the two acts are widely and reasonably regarded as quite distinct. In Cruzan itself, we recognized that most States outlawed assisted suicide—and even more do today— and we certainly gave no intimation that the right to refuse unwanted medical treatment could be somehow transmuted into a right to assistance in committing suicide" [1997 U.S. LEXIS 4039 at 40].

Similarly, the Court said that its *Casey* decision did not support the challenge.

Respondents also rely on Casey. There, the Court's opinion concluded that "the essential holding of Roe v. Wade should be retained and once again reaffirmed. . . ." In reaching this conclusion, the opinion discussed in some detail this Court's substantive-due-process tradition of interpreting the Due Process Clause to protect certain fundamental rights and personal decisions relating to marriage, procreation, contraception, family relationships, child rearing, and education, and noted that many of those rights and liberties involve the most intimate and personal choices a person may make in a lifetime.

The Court of Appeals, like the District Court, found Casey "highly instructive" and "almost prescriptive" for determining "what liberty interest may inhere in a terminally ill person's choice to commit suicide": "Like the decision of whether or not to have an abortion, the decision how and when to die is one of 'the most intimate and personal choices a person may make in a lifetime,' a choice 'central to personal dignity and autonomy.'" [79 F.3d, at 813–814]

By choosing this language, the Court's opinion in Casey described, in a general way and in light of our prior cases, those personal activities and decisions that this Court has identified as so deeply rooted in our history and traditions, or so fundamental to our concept of constitutionally ordered liberty, that they are protected by the Fourteenth Amendment. The opinion moved from the recognition that liberty necessarily includes freedom of conscience and belief about ultimate considerations to the observation that "though the abortion decision may originate within the zone of conscience and belief, it is more than a philosophic exercise." That many of the rights and liberties protected by the Due Process Clause sound in personal autonomy does not warrant the sweeping conclusion that any and all important, intimate, and personal decisions are so protected, and Casey did not suggest otherwise. [1997 U.S. LEXIS 4039, at 41–42]

While not foreclosing future challenges to these laws to permit physicians to assist terminally ill patients in suicide, the judges suggested such challenges had a substantial burden to overcome. In a footnote, they observed: "We emphasize that we today reject the Court of Appeals' specific holding that the statute is unconstitutional 'as applied' to a particular class. Justice Stevens agrees with this holding, but would not 'foreclose the possibility that an individual plaintiff seeking to hasten her death, or a doctor whose assistance was sought, could prevail in a more particularized challenge.' Our opinion does not absolutely foreclose such a claim. However, given our holding that the Due Process Clause of the Fourteenth Amendment does not provide heightened protection to the asserted liberty interest in ending one's life with a physician's assistance, such a claim would have to be quite different from the ones advanced by respondents here" [1997 U.S. LEXIS 4039 at 55].

PRIVACY OF SEXUAL CONDUCT

In *Stanley v. Georgia,* 394 U.S. 557 (1969), the Court held that a person's conduct in his own home was protected by a right of privacy. There the Court was faced with a case where the police had entered the defendant's house with a warrant, but then searched beyond the scope of the warrant, finding some films, playing them on the defendant's projector, and judging them to be obscene. The defendant was arrested and convicted for possessing pornography. Overturning the conviction, the Court said: "Whatever may be the justifications for other statutes regulating obscenity, we do not think they reach into the privacy of one's home. If the First Amendment means anything, it means that a State has no business telling a man, sitting alone in his own house, what books he may read or what films he may watch. Our whole constitutional heritage rebels at the thought of giving government the power to control men's minds" [394 U.S. 557, 565 (1969)].

However, in a 1986 Supreme Court decision, *Bowers v. Hardwick,* 478 U.S. 186 (1986), the Court upheld state limitations on sexual relations in the privacy of one's home. There, Hardwick was arrested for committing homosexual sodomy in the privacy of his own bedroom, despite the fact that the sexual activity was consensual and both partners were adults. According to the Georgia statute, the act of sodomy performed by any two persons, male or female, is a felony criminal offense: "(a) A person commits the offense of sodomy when he performs or submits to any sexual act involving the sex organs of one person and the mouth or anus of another. . . . (b) A person convicted of the offense of sodomy shall be punished by imprisonment for not less than one nor more than 20 years" [Georgia Code Ann. §16-6-2].

While the prohibition was not enforced against heterosexual couples, it was used against Hardwick, a homosexual. Hardwick challenged his arrest, arguing that his privacy was invaded and he, a homosexual, was being treated differently from heterosexuals. In a five to four decision, the Supreme Court upheld the statute, finding no invasion of privacy:

> We first register our disagreement with the Court of Appeals and with respondent that the Court's prior cases have construed the Constitution to confer a right of privacy that extends to homosexual sodomy and for all intents and purposes have decided this case. . . . [W]e think it evident that none of the rights announced in those cases bears any resemblance to the claimed constitutional right of homosexuals to engage in acts of sodomy that is asserted in this case. No connection between family, marriage, or procreation on the one hand and homosexual activity on the other has been demonstrated. . . . Precedent aside, however, respondent would have us announce, as the Court of Appeals did, a fundamental right to engage in homosexual sodomy. This we are quite unwilling to do. [478 U.S. 186, 190 (1986)]

Justice Blackmun, writing for the dissent, responded:

> This case is no more about "a fundamental right to engage in homosexual sodomy," as the Court purports to declare, than Stanley v. Georgia was about a fundamental right to watch obscene movies, or Katz v. United States was about a fundamental right to place interstate bets from a telephone booth. Rather, this case is about "the most comprehensive of rights and the right most valued by civilized men," namely, "the right to be let alone."
>
> The statute at issue denies individuals the right to decide for themselves whether to engage in particular forms of private, consensual sexual activity. The Court concludes that [it] is valid essentially because "the laws of . . . many States . . . still make such conduct illegal and have done so for a very long time." But the fact that the moral judgments expressed by statutes like §16-6-2 may be "natural and familiar . . . ought not to conclude our judgment upon the question whether statutes embodying them conflict with the Constitution of the United States." Like Justice Holmes, I believe that "[it] is revolting to have no better reason for a rule of law than that so it was laid down in the time

of Henry IV. It is still more revolting if the grounds upon which it was laid down have vanished long since, and the rule simply persists from blind imitation of the past." I believe we must analyze respondent Hardwick's claim in the light of the values that underlie the constitutional right to privacy. If that right means anything, it means that, before Georgia can prosecute its citizens for making choices about the most intimate aspects of their lives, it must do more than assert that the choice they have made is an "abominable" crime not fit to be named among Christians. . . . . Michael Hardwick's standing may rest in significant part on Georgia's apparent willingness to enforce against homosexuals a law it seems not to have any desire to enforce against heterosexuals. But his claim that §16-6-2 involves an unconstitutional intrusion into his privacy and his right of intimate association does not depend in any way on his sexual orientation. . . . The Court claims that its decision today merely refuses to recognize a fundamental right to engage in homosexual sodomy; what the Court really has refused to recognize is the fundamental interest all individuals have in controlling the nature of their intimate associations with others. [478 U.S. 186, 199 (1986)][4]

Personal Privacy: Freedom From Surveillance, Search, and Intrusion

SEARCH WARRANTS AND REASONABLE SEARCHES

Under common law, search warrants had to specify in detail what was to be searched and what was to be seized. However, for the American colonies in the eighteenth century the English Parliament authorized writs of assistance to enforce the Trade Acts. Under these, customs officials could search and seize property without limitation. In reaction to this, the Fourth Amendment was adopted as part of the Bill of Rights, specifying: "The right of the people to be secure in their persons, houses, papers, and effects, against unreasonable searches and seizures shall not be violated, and no Warrants shall issue, but upon probable cause, supported by Oath or affirmation, and particularly describing the place to be searched, and the persons or things to be seized." A legal search under the Fourth Amendment must be reasonable, and if a search warrant is issued by a court, it must be based upon probable cause, describing with particularity the subject of the search. Evidence obtained in an illegal search generally may not be used in a subsequent trial.[5]

The rationale for a court-issued search warrant is that the search then must be approved by an independent, unbiased authority who is not part of the state's law enforcement system. Although many searches, particularly property searches and wiretaps, are accompanied by a search warrant and have court approval, there are a number of situations where a search need not be accompanied by a search warrant. Often these warrantless searches are found reasonable because in a particular situation waiting for a warrant might result in destruction or hiding of evidence. More recently, however, there has been a judicial trend toward accepting the legality of warrantless searches of persons or property even though there was no risk of lost evidence as long as the search itself is reasonable. Included here are warrantless searches incident to a lawful arrest and warrantless searches of automobiles. In *U.S. v. Rabinowitz,* 339 U.S. 56 (1950), the Court upheld the search of a desk and file cabinet incident to an arrest although there was time to obtain a search warrant prior to the search, stating, "It is not disputed that there may be reasonable searches, incident to an arrest without a search warrant. . . . The relevant test is not whether it is reasonable to procure a search warrant but whether . . . the search was reasonable." In *Harris v. U.S.,* 390 U.S. 234 (1968), the Court upheld the introduction into evidence of an item obtained from an automobile without a search warrant, where the item was visible from outside the car—the "plain view" doctrine. In *Florida v. Bostwick,* 501 U.S. 429 (1991), the U.S. Supreme Court approved a suspicionless, warrantless search and seizure procedure used in drug interdiction, where armed investigating officers entered an interstate bus, requested identification from passengers at random, and then requested their consent to open and examine their baggage.

PROPERTY SEARCHES

The legality of many warrantless property searches, ranging from homes and offices to open fields, has turned upon the degree of invasiveness and the individual's expectation of privacy. Under common law, the privacy of one's home extended to the property within one's "curtilage," defined as "a small court, yard, garth, or piece of ground attached to a dwelling-house, and forming one enclosure with it, or so regarded by the law; the area attached to and containing a dwelling-house and its out-buildings" [*Oxford English Dictionary*, 2:1278 (1933), quoted in *California v. Ciraolo*, 474 U.S. 207, 221 n.6 (1986)].

Whether or not property lies within the curtilage depends on a number of factors. Among them, the Supreme Court has said, are proximity to the home, whether it is included in an enclosure surrounding the home, its use, and the steps taken to protect it from observation. However, "these factors are useful analytical tools only to the degree that, in any given case, they bear upon the centrally relevant consideration—whether the area in question is so intimately tied to the home itself that it should be placed under the home's 'umbrella' of Fourth Amendment protection" [*U.S. v. Dunn*, 480 U.S. 294, 301 (1987)].

Searches of property outside the homeowner's curtilage are generally permissible. Under the "open fields" doctrine, warrantless searches of property not within one's curtilage have been held to be legal, even if the property was surrounded by fences and locked gates [*Oliver v. U.S.*, 466 U.S. 170 (1984)].

Even if the property lies within the curtilage, there is no absolute protection from warrantless searches. Instead, the legality of the search will depend upon the property owner's expectation of privacy and whether that expectation is reasonable.[6] Relying again on whether or not there is an expectation of privacy, recent decisions have also upheld the warrantless search of garbage left on the street, shredded paper placed in garbage bags, and garbage cans left near a home.[7] Conversely, the Connecticut Supreme Court found the search of a homeless man's possessions, left unattended beneath a bridge where he had been living, to be unconstitutional because he had an expectation of privacy in his belongings, a closed cardboard box and a closed duffel bag [*State v. Mooney*, 588 A.2d 145 (Conn. 1991)]. In New Jersey, a federal court held that the nighttime search of a guidance counselor's desk by a school board member was illegal and actionable because of the counselor's expectation that materials in his office would remain private [*Gillard v. Schmidt*, 579 F.2d 825 (3d Cir. 1978). (See Chapter 5.)

PERSONAL SEARCHES

Individuals also have the expectation of privacy in searches of their person, but again the reasonableness of the search and the individual's expectation of privacy are critical. An important consideration for the court is the intru-siveness of the search. For example, the use of voice patterns, handwriting, fingerprints, and scrapings from fingernails obtained without warrant has been upheld as not overly intrusive.[8]

In *Schmerber v. California,* 384 U.S. 757 (1966), the Supreme Court upheld the involuntary withdrawing of a person's blood to test for blood-alcohol levels on the grounds that such a search was not unreasonable, overly intrusive, or dangerous to the health of the individual. (In compari-son, in *Winston v. Lee,* 470 U.S. 753 [1985], the court held that a surgical removal of a bullet from a suspect without his consent did constitute an il-legal search.) Governmental drug testing of urine has been upheld by courts in a number of situations that implicate public safety. Testing federal cus-toms inspectors and railway, military, law enforcement, and corrections per-sonnel have all been upheld. However, unannounced, suspicionless blanket urine testing of firemen has been found to be an illegal search. (See generally Chapter 5.)

The mandatory withdrawing of blood from convicted criminals to create a DNA data bank has been upheld in a number of cases. (See page 114.) Sus-picionless, mandatory random urine testing of grade and high school athletes—including a urine gathering procedure whereby monitors watched the children urinate—was upheld recently by the Supreme Court. (See Chapter 8.)

EAVESDROPPING AND ELECTRONIC SURVEILLANCE

In *Silverman v. United States,* 365 U.S. 505 (1961), the Supreme Court held that eavesdropping with an electronic probe that penetrated the wall of the premises occupied by the petitioner was a violation of the Fourth Amend-ment. That case established that interception of conversations reasonably intended to be private could constitute a "search and seizure," and that the examination or taking of physical property was not required.

In *Katz v. U.S.,* 389 U.S. 347 (1967), the Court held that an illegal search was conducted when the government listened to telephone conversations by attaching a listening device to the outside wall of a telephone booth. In that decision, Justice Harlan wrote a concurring opinion often quoted as estab-lishing the basis for determining whether or not a search is constitutionally acceptable: "My understanding of the rule that has emerged from prior de-cisions is that there is a twofold requirement, first that a person have exhibited an actual (subjective) expectation of privacy and, second, that the expectation be one that society is prepared to recognize as 'reasonable.' Thus a man's home is, for most purposes, a place where he expects privacy, but objects, activities, or statements that he exposes to the 'plain view' of outsiders are not 'protected' because no intention to keep them to himself has been exhibited. On the other hand, conversations in the open would not be protected against being overheard, for the expectation of privacy under the circumstances would be unreasonable" [389 U.S. 347, 360 (1967)]. (For a discussion of surveillance and searches in the workplace, see Chapter 5.)

Intentional Privacy: Preventing Unauthorized Disclosure

The third—and perhaps most tenuous—type of constitutional privacy lies in the individual's right to keep personal information private, free from disclosure by the government. The Supreme Court decision most often cited as supporting this right is *Whalen v. Roe*, 429 U.S. 589 (1977). *Whalen* was a constitutional challenge to a state law requiring that all prescriptions of certain drugs be recorded by drug, dosage, physician, and patient name and address in a centralized state computer system. The Court upheld the constitutionality of disclosing the private information:

> Even without public disclosure, it is, of course, true that private information must be disclosed to the authorized employees of the New York Department of Health. Such disclosures, however, are not significantly different from those that were required under prior law. Nor are they meaningfully distinguishable from a host of other unpleasant invasions of privacy that are associated with many facets of health care. Unquestionably, some individuals' concern for their own privacy may lead them to avoid or to postpone needed medical attention. Nevertheless, disclosures of private medical information to doctors, to hospital personnel, to insurance companies, and to public health agencies are often an essential part of modern medical practice even when the disclosure may reflect unfavorably on the character of the patient. Re-

quiring such disclosures to representatives of the State having responsibility for the health of the community, does not automatically amount to an impermissible invasion of privacy. [429 U.S. 589, 602 (1977)]

Later in the decision, the Court acknowledged the issue it was not addressing, the potential for constitutional privacy violations in computerized data collection and storage:

A final word about issues we have not decided. We are not unaware of the threat to privacy implicit in the accumulation of vast amounts of personal information in computerized data banks or other massive government files. The collection of taxes, the distribution of welfare and social security benefits, the supervision of public health, the direction of our Armed Forces, and the enforcement of the criminal laws all require the orderly preservation of great quantities of information, much of which is personal in character and potentially embarrassing or harmful if disclosed. The right to collect and use such data for public purposes is typically accompanied by a concomitant statutory or regulatory duty to avoid unwarranted disclosures. Recognizing that in some circumstances that duty arguably has its roots in the Constitution, nevertheless New York's statutory scheme, and its implementing administrative procedures, evidence a proper concern with, and protection of, the individual's interest in privacy. We therefore need not, and do not, decide any question which might be presented by the unwarranted disclosure of accumulated private data—whether intentional or unintentional—or by a system that did not contain comparable security provisions. We simply hold that this record does not establish an invasion of any right or liberty protected by the Fourteenth Amendment. [429 U.S. 589, 605 (1977)]

This concern was echoed by Justice Brennan in a concurring opinion:

What is more troubling about this scheme, however, is the central computer storage of the data thus collected. Obviously, as the State argues, collection and storage of data by the State that is in itself legitimate is not rendered unconstitutional simply because new technology makes the State's operations more efficient. However, as the example of the Fourth Amendment shows, the Constitution puts limits not only on the type of information the State may gather, but also on the means it may use to gather it. The central storage and easy accessibility of computerized data vastly increase the potential for abuse of that information, and I am not prepared to say that future developments will not demonstrate the necessity of some curb on such technology. [429 U.S. 589, 606 (1977)]

These passages are often quoted as establishing a constitutional basis for a right of informational privacy. However, they were not central to the Court's decision and legally are regarded as *dicta*—literally "words"—and are not binding on other courts.[9] Since *Whalen* in 1977, the Supreme Court has rarely dealt with the informational privacy issue.[10] A number of lower court decisions have addressed these issues, some relying on the *Whalen dicta*. Several will be reviewed here, but the social work professional and student must keep in mind that there is no final legal authority in this matter at this time, and the legal landscape could change dramatically.

In *Doe v. Borough of Barrington*, 729 F.Supp. 376 (D.N.J. 1990), a federal district court held that there was a constitutional right of privacy under *Whalen* that protected the disclosure of the plaintiff's AIDS status to the public. (See Chapter 9.) In *U.S. v. Westinghouse*, 638 F.2d 570 (3d Cir. 1980), the issue was access by a federal health agency to confidential employee medical records. The court held that the employees had a constitutional privacy interest in these records, citing the *Whalen dicta*. In determining that the government could access those records, the court balanced the competing interests:

Thus, as in most other areas of the law, we must engage in the delicate task of weighing competing interests. The factors which should be considered in deciding whether an intrusion into an individual's privacy is justified are the type of record requested, the information it does or might contain, the potential for harm in any subsequent nonconsensual disclosure, the injury from disclosure to the relationship in which the record was generated, the adequacy of safeguards to prevent unauthorized disclosure, the degree of need for access, and whether there is an express statutory mandate, articulated public policy, or other recognizable public interest militating toward access. [638 F.2d 570, 578 (1980)]

The *Westinghouse* factors have been used in some subsequent informational privacy cases to determine whether access by the state to confidential information is permissible or not. In *Woods v. White*, 689 F.Supp. 874 (W.D.Wis. 1988), a prisoner brought an action for an invasion of privacy for the wrongful release of his HIV-positive status to staff and fellow inmates. The court upheld his lawsuit, holding that an individual's privacy rights remain even though the individual is incarcerated.

The right of privacy suggested by *Whalen* was questioned in *J.P. v. De-Santi*, 653 F.2d 1080 (6th Cir. 1981). That case was a challenge to an Ohio statute that, among other things, permitted a juvenile judge to review a juvenile's social history prior to making an adjudication of delinquency and then allowed disclosure to any of fifty-five government, social, and religious agencies that belong to a "social services clearinghouse."[11] The circuit court held that there was no invasion of a constitutional privacy right, and questioned whether such a general right actually existed.

While *DeSanti* reflects a minority view, in the absence of a Supreme Court ruling directly on the issue, a constitutional right of informational privacy remains tenuous. Lower courts are relatively free to accept or reject the *Whalen dicta*, embracing an informational privacy right implicit in the constitution or finding no such right.

PRIVACY AND SOCIAL WORK

It is clear that privacy law impacts social workers—both professionals and students—as well as their patients and clients to a great extent. The concepts are broad, encompassing much of one's daily life: decisions, personal integrity, and personal information. At the same time, the legal protections of privacy are still being developed, and in computer technology, electronic surveillance, DNA testing, and life support systems, for example, the law follows rather than leads technological developments. These themes are developed in succeeding chapters.

CHAPTER FOUR

PRIVACY, CONFIDENTIALITY, *and the* SOCIAL WORKER'S ETHICAL RESPONSIBILITIES

Professional codes of ethics are prescriptive rules of conduct, describing how certain professionals should act with clients, agencies, other professionals, and the community at large. As such, they are not legally binding, although some provisions may incorporate legal requisites. (For example, the description of sexual harassment in the American Psychological Association Code of Ethics standard 1.11, which states that sexual harassment is unethical conduct, is very similar to that found in case and statutory law.)[1] A code of ethics differs from an individual's moral code in that it applies to professional rather than personal conduct, and has as its source a professional body which has established it as a set of standards for its members.

Violations of codes of ethics—unethical conduct—may be penalized by the professional association, and can result in an admonishment, a temporary suspension from practice, or an expulsion from the profession. However, conduct violating an ethical prescription need not be illegal and does not necessarily constitute a violation of law. Nonetheless, unethical conduct may form a basis for a legal action, such as malpractice, breach of contract, or breach of a fiduciary duty. Here a code of ethics may establish a standard of care against which professional performance may be compared.

Van Hoose and Kottler (1985) have identified several purposes of a code of ethics. A main function is to provide guidance for professional conduct and decision making. Another function is to legitimate the profession in the eyes of the public, and a third is to preempt governmental regulation and the imposition of external standards. A fourth function is to establish a standard by which professional conduct can be compared, either to protect professionals whose practice comports with an ethical code or to discipline professionals who violate that code.

The National Association of Social Workers (NASW) Code of Ethics states that the code serves six purposes:

1. Identifies core values of the profession.
2. Summarizes broad ethical principles that reflect core values and establishes a set of ethical standards.
3. Helps social workers to identify considerations when there is a conflict of professional obligations or there are ethical uncertainties.
4. Provides standards which can be used to hold social workers accountable to the general public.
5. Socializes practitioners new to the field.
6. Articulates standards which the profession can use to determine if social workers have engaged in unethical conduct. [NASW, 1996:2][2]

In this chapter we will first contrast standards of ethical behavior with legal requirements, making the general point that although the two overlap, they are different and may be in conflict, at times posing difficult choices for the social worker. Then the major portion of the chapter is devoted to tracing the development and change in the NASW standards for ethical conduct with respect to confidentiality and privacy. While the 1960 Code of Ethics contained two very general standards, the 1979 revised code contained at least five somewhat more specific standards. Recognizing the importance of confidentiality and privacy in social work practice, the revised 1996 code includes no less than eighteen separate provisions relating to confidentiality and privacy. The three codes are described, with particular attention given to the 1996 NASW Code of Ethics.

Codes of Ethics and the Law

It is important to remember that law and ethics are distinct—each has a separate source, each serves a different function. Consequently, while the two substantially overlap, they are not coterminous. Most professional conduct of social workers is both ethical and legal. But it is logically possible and does happen that professional conduct that is ethical can at times be illegal; that professional conduct that is unethical can nonetheless at times be perfectly legal; and, as occasionally happens, conduct by a professional may be both unethical and illegal [Dickson, 1995].

Preserving patient or client confidentiality, respecting privacy, requiring an informed consent before releasing information—all are examples of conduct that both follows ethical standards and comports with the law. Conversely, a breach of confidentiality may be both illegal and unethical. A release of confidential patient information from a federally funded substance abuse program violates legal protections and is actionable. Similarly, such conduct would be in violation of confidentiality provisions in the NASW Code of Ethics.

The other two possibilities—ethical yet illegal conduct and unethical yet legal conduct—may not be as obvious, but certainly may occur in practice. Most states have no requirement that a professional inform a patient or client about the legal limits of professional confidentiality, such as the legal requirement in all states to report suspected child abuse, or in many states the duty to breach confidentiality to protect another from harm. However, the NASW Code of Ethics includes a provision stating that it is ethical practice to inform a client wherever possible of the limits of confidentiality [NASW, Code of Ethics standard 1.07(d) (1996)]. Conduct that is ethical but nonetheless illegal can occur in the broader areas of social work practice, such as social or political action. Participation in sit-ins, disruptions, and demonstrations to take an ethical stand on an issue, such as condemning discrimination or promoting integration or social justice, is in keeping with the social work Code of Ethics, although the conduct may be in violation of law and result in fines or imprisonment. Within the confines of confidentiality and privacy, it is illegal in many states to reveal the HIV/AIDS status of a patient or client without his or her informed consent, but faced with a situation where the professional knows another is at risk and the patient or client refuses to inform the other party or change his or her high-risk behavior, the social worker may decide to warn the other party, thus violating the law.[3]

Ethical Standards
in Confidentiality and Privacy
for Social Workers

In the following discussion, we shall look at specific ethical standards of conduct for social workers as they pertain to confidentiality and privacy. The reader should keep in mind that other codes of ethics may also be applicable for those social workers who are members of more than one professional society, such as codes of ethics for marriage and family therapists, counselors, and school counselors.

In the area of confidentiality and privacy, just as the law has changed markedly in recent years, so too have ethical codes undergone major transformations. Here we will briefly review how all three versions of the NASW Code of Ethics have dealt with confidentiality and privacy. Over time, the codes of ethics have become far more detailed and far more inclusive, reflecting the complexity of law and practice in these areas.

THE 1960 NASW CODE OF ETHICS

Two of the fifteen principles in the 1960 code related to confidentiality and privacy: "I respect the privacy of the people I serve." "I use in a responsible manner information gained in professional relationships" [Wilson, 1978:232].

While unassailable as principles, neither provides much guidance to the social worker as an ethical basis for decision making. A social worker should respect privacy and use information responsibly, but beyond that both the subject addressed and the actions to be taken are not clear. Of what privacy consists is undefined; what kind of information is unclear. As important, what conduct comports with respecting privacy and how one uses this information in a responsible manner are unspecified. Presumably, disclosure of confidential client information to one who had no need to know it would be irresponsible. But harder questions are left unanswered. For example, a social worker seeking ethical guidance about what he or she should do when faced with any of the myriad difficult decisions about maintaining, using, or releasing confidential or privileged information would have found these standards of little help. Nor are the principles particularly useful as a standard to judge whether or not a social worker's conduct was ethical, since no ethically appropriate rules of conduct are specified.

THE 1979 NASW CODE OF ETHICS

The 1979 National Association of Social Workers Code of Ethics (with minor later revisions) devoted one section to confidentiality and privacy (section H), which included five provisions that dealt with revealing confidentiality information, informing clients about the limits of their confidences, providing client access to records, and obtaining clients' informed consent in certain situations. The code specified:

H. Confidentiality and Privacy—The social worker should respect the privacy of clients and hold in confidence all information obtained in the course of professional service.

1. The social worker should share with others confidences revealed by clients, without their consent, only for compelling professional reasons.
2. The social worker should inform clients fully about the limits of confidentiality in a given situation, the purposes for which information is obtained, and how it may be used.
3. The social worker should afford clients reasonable access to any official social work records concerning them.
4. When providing clients with access to records, the social worker should take due care to protect the confidences of others contained in those records.
5. The social worker should obtain informed consent of clients before taping, recording or permitting third party observation of their activities. [NASW, 1979]

Two of the provisions apply directly to confidentiality, two more to records, and one to informed consent. The first provision continues to suffer from the vagueness of its predecessor. Instead of respecting privacy and behaving in a responsible manner, the social worker should share with others confidential patient or client information without consent for unspecified "compelling professional reasons." What is involved in "sharing," who "others" might be, and what the compelling reasons might include are unknown.

The second provision is far more specific, requiring the social worker to inform the patient/client "fully" about the limits of confidentiality, the purposes of gathering information, and its future uses. This is far more useful and gives specific guidance to the social worker. However, there are some difficulties. Informing a patient or client fully about the limits of confidentiality is laudable, but probably not possible, given the complications of the law. Moreover, it is not clear when such information should be offered—at the outset of a professional relationship, when the social worker believes the client is about to make a revelation that cannot be held in confidence, or after such a revelation has been made. Moreover, there may be times when it is unwise to inform the client about the limits, for example, if the social worker feared the client would be a danger to him or her. Finally, different patients and clients will have different capacities, requiring different kinds of information if they are to understand these limits. Similarly, informing the patient or client of the future uses of the information may be an impossible task, requiring uncommon prescience on the part of the social worker.

The remaining provisions are less troublesome. The third, client access to records, is generally laudable. Note that the provision applies to "official records" and not other records the worker or agency might maintain. Note also that the provision does not address a situation where the client is a minor or a person who needs help in understanding the record, nor does it acknowledge the possibility that some clients should not have access to some records for sound practice reasons. The fourth provision protects other confidences; the fifth provides for informed consent in some situations. Again it does not address a patient or client's limited understanding or need for a guardian to make that decision.

THE 1996 NASW CODE OF ETHICS

A revised Code of Ethics was adopted by the NASW Delegate Assembly in 1996. The provisions relating to privacy and confidentiality are far more detailed than before. Eighteen separate paragraphs deal with privacy and confidentiality, including protections, limitations, disclosure, and consent, and others deal with records and their access. Along with individual clients, the provisions address confidentiality and privacy considerations when dealing with groups, families or couples, third party payors, courts, and the media. Other sections deal with privacy considerations in electronic records, e-mail, faxes, and computer transmissions.

As compared with previous versions, the code goes beyond general principles and often provides specific guidance to social workers in specific situations. For example, in standard 1.07(c), the code addresses the duty to protect and mandatory reporting limitations to confidentiality. In this, it comes close to tracking the existing law in many jurisdictions by stating that the general principle of confidentiality does not apply when "disclosure is necessary to prevent serious, foreseeable, and imminent harm to a client or other identifiable person or when laws or regulations require disclosure without a client's consent."

Standard 1.07(a) of the code provides: "Social workers should respect clients' right to privacy. Social workers should not solicit private information from clients unless it is essential to providing service or conducting social work evaluation or research. Once private information is shared, standards of confidentiality apply." This standard not only states that a client's privacy should be respected—a longtime ethical standard—but that private information should not be gathered unless it is essential to the work being done. At that point, confidentiality considerations apply.

The next two standards deal with disclosure. Standard 1.07(b) states: "Social workers may disclose confidential information when appropriate with a valid consent from a client, or a person legally authorized to consent on behalf of a client." Standard 1.07(c) elaborates on a provision in the 1979 ethics code, which stated it was ethically permissible for a social worker to reveal confidential client information "for compelling professional reasons." While the extent of such reasons remains unclear, in particular this section addresses the "duty to protect" situation. It states, in part: "The general expectation that social workers will keep information confidential does not apply when disclosure is necessary to prevent serious, foreseeable, and imminent harm to a client or other identifiable person or when laws or regulations require disclosure without a client's consent." In addition, this section cautions the social worker to strictly limit any such disclosure: "In all instances, social workers should disclose the least amount of confidential information necessary to achieve the desired purpose; only information that is directly relevant to the purpose for which the disclosure is made should be revealed" [standard 1.07(c)].

When such a disclosure does occur, the following ethical standard calls for informing the client: "Social workers should inform clients, to the extent possible, about the disclosure of confidential information and the potential consequences and, when feasible, before the disclosure is made" [standard 1.07(d)].

An important provision is found in standard 1.07(e), which states: "Social workers should discuss with clients and other interested parties the nature of confidentiality and the limitations of clients' right to confidentiality. Social workers should review with clients circumstances where confidential information may be requested and where disclosure of confidential information may be legally required. This discussion should occur as soon as possible in the social worker–client relationship and as needed throughout the course of the relationship."

As noted elsewhere in the text, this standard reflects the law in some states, and would seem to be inherent in the legal doctrine of informed consent, where a person giving an informed consent is entitled to an adequate disclosure of material facts so they can make an informed decision. (See Dickson, 1995.)

The standards also address the problems of confidentiality in settings with multiple clients—groups, couples, or families. Along with encouraging the social worker to obtain prior agreements among members about the confidential treatment of group information, the standards also acknowledge the limits of such promises of confidentiality: "Social workers should inform participants in families, couples, or group counseling that social workers cannot guarantee that all participants will honor such agreements" [standard 1.07(f)].

Standard 1.07(j) addresses the sometimes difficult ethical issue when the worker is faced with a court order to reveal confidential information: "When a court of law or other legally authorized body orders social workers to disclose confidential or privileged information without a client's consent and such disclosure could cause harm to the client, social workers should request that the court withdraw or limit the order as narrowly as possible and/or maintain the records under seal, unavailable for public inspection."

Remaining ethical provisions addressing confidentiality include prohibitions on disclosure of confidential information to third party payors without a client's consent, standard 1.07(h); prohibiting the discussion of confidential information in a variety of settings where it might be overheard, standard 1.07(i); confidentiality in responding to requests by the media, standard 1.07(k); confidentiality of records, standard 1.07(l); confidentiality in the electronic transmission of information, standard 1.07(m); disposal of records, standard 1.07(n); confidentiality protections needed when a social worker withdraws from practice, becomes incapacitated, or dies, standard 1.07(o); confidentiality issues in teaching, training, or consulting, standards 1.07(p)–(q); and confidential information of deceased clients, standard 1.07(r).

Standard 1.08 deals with access to records. Along with the general rule that clients should be allowed access to their records, standard 1.08(a) addresses the ethical—and practice—problem of when access should be limited: "Social workers who are concerned that clients' access to their records could cause serious misunderstanding or harm to the client should provide assistance in interpreting the records and consultation with the client regarding the records. Social workers should limit client access to social work records, or portions of clients' records, only in exceptional circumstances when there is compelling evidence that such access would cause serious harm to the client. Both the client's request and the rationale for withholding some or all of the record should be documented in the client's file."

This is the ethical aspect of "therapeutic privilege," a legal construct that permits the professional not to disclose information to a client or patient for sound professional reasons. (See Rozovsky, 1990; Dickson, 1995.) As a legal matter, one should carefully document what information was not disclosed and the reasons for withholding it. Another provision, standard 1.08(b), is similar to one in the 1979 code: "When providing clients with access to their records, social workers should take steps to protect the confidentiality of other individuals identified or discussed in such records."

ETHICS IN SOCIAL WORK PRACTICE

At this time, the provisions concerning privacy, confidentiality, and record keeping in the National Association of Social Workers Code of Ethics are among the most detailed of any professional group. Going beyond generalities, they give specific information on how the professional should act to deal ethically with particular situations. Students and practitioners have both an ethical and legal obligation to review these principles and incorporate them in their daily practice.

PART TWO

LAW *and* PRACTICE

Part II addresses confidentiality and privacy in a number of areas of social work practice. Chapter 5 discusses select topics in workplace privacy. Workplace privacy is a broad area, encompassing a great many issues. Here the discussion is necessarily limited, and the reader wishing other information is urged to consult the references provided. In particular, Kurt Decker's *Privacy in the Workplace: Rights, Procedures, and Policies* presents a thorough treatment of many workplace privacy issues, and Sandra Nye's *Employee Assistance Law Answer Book* contains a thorough discussion of the law in this area. Topics addressed in Chapter 5 include workplace searches and surveillance, monitoring employees on and off the job, public and private sector drug testing, sexual harassment and related limitations on speech and conduct, and confidentiality in employee assistance programs (EAPs). Searches of persons, offices, and desks and monitoring employee behavior are not limited to business and industry, but occur in state and private health and human service agencies as well, making the topic particularly salient for the social work professional and student. The privacy of electronic communications, e-mail, and computerized records is a growing concern. Drug testing is not only commonplace in business and industry but is increasing in health and social service agencies. While the legal recognition of sexual harassment is fairly recent, the behavior is not new, and has been documented in a range of health and human service agencies. Sexual harassment involves privacy considerations because the behavior impinges on a worker's personal privacy. Employee assistance programs are expanding in public and private organizations and are becoming a significant employer of social workers. Their status as part of a larger organization or as an independent contractor has implications for confidentiality and privacy.

Chapter 6 considers confidentiality and privacy in relation to files and records, a particularly salient topic today. With technological changes, particularly the growth of computer technology, the amount of information recorded, stored, and transmitted and the potential for access have grown markedly. Records and record keeping are discussed, with particular attention to client access and court-ordered access to confidential child protective service records and sexual assault victim records. The practice of maintaining dual sets of records is discussed, and several statutes that specifically permit dual record keeping are examined. The chapter then turns to disclosure of records with an informed consent, subpoenas of records, and record retention and destruction. Probably the single most important law protecting the privacy of federal government records and files is the Privacy Act of 1974. Much of the chapter discusses this law and its later amendments addressing computer matching. Although the law contains significant penalties for willful violations, it also contains exceptions that severely limit its effectiveness. Finally, the chapter addresses privacy in health records and the potential benefits and costs of developing a single lifetime record with a unique identifier for each individual receiving treatment and services. Here records in managed care and DNA data banks are examined.

Chapter 7 returns to a topic introduced earlier, the ever-troublesome duty of a social worker to breach confidentiality to protect an individual from harm. First established in the California *Tarasoff* decision, this obligation has become law for some professionals in many states, and has been extended to social workers in some jurisdictions. At the same time, the nature of the duty, when harm is foreseeable, and what must be done vary across the states. Here the discussion is limited to confidentiality and privacy issues rather than a broader discussion of the professional's standard of care or liability. Readers who wish to pursue these topics should consult the Bibliography. In particular, Michael Perlin's *Mental Disability Law: Civil and Criminal* is a comprehensive treatment.

In Chapter 8, the laws concerning minors and privacy are discussed. Here minors' decision-making rights and rights to personal and informational privacy are examined. Minors themselves as legal incompetents have only limited legal rights, and in many cases the power to make decisions or access records resides with the parent or state. Yet minors do have legal rights, and may be as able to make independent, competent decisions as are adults. This dichotomous view of minors in need of protection yet able to act independently is reflected in privacy law, which at times reinforces independent decision making, and at times refuses to recognize it. A minor's privacy rights to an abortion, to contraception, and to consent to treatment for addiction and sexually transmitted diseases are discussed in this context.

The public schools reflect the tension between a minor's ability to make decisions and the need for adult authority. The courts have held that within the public schools, minors have fewer rights than outside. Both because school issues illustrate the tensions that exist within the law and because of their importance to social workers, a significant portion of the chapter is devoted to them. First, school searches of the minor's person and property are addressed. Then the discussion turns to a particular type of search, mandatory drug testing in the public schools. In a recent decision, a majority of the U.S. Supreme Court upheld such mass testing for grade and high school students who participate in athletics, making this an exception to Fourth Amendment constitutional prohibitions of warrantless and suspicionless searches. Both majority and minority opinions are discussed.

Finally, another important topic in school privacy, educational records, is examined. Although the federal Family Educational Rights and Privacy Act (FERPA) applies to adult students as well as minors, it is included here because of its significant implications for children. Finally, minors and their confidences are addressed. At times it is possible—or even mandatory—for the social worker to keep confidential a minor's disclosures, but at times it is not. Here disclosures about child abuse or intended suicide are important areas where the social worker cannot keep a confidence but must take further action.

In Chapter 9 the complex, timely, rapidly changing topic of confidential, privacy, and persons with AIDS is addressed. Arriving late on the legal scene, subject to a variety of political pressures and public uncertainties, AIDS law presents a host of privacy and confidentiality difficulties. After briefly summarizing the incidence, prevalence, and known means of transmission of AIDS, the discussion turns to voluntary and mandatory testing for AIDS and access to test results.

Here the law is in flux, and many states have modified original AIDS confidentiality statutes to include exceptions such as mandatory testing of newborns, children going into foster care, prison inmates, and health care workers or patients. Similarly, confidential test results may be revealed to certain individuals in some states, including patients, spouses, and sexual partners. An important point made here is that merely the release of an individual's HIV-positive status may result in significant harm to that individual in terms of discrimination or loss of friends and personal contacts, and there may be significant legal liabilities attached for a wrongful release or release without informed consent.

Chapter 10 concludes the text, covering a range of social work confidentiality and privacy issues not easily categorized. The chapter is organized into two main parts, confidentiality of types of records and confidentiality with groups of individuals. For records, the chapter first examines records in federally funded substance abuse programs. Here, as many social workers are aware, are some of the most stringent privacy protections, coupled with substantial penalties for violations. The federal statute and related rules are discussed in detail. Next, confidentiality of child protective service records is examined. Long protected by confidentiality laws, these records—or parts of them—are now subject to access by attorneys and parents in some situations. One of the consequences of the strict confidentiality laws has been that it is difficult, if not virtually impossible in some states, to ascertain, amend, correct, or expunge the child abuse records, even when there has been no court finding of abuse. As the discussion shows, this can have significant consequences since some employers are required to search these confidential records before hiring a job applicant and must justify hiring an individual whose records are contained in the central registry. On the other hand, while information contained in the protective services records may have been obtained under a promise of confidentiality, a 1987 Supreme Court decision held that access to these confidential records by defendants in criminal child abuse proceedings may be permitted after a court inspection. Similarly, juvenile court records are confidential, yet here many agencies and individuals are permitted access—in one example, up to fifty-five community and state agencies. Again, correcting or expunging these records is very difficult, and in some states they may be used by employers making hiring decisions.

Then the chapter addresses confidentiality of adoption records, an area of growing controversy. Here the interests of three separate parties may collide: the birth parents, the adoptive parents, and the adoptee. The birth and adoptive parents often have been promised that the original birth certificate of the child to be adopted will remain under court seal and may have agreed to the adoption on that condition. However, the adopted child, as he or she grows to adulthood, may want or need access to information about biological parentage. While nonidentifying information has long been provided in many states, increasingly the adult adoptee's psychological need to locate birth parents has become an issue. States are grappling with this problem and have come to various formulations intended to further the privacy rights of the adoptees, yet protect the privacy of the birth parents and the original promises of confidentiality. A number of states now have systems in place where adult adoptees who wish to contact their birth parents and birth parents who want to contact their children placed for adoption can register; if there is a corresponding match, they may contact each other. Some states have instituted a more proactive system, whereby upon registration of the adult adoptee, there is an attempt by the state or agency to locate and contact the birth parent or parents to ascertain if a meeting with the birth child is acceptable. Finally, a few states have recently enacted laws that essentially void prior promises of confidentiality and permit the release of identifying information to any adult adoptee who applies.

Chapter 10 then turns to confidentiality and privacy with groups. An important part of social work is working with couples, families, or groups. While an individual patient or client often can be assured of confidentiality—with the limitations discussed throughout this book— this is less true in a multiple-person setting. A few states specifically protect confidentiality in family, joint, or group therapy, but many do not, and social workers need to make this limitation clear to their patients and clients. In the concluding part of the chapter, confidentiality in self-help groups is examined. Here legal protections are minimal, since they often would require that the leader be a professional covered by a confidentiality statute and that the information divulged be used for purposes of diagnosis and treatment. However, as in Alcoholics Anonymous, confidentiality may be a cornerstone of the self-help program. Here a social worker must make it very clear that although confidentiality is encouraged, and individuals may be morally bound to maintain it, there is little in the law to protect the confidentiality of disclosures in self-help groups.

CHAPTER FIVE

WORKPLACE PRIVACY: SELECTED ISSUES

Privacy concerns in the workplace are receiving increased attention due to technological advances, widespread testing for substance abuse, and concern over acceptable workplace speech and conduct, among other factors. While technological advances may have resulted in workplace efficiencies, they have also provided more possibilities for employee monitoring and surveillance. Concerns over substance abuse have resulted in banning drugs, alcohol, and in some cases cigarettes from the workplace, and have led to widespread drug testing of job applicants and current employees. Concern over sexual harassment in the workplace has produced policies and training designed to eradicate sexually offensive conduct and speech, but has also resulted in increased employer regulation of employees' speech and conduct both on and off the job.

Due to space limitations this chapter focuses primarily on topics particularly salient for social worker professionals and students in practice and administration: workplace searches and surveillance; monitoring employees on and off the job; public and private sector drug testing of job applicants and employees; confidentiality in employee assistance programs (EAPs); and sexual harassment and related limitations on speech and conduct. While employee surveillance, monitoring, drug testing, and sexual harassment are most often thought of as issues for business and industry, they are not uncommon in the health and human services. Employee searches, surveillance, and monitoring are increasing in mental hospitals, general hospitals, social service programs, and state agencies. Sexual harassment complaints have been filed in virtually every type of health, human service, and educational organization. Employee drug testing occurs in corrections, drug treatment programs, social service programs, and institutions, and has been proposed for various hospitals and schools.

As with many of the topics in this text, an important consideration in workplace privacy is whether the agency is public—thereby implicating U.S. constitutional privacy protections—or private, where federal constitutional limitations on governmental action do not apply, thereby allowing employers far greater latitude in testing, monitoring, and surveillance. For example, courts have held that public sector drug testing that requires an employee to urinate under observation, producing a sample which is then sent for analysis, raises Fourth Amendment search and seizure issues, and may or may not be permissible depending upon a number of factors—while similar testing in the private sector workplace is permissible under the federal constitution. However, as shall be seen, private action is not without legal limits, and may be governed by federal statutes, state statutes, or state constitutions. For example, laws limiting sexually offensive workplace behavior (sexual harassment) consist of federal and state statutes and regulations, rather than broad constitutional protections. Similarly, private sector drug testing does not implicate the federal constitution, but in some states such as California courts have held that it does come within state constitutional privacy provisions.[1] In general, however, courts have reasoned that in nongovernmental settings where the federal constitution is not involved, many privacy issues should be the subject of employer-employee negotiation and collective bargaining.

Workplace Searches, Surveillance, and Monitoring

PERSONAL SEARCHES OF EMPLOYEES

Employees have more legal protection against personal searches than property searches since searches of the body are seen as involving greater invasions of privacy.[2]

> In general, courts and arbitrators distinguish between searching people (bodily searches) and searching property. Personal or body searches are afforded more protection than property searches. In most cases, a search is acceptable if there is "reasonable suspicion," for example, where a specific individual is suspected of improper behavior. On the other hand, employers sometimes undertake random searches when a crime has been committed but no specific individual is implicated. Courts generally view a random search as a greater intrusion on an individual's Fourth Amendment rights; a more compelling employer interest is necessary to justify such searches. [Gerhart, 1995:200]

Personal searches may be upheld, however, particularly when they are reasonable, based on a reasonable suspicion, conducted with prior consent, or are an agreed-to condition of work.

SEARCHES OF OFFICES, LOCKERS, AND DESKS

> The workplace includes those areas and items that are related to work and are generally within the employer's control. At a hospital, for example, the hallways, cafeteria, offices, desks, and file cabinets, among other areas, are all part of the workplace. These areas remain part of the workplace context even if the employee has placed personal items in them, such as a photograph placed in a desk or a letter posted on an employee bulletin board. Not everything that passes through the confines of the business address can be considered part of the workplace context, however. An employee may bring closed luggage to the office prior to leaving on a trip, or a handbag or briefcase each workday. While

whatever expectation of privacy the employee has in the existence and the outward appearance of the luggage is affected by
its presence in the workplace, the employee's expectation of privacy in the contents of the luggage is not affected in the same
way. The appropriate standard for a workplace search does not
necessarily apply to a piece of closed personal luggage, a hand-
bag, or a briefcase that happens to be within the employee's business address. [*O'Connor v. Ortega* 480 U.S. 709, 715 (1987)]

Office spaces, restrooms, break rooms, and their contents are generally
the property of the employer, not the employee, and this alone may provide
a sufficient legal basis to justify a search. However, other factors may come
into play: for the employer, a reasonable suspicion for the search, such as
misfeasance, or a policy that clearly states the conditions under which
searches may take place; for the employee, a legitimate expectation of privacy. For example, if the employer specifies in a written policy that lockers,
desks, and file cabinets are the property of the employer and can be subject
to search at any time, this would support the legality of the search. Conversely, if the office space contains confidential material, such as medical or
counseling records, which may be seen or inspected only by certain other
employees, this might lead a court to find the search illegal.

Searches of property may be searches of physical property owned by the
employee—such as bags, purses, etc.—or physical property owned by the
employer but used by the employee, such as lockers, desks, office space, and
file cabinets. Property searches may also consist of searches of computer files
and databases. While there may be greater privacy protections for property
owned by the individual employee than property owned by the employer—
based on the employee's greater expectation of privacy—the Supreme Court
has noted: "Government offices are provided to employees for the sole purpose of facilitating the work of an agency. The employee may avoid expos-
ing personal belongings at work by simply leaving them at home" [480 U.S.
709, 725 (1987)].

Probably the most important court decision in workplace property
searches in the public sector is *O'Connor v. Ortega,* 480 U.S. 709 (1987),
where the U.S. Supreme Court established a standard for constitutionally
acceptable searches. Napa State Hospital, a public hospital, became concerned over possible fiscal irregularities and sexual harassment charges filed

against an employee psychiatrist, Dr. Ortega. He was placed on administrative leave while the charges were investigated. While he was on leave, several Napa employees entered Ortega's office, searched his desk and file cabinet, and removed some items, including some of a personal nature. Ortega filed suit, claiming the hospital's actions constituted an illegal search under the Fourth Amendment. The Court relied on prior decisions where searches conducted by non–law enforcement government officials (such as housing inspectors and school administrators) were found to come within Fourth Amendment requirements, and held that the actions of Napa State Hospital and its director, O'Connor, constituted a search protected by the Fourth Amendment.[3] Critical to this part of the decision was that Ortega had an expectation of privacy in his office and papers. The Court said:

> Within the workplace context, this Court has recognized that employees may have a reasonable expectation of privacy against intrusions by police. As with the expectation of privacy in one's home, such an expectation in one's place of work is "based upon societal expectations that have deep roots in the history of the Amendment. . . ."
>
> But regardless of any legitimate right of access the Hospital staff may have had to the office as such, we recognize that the undisputed evidence suggests that Dr. Ortega had a reasonable expectation of privacy in his desk and file cabinets. The undisputed evidence discloses that Dr. Ortega did not share his desk or file cabinets with any other employees. Dr. Ortega had occupied the office for 17 years and he kept materials in his office, which included personal correspondence, medical files, correspondence from private patients unconnected to the Hospital, personal financial records, teaching aids and notes, and personal gifts and mementos. The files on physicians in residency training were kept outside Dr. Ortega's office. Indeed, the only items found by the investigators were apparently personal items because, with the exception of the items seized for use in the administrative hearings, all the papers and effects found in the office were simply placed in boxes and made available to Dr. Ortega. Finally, we note that there was no evidence that the Hospital had established any reasonable regulation or policy discouraging employees such

as Dr. Ortega from storing personal papers and effects in their desks or file cabinets, although the absence of such a policy does not create an expectation of privacy where it would not otherwise exist.[4] [480 U.S. 709, 715–717 (1987)]

Having determined that the Fourth Amendment was applicable, the Court then addressed the requirements of a search warrant and probable cause. The Court held that as in a number of other non–law enforcement situations, a search warrant requirement was unreasonable and unnecessary. Similarly, as in its *New Jersey v. T.L.O.* decision (see page 182), the Court dispensed with the probable cause standard, holding that the standard should be whether the search was "reasonable."

A determination of reasonableness, the Court said, has two dimensions: whether the search was justified to begin with ("justified at its inception"), and whether the search that was conducted was reasonably related to its initial purpose:

> Ordinarily, a search of an employee's office by a supervisor will be "justified at its inception" when there are reasonable grounds for suspecting that the search will turn up evidence that the employee is guilty of work-related misconduct, or that the search is necessary for a noninvestigatory work-related purpose such as to retrieve a needed file. Because petitioners had an "individualized suspicion" of misconduct by Dr. Ortega, we need not decide whether individualized suspicion is an essential element of the standard of reasonableness that we adopt today. The search will be permissible in its scope when "the measures adopted are reasonably related to the objectives of the search and not excessively intrusive in light of . . . the nature of the [misconduct]." [480 U.S. 709, 726 (1987)]

Since the case came to the Supreme Court as an appeal prior to trial testimony, the Court returned it to the trial court for a determination whether or not the search was reasonable under the Court's standard.

In *Gillard v. Schmidt,* 579 F.2d. 825 (3rd Cir. 1978), a board of education member entered a guidance counselor's locked office at night and searched the counselor's desk for evidence that the counselor had drawn a cartoon critical of the board. The counselor sued. The circuit court reversed a lower court dismissal of the action, holding that the counselor had an expectation of privacy:

> As a guidance counselor, Gillard dealt daily with students' private, personal problems. Working in an office secured by a locked door at a desk containing psychological profiles and other confidential student records, Gillard had a reasonable expectation that papers in his desk would remain safe from prying eyes. Gillard's privacy expectation was by no means atypical, for as the Fair Lawn Superintendent of Schools testified at trial: "Speaking not only as superintendent of schools, but as a former teacher, my desk as a teacher was probably the only place within the classroom or within a department that you could keep private. . . . I think it is reasonable for any teacher or any administrator to assume that if they would put something in their desk, that it would be for their eyes only and not accessible to anyone else. . . ."
>
> We therefore hold that a guidance counselor, charged with maintaining sensitive student records, in the absence of an accepted practice or regulation to the contrary, enjoys a reasonable expectation of privacy in his school desk. Defendant's contention that Gillard cannot claim a fourth amendment violation because the desk belonged to the school system is unsupported by the case law. Applicability of the fourth amendment does not turn on the nature of the property interest in the searched premises, but on the reasonableness of the person's privacy expectation. [579 F.2d 825, 828 (1978)]

The legality of private sector searches, not protected by the Fourth Amendment, still involves balancing employer interests with employee expectations of privacy. For example, in *K-Mart v. Trotti,* 677 S.W.2d 632 (Tex.Ct.App. 1984), the employer conducted an unannounced search of employee lockers, including a search of Trotti's locker—which was locked with her own padlock—and her purse and personal belongings within it. Although the appellate court reversed a jury award of $8,000 in actual damages and $100,000 in exemplary (punitive) damages because of faulty instructions by the trial judge, the court indicated that with proper instructions an invasion of privacy claim could be successful:

> The lockers undisputably were the appellants' [K-Mart's] property, and in their unlocked state, a jury could reasonably infer that those lockers were subject to legitimate, reasonable searches by the appellants. This would also be true where the employee used a lock provided by the appellants, because in retaining the lock's combination or master key, it could be inferred that the appellants manifested an interest both in maintaining control over the locker and in conducting legitimate, reasonable searches. Where, as in the instant case, however, the employee purchases and uses his own lock on the lockers, with the employer's knowledge, the fact finder is justified in concluding that the employee manifested, and the employer recognized, an expectation that the locker and its contents would be free from intrusion and interference. . . . It is sufficient that an employee in this situation, by having placed a lock on the locker at the employee's own expense and with the appellant's consent, has demonstrated a legitimate expectation to a right of privacy in both the locker itself and those personal effects within it. [677 S.W.2d 632, 638 (1984)][5]

Finally, even if the search is justifiable, the employer must be careful that the search doesn't extend beyond the items searched for and intrude into private matters.

EMPLOYEE SURVEILLANCE AND MONITORING

"Surveillance" and "monitoring" here refer to the various means used by employers to observe, listen to, and record employee performance and behavior. While supervisors have traditionally monitored employees by direct visual or aural means, modern technology has expanded the means of surveillance to include video cameras; tape recorders; and electronic monitoring of telephones, data transmission, files, and computer screens, to name only a few. An employee may or may not be aware of the surveillance, and the surveillance may occur at the workstation or away from it, perhaps in hallways, elevators, dining rooms, or restrooms.

Employer surveillance of employees on the job has long been used to prevent theft, monitor production, and insure quality. Such surveillance generally has been found acceptable by courts, particularly if the employee knows that the surveillance is taking place. "Surveillance is not actionable if conducted in a 'reasonable and non-obtrusive manner'" [Cavico, 1993:1285]. However, unreasonable surveillance was found in *State of Hawaii v. Bonnell*, 856 P.2d 1265 (Haw. 1993), where employees were unaware they were being videotaped. Acting on anonymous reports of gambling by postal employees, a postal inspector with local police secretly installed four video cameras in the post office, including one in a smoke detector in an employee break room. Employees were videotaped 24 hours a day over an entire year, and three employees were prosecuted for misdemeanor gambling charges. The Hawaii Supreme Court upheld a lower court decision not to allow the videotapes into evidence, basing its decision on the Fourth Amendment and an employee expectation of privacy in the break room. The court said: "To measure the government's intrusion we must consider the expectations of society. We agree with the United States Court of Appeals for the Fifth Circuit that 'this type of surveillance provokes an immediate negative visceral reaction: indiscriminate video surveillance raises the specter of the Orwellian state. . . .' And we likewise believe it to be 'unarguable that television surveillance is exceedingly intrusive . . . and inherently indiscriminate, and that it could be grossly abused'" [856 P.2d 1265, 1276 (1993)].[6]

To avoid liability, Decker suggests the following guidelines for employers wishing to conduct employee surveillance:

1. review applicable federal or state statutes regulating the proposed surveillance;
2. ensure that the surveillance is job-related;
3. clearly notify employees that they may be subject to surveillance;
4. obtain employee's written consent to surveillance as a condition of employment;
5. disclose to employees what mechanical, electronic, or other devices may be used for surveillance;
6. disclose to employees when, where, and how these mechanical, electronic, or other devices may be used for surveillance. [Decker, 1994: sec. 6:20]

Electronic Monitoring. More complex, perhaps, is electronic workplace surveillance in the computer age.

MacWorld recently described a survey of executives at 301 American companies concerning employee monitoring and surveillance. The survey revealed that twenty-two percent of firms reported engaging in searches of employee computer files, voice mail, e-mail, and other forms of networked communications; in companies with one thousand or more employees, the proportion of respondents engaging in such conduct rose to thirty percent. *MacWorld* estimated that approximately twenty million workers were subject to electronic computer monitoring. The survey further found that only eighteen percent of all respondents reported having written policies regarding electronic privacy for employees, indicating that most employees have no idea how, when, where, or for what purposes their supervisor may be monitoring them. [Gerhart, 1995:175]

Technological advances, particularly the computerization of the workplace, have presented many new challenges to privacy. In addition to video surveillance, electronic monitoring may include "service observation" ("the practice of electronically monitoring employee job performance—most common through the use of telephones or other listening devices") and "computer-based monitoring" ("the practice of monitoring an employee's computer screen as he or she works and collecting data about the employee's work performance for later review") [Jenero and Mapes-Riordan, 1992:72].

At present, the law is only beginning to address recent developments in electronic surveillance and monitoring. Along with Fourth Amendment protections—which apply only in case of governmental surveillance—the only federal law that applies to electronic monitoring of employees is a federal anti-wiretap statute, amended by the Electronic Communications Privacy Act (ECPA), 18 U.S.C. §§2510–2520, which provides for criminal penalties and civil liability for anyone who "intentionally intercepts, endeavors to intercept, or procures any other person to intercept or endeavor to intercept, any wire, oral or electronic communication." While violations can be penalized by fines exceeding $10,000, along with compensatory damages, punitive damages, and attorneys' fees, the act has important exceptions that limit its effectiveness.

The statute primarily deals with unauthorized access to electronic communications by outsiders, rather than employers. In addition, it contains exceptions that allow access when (1) there is consent by one of the parties; (2) providers of the electronic service need to monitor their lines for adequate service; and (3) the interception is "in the ordinary course of business." In general, where monitoring was conducted for a business purpose and personal calls were not listened to, the monitoring has been upheld as within the "ordinary course of business" exception. When the monitoring has extended to listening to personal conversations, violations have been found.[7]

Privacy of Employee E-mail. "Recent estimates speculate that more than twenty million Americans regularly use E-mail at work, with E-mail being used in some capacity by all Fortune 1000 companies and by seventy-five percent of all large companies in America. Commentators predict that by the year 2000, an estimated forty million users will send sixty billion E-mail messages a year. Especially in companies in which much work is performed on computers, E-mail has become a strategic communications backbone" [Natt Gantt, 1995:348].

While various federal statutes limit access to telephone or U.S. mail communications, none currently applies directly to e-mail. In that business e-mail has become a routine mode of communication, an employer might reasonably argue that it should be accessible for business reasons—to insure accuracy, to insure that the communication took place, to insure that it was sent to an appropriate party, and to insure that an employee's e-mail is not being used for nonbusiness or illegal purposes which might harm the business. Conversely, an employee might reasonably argue that it is a legitimate means of communication, much like telephone or regular mail, and for another to access it without notice and permission is a clear violation of privacy. To date, what little law there is seems to support the business necessity approach, particularly if the employer makes clear that e-mail is not private and may be accessed.

While various federal statutes limit access to telephone conversations or U.S. mail, the only one that arguably applies to e-mail is the aforementioned Electronic Communications Privacy Act, 18 U.S.C. §§2510–2520. E-mail is not specifically mentioned, but the act applies to electronic communications, defined as "any transfer of signs, signals, writing, images, sounds, data, or intelligence of any nature transmitted in whole or part by a wire, radio, electromagnetic, photoelectronic, or photooptical system that affects interstate or foreign commerce" [18 U.S.C. §2510(12)]. Assuming e-mail comes within this definition, one limitation is that the statute applies only to a communication that "affects interstate or foreign commerce." This might exclude from coverage an e-mail system solely within an organization, but presumably would include e-mail carried by the large Internet providers.[8]

Other previously discussed exceptions to the ECPA would apply as well: the prior consent exception, where consent by one of the parties would be sufficient for the employer to read e-mail; and the business use exception, allowing employer access with a business justification. To date, the law seems to support these exceptions, particularly if it is clear that employee e-mail is not private and is subject to inspection by the employer.[9] An employee's expectation of privacy could be a countervailing factor. Where an employee is allowed to select her or his own password or is otherwise assured confidentiality, this might lead to a reasonable expectation of privacy. Conversely, if the employer keeps a directory of passwords and routinely makes backup copies of all computer work products, and employees are so informed, this would diminish any privacy expectation.

Privacy and Employee Off-Duty Conduct. As we have seen, in the workplace an employer may make significant intrusions into a worker's privacy as long as they meet the standard of reasonableness. While most off-duty employee conduct is beyond the purview of employers—as indeed probably most employers would prefer—at times, employers do have a stake, and a legal right, in controlling employee off-duty conduct. Since a positive drug test may result from the presence of a substance used days or weeks earlier—typical of marijuana, for instance—the test may function more as a measure of employee off-duty behavior than current conduct. Recently, employer concerns about smoking have been expanded from a smoke-free workplace to rewards for employees not smoking away from the workplace, in the belief that this will reduce employer medical expenses.

In other areas of employee off-duty behavior, the law is less clear. Surveillance of off-duty employees has been upheld when there was a reasonable suspicion of fraudulent conduct or malingering, as long as the surveillance was of public behavior—that which was apparent to anyone. Depending on the type of work, a conviction of a crime away from the workplace could be cause for employer dismissal of an employee on the grounds that the unfavorable publicity would harm the organization. Depending on work rules, an employee who violates them in off-duty conduct may be disciplined or dismissed. If an agency has a policy that employees

may not date residents or former clients, a dismissal based on these rules—
if they are reasonable—would probably be upheld.

In *Patton v. J. C. Penney,* 719 P.2d 854 (Ore. 1986), the Oregon court upheld the dismissal of an employee because he dated a co-worker. Basing the
decision on the concept that one who is an "employee at will" can be discharged for any reason or no reason, except for a discriminatory or illegal
reason, the court said:

> Even if defendant fired plaintiff for refusing to break off a rela-
> tionship with a co-employee and this was intended to, and in fact
> did, inflict severe emotional distress, the act of firing is not be-
> yond the bounds of socially acceptable behavior. We have just
> held that the act of discharging the plaintiff because his supervi-
> sor did not approve of plaintiff's private relationship with a co-
> employee is not actionable on a theory of wrongful discharge.
>
> Of course, the fact that an act is lawful does not mean that it
> is not actionable if the legal right is improperly manipulated or
> abused. But here, the employer had the right to discharge the em-
> ployee at will; he warned the employee that he would be dis-
> charged if he pursued a private right and he did in fact discharge
> him. This may be bad conduct or offensive conduct, but it is not
> an "extraordinary transgression of the bounds of socially tolera-
> ble" behavior. Private employers who engage in the free enter-
> prise system and risk their own capital can fire employees at any
> time and at will. [719 P.2d 854, 857 (1986)]

In a case where the employer had a written policy of noninterference in
employee off-duty conduct as long as it did not affect workplace performance, a court upheld a substantial damage award to an employee who was
fired because she refused to break off a relationship with a former employee
who had left for a job with a competitor. The company had argued that the
relationship constituted a conflict of interest and as such dismissal was appropriate [*Rulon-Miller v. I.B.M.,* 162 Cal.App.3d 241 (1984)].

Substance Abuse Testing
in the Workplace

The growing concern over alcoholism and drug abuse has had a significant impact on workplace privacy. While mandatory substance abuse testing for some groups, such as members of the armed forces, has been in effect for some time, only recently has widespread testing of employees and job applicants become a common practice.[10] A major impetus to mandatory drug testing of federal employees came from President Reagan's Executive Order No. 12,564, calling for a "drug-free federal workplace" [51 *Fed. Reg.* 32,889 (Sept. 17, 1986)]. This order required federal executive department agencies to establish drug testing programs for certain employees, including those in "sensitive positions." As various agencies developed drug testing policies, many were challenged as invasions of privacy, usually on the grounds that they constituted illegal government searches under the Fourth Amendment. Within the Fourth Amendment context, governmental employees argued that the drug tests constituted warrantless and unreasonable searches, and were not based on probable cause or even a reasonable suspicion that drug abuse had occurred. The government argued that search warrants for drug tests were unnecessary, the tests were not invasive, were required for public safety, and were a reasonable accommodation in light of the widespread use of alcohol and drugs across the country.

DRUG TESTS AND THE TESTING PROCESS

The United States Supreme Court has observed: "There are few activities in our society more personal or private than the passing of urine. Most people describe it by euphemisms if they talk about it at all. It is a function traditionally performed without public observation; indeed, its performance in public is generally prohibited by law as well as social custom" [*Skinner v. Railway Labor Executives' Ass'n*, 489 U.S. 602, 617 (1989)]. While different testing procedures are in use, the Supreme Court described those used by the federal government to test customs agents:

> On reporting for the test, the employee must produce photographic identification and remove any outer garments, such as a coat or a jacket, and personal belongings. The employee may produce the sample behind a partition, or in the privacy of a

bathroom stall if he so chooses. To ensure against adulteration of the specimen, or substitution of a sample from another person, a monitor of the same sex as the employee remains close at hand to listen for the normal sounds of urination. Dye is added to the toilet water to prevent the employee from using the water to adulterate the sample.

Upon receiving the specimen, the monitor inspects it to ensure its proper temperature and color, places a tamper-proof custody seal over the container, and affixes an identification label indicating the date and the individual's specimen number. The employee signs a chain-of-custody form, which is initialed by the monitor, and the urine sample is placed in a plastic bag, sealed, and submitted to a laboratory.

The laboratory tests the sample for the presence of marijuana, cocaine, opiates, amphetamines, and phencyclidine. Two tests are used. An initial screening test uses the enzyme-multiplied-immunoassay technique (EMIT). Any specimen that is identified as positive on this initial test must then be confirmed using gas chromatography/mass spectrometry (GC/MS). [489 U.S. 656, 661 (1989)]

When the combination of EMIT and gas chromatography tests is used, the results are apparently quite accurate in indicating the presence of certain drugs in the body [O'Donnell, 1988]. However, unlike blood alcohol level testing, which shows current impairment, drug testing will indicate minute traces of drugs consumed days or weeks before. Justice Marshall in his dissent in *Skinner* wrote: "The majority also overlooks needlessly intrusive aspects of the testing process itself. Although the FRA [the federal agency] requires the collection and testing of both blood and urine, the agency concedes that mandatory urine tests—unlike blood tests—do not measure current impairment and therefore cannot differentiate on-duty impairment from prior drug or alcohol use which has ceased to affect the user's behavior. See 49 C.F.R. §219.309(2) (urine test may reveal use of drugs or alcohol as much as 60 days prior to sampling)" [489 U.S. 602, 651 (1989)].

Thus rather than indicating current drug use, the test may be an indicator of previous off-duty conduct which may have no bearing on current behavior. Another problem with drug testing is that the urinalysis may be used to test for other medications or other conditions. Justice Marshall observed in *Skinner*:

> Technological advances have made it possible to uncover, through analysis of chemical compounds in these fluids, not only drug or alcohol use, but also medical disorders such as epilepsy, diabetes, and clinical depression. As the Court of Appeals for the District of Columbia Circuit has observed: "[S]uch tests may provide Government officials with a periscope through which they can peer into an individual's behavior in her private life, even in her own home." The FRA's requirement that workers disclose the medications they have taken during the 30 days prior to chemical testing further impinges upon the confidentiality customarily attending personal health secrets. [489 U.S. 602, 647 (1989)]

In addition, the tests may be unable to differentiate between illegal drug use and consumption of poppy seeds, some herbal teas, and legitimate medications.[11]

PUBLIC SECTOR DRUG TESTING

The U.S. Supreme Court decided two workplace drug testing cases in 1989, upholding the tests in most respects. In *Skinner v. Railway Labor Executives' Ass'n*, 489 U.S. 602 (1989), the Court upheld federal regulations mandating breath and urine testing of railway employees who were involved in accidents or violated certain safety rules. In its decision, the Court held that the Fourth Amendment did apply to a private employer drug testing program where the government had required its implementation. Citing governmental statistics pointing to twenty-one serious railway accidents in twelve years where alcohol or drug abuse may have been a factor, the Court concluded that there was a valid governmental interest in insuring safety which justified prohibiting employees from using drugs or alcohol on duty or while subject to being called for duty. The Court went on to hold that in these instances, a search warrant was unnecessary, as was a requirement that there be a suspicion of drug abuse before testing.

Although the collection of urine could be seen as an invasion of privacy, the Court said workers in the heavily regulated railroad industry had diminished expectations of privacy: "More importantly, the expectations of privacy of covered employees are diminished by reasons of their participation in an industry that is regulated pervasively to ensure safety, a goal dependent, in substantial part, on the health and fitness of covered employees" [489 U.S. 602, 627 (1989)].

Thus in *Skinner,* the Court held that governmentally mandated private sector drug testing was reasonable within the Fourth Amendment—although there was no suspicion of abuse by a particular person—based on special needs, primarily safety considerations, the degree of governmental regulation, and the limited intrusion of the tests.

In *Treasury Employees v. Von Raab,* 489 U.S. 656 (1989), decided the same day, the Court upheld a U.S. Customs drug testing program for those employees involved in drug interdiction or law enforcement and those carrying firearms:

> We think Customs employees who are directly involved in the interdiction of illegal drugs or who are required to carry firearms in the line of duty likewise have a diminished expectation of privacy in respect to the intrusions occasioned by a urine test. Unlike most private citizens or government employees in general, employees involved in drug interdiction reasonably should expect effective inquiry into their fitness and probity. Much the same is true of employees who are required to carry firearms. Because successful performance of their duties depends uniquely on their judgment and dexterity, these employees cannot reasonably expect to keep from the Service personal information that bears directly on their fitness. While reasonable tests designed to elicit this information doubtless infringe some privacy expectations, we do not believe these expectations outweigh the Government's compelling interests in safety and in the integrity of our borders. [489 U.S. 656, 672–677 (1989)]

In 1989, the Drug Free Work Place Act, 41 U.S.C. §701, went into effect. The act applies to certain federal contractors and direct recipients of federal grants, and requires those who are covered to agree to provide a drug-free workplace. The act calls for workplace drug information, drug awareness programs, and notification to employers of employees' criminal drug convictions occurring at work. However, the act does not require workplace drug testing or even prohibit workers from coming to work under the influence of drugs.

Over time, a number of federal and state statutes and regulations requiring either random or mass testing of applicants or current employees in various occupations have been upheld, including airline employees [*Bluestein v. Skinner*, 908 F.2d 451 (9th Cir. 1990)]; civilian defense department employees who carry weapons, are firefighters or nurses, or handle hazardous waste [*Plane v. U.S.*, 750 F.Supp. 1358 (W.D. Mich. 1990)]; corrections employees [*Taylor v. O'Grady*, 888 F.2. 1189 (7th Cir. 1989)]; jockeys and related horse-racing employees [*Shoemaker v. Handel*, 795 F.2d 1136 (3d Cir. 1989), *Dimeo v. Griffin*, 943 F.2d 679 (7th Cir. 1991)]; and mass transit personnel [*Burka v. New York City Transit Auth.*, 739 F.Supp. 814 (S.D.N.Y. 1990)]. Some courts have upheld testing of police and firefighters, relying on public safety needs; others have found such testing unconstitutional invasions of privacy.[12]

In *Kemp v. Claiborne County Hospital*, 763 F.Supp. 1362 (S.D.Miss. 1991), the court upheld mass testing of all county hospital employees who had patient contact on the grounds that they were in safety-related "sensitive positions." Kemp, who functioned at times as a "scrub tech," was dismissed because she refused to totally undress as part of the testing procedure. The court observed that being a scrub tech

> . . . involves direct, hands-on patient care, including bringing the patient from the hospital room to the operating room for surgery and being present and assisting during surgery. . . . The undisputed described tasks of Plaintiff in her capacity as a scrub tech in surgery mandates that her position be deemed "safety sensitive." An employee responsible for bringing a patient from his hospital room to the operating room whose judgment is impaired by drugs or alcohol could do irremediable harm by allowing such patient to fall from the gurney or operating table. Even under the supervision of a physician and registered nurse, a scrub tech could cause harm to a patient which could not be rectified. Examples would be bumping the surgeon or patient at a

critical moment during the surgery or the failure to properly count surgical sponges or instruments. [763 F.Supp 1362, 1367 (1991)]

Courts have held that mandatory drug testing of federal prosecutors, schoolteachers, state employees, county health inspectors, and postal workers, among others, is unconstitutional generally because there is no risk to public safety.[13] For example, in *American Postal Workers Union v. Frank,* 725 F.Supp. 87 (D. Mass. 1989) (reversed on other grounds, 968 F.2d 1373 (1992), the court found that mandatory testing of all applicants for postal positions did not fall within the Supreme Court's highly regulated, public safety rationale for worker testing. (While the testing was for research purposes, any applicants testing positive who were hired would be closely monitored.)

The Supreme Court predicated both Skinner and Von Raab on the government's compelling need to protect public safety within the highly regulated industry of railroads, and to maintain the integrity of the United States Customs Service. That is not the case here. The United States Postal Service is not a highly regulated industry like the railroads. We are not dealing here with the compelling need to provide safe public transportation. Major accidents with high fatalities just do not occur within the Postal Service. Although some of plaintiff union members do operate special delivery crafts, and others maintain vehicles which requires precision and alertness, the government does not set forth a good enough reason to intrude upon each applicant's privacy interests. APWU workers are not required to carry firearms, nor are they involved in drug interdiction. Furthermore, a review of the law, albeit scanty, on the distinction between prospective employees and current employees does not convince me that job applicants should be accorded lesser Fourth Amendment protections. In addition, urinalysis drug screening when part of a medical examination is not doctrinally distinct from a compelled urinalysis. In sum, I simply cannot extend the breadth of the recent Supreme Court decisions to persons seeking employment in an industry such as the Postal Service for the sake of research. [725 F.Supp. 87, 89 (1989)][14]

PRIVATE SECTOR DRUG TESTING

In a 1993 survey by the American Management Association of 630 major companies, 85 percent reported they tested job applicants for drug use [Norwood, 1994:734]. Since the testing occurs in the private sector, Fourth Amendment constitutional prohibitions on governmental searches are not involved. A private sector employer can refuse to hire an applicant or, if the workers are legally employees at will, can discharge an employee for no reason or any reason, as long as it is not a discriminatory reason or in retaliation for legally protected conduct. Thus private sector employers have significant freedom to refuse to hire or to fire employees who either refuse to take drug tests or fail them.

However, there are some limits. A number of states have enacted drug testing laws, which range from significantly limiting private sector testing to generally endorsing it. In general, tests of job applicants, tests in safety-sensitive positions, or tests where there is a reasonable suspicion of drug abuse are more likely to be permitted. Mandatory mass or random testing of current employees who are not in safety-sensitive positions, where there is no reasonable suspicion of drug abuse, is more likely to be prohibited. Rhode Island typifies states restricting drug testing;[15] Florida is typical of states generally permitting private sector testing.[16] In addition, some state constitutional privacy protections may impact private sector testing, and in a few instances courts have looked to broader public policy considerations. Several recent decisions are indicative of these issues. In *Wilkinson v. Times Mirror,* 264 Cal.Rptr. 194 (Cal.App. 1989), the California appellate court held that mandatory testing of private sector job applicants was not a violation of the California constitution privacy provisions. The court wrote in part:

> When selecting employees, private employers must comply with applicable federal and state statutes prohibiting discrimination based on race, color, religion, sex, national origin, age, physical handicap, or medical condition. Subject to these and other statutory restrictions, however, a private employer has considerable discretion in setting job-related hiring standards. A private employer unquestionably has a legitimate interest in a drug- and alcohol-free work environment, and in excluding from employment those individuals whose drug and alcohol use may affect their job performance or threaten harm to themselves. . . .

. . . [W]e hold that Matthew Bender does not violate article I, section 1 of the California Constitution when it asks job applicants to consent to a urinalysis which tests for alcohol and other drugs as a condition of a job offer, given the notice provided to prospective employees of the testing program, the limited intrusiveness of the collection process, and the procedural safeguards which restrict access to the test results. [264 Cal.Rptr. 194, 205 (1989)]

The Matthew Bender drug testing was for applicants who sought work as legal writers and copy editors. In that decision and in others, factors that courts considered in approving testing have included advance notice, privacy and confidentiality protections, limiting the testing to specific drugs, and minimal intrusiveness of the testing procedures. Public and worker safety considerations were particularly important to courts upholding company dismissals of workers in oil drilling, machine tool, and refinery work who refused to submit to drug testing.[17]

Substance abuse testing is a growing phenomenon in the workplace, for both public and private employees. Public sector testing is more limited in scope, since constitutional privacy protections are implicated. However, under the special needs doctrine of the Supreme Court, an increasing number of public sector substance abuse programs are being upheld despite the fact there is no reasonable suspicion for the testing. Private sector drug testing is more pervasive, but recently is being limited in some states by statutory law or court decisions that find it in violation of state constitutional law or perhaps, more broadly, in violation of public policy. Other issues that have been raised are the accuracy of the testing, the degree to which a person's privacy is invaded by the testing, the use of the results, the reasonableness of the testing program, whether the testing is mass or random, for only new hires or everyone, and whether the positions being tested for are particularly in need of individuals who don't have a drug problem.

Other Workplace Testing

Job applicant polygraph testing is forbidden by federal law; however, when there is a reasonable suspicion, polygraph testing of current employees is permissible.[18] Psychological testing may or may not be acceptable. In *Soroka v. Dayton Hudson Corp.*, 1 Cal.Rptr.2d 77 (1991), applicants for a position of store security officer (SSO) were required to take a psychological test that included questions about religious beliefs and sexual orientation:

> The test includes questions about an applicant's religious attitudes, such as: "67. I feel sure that there is only one true religion.... 201. I have no patience with people who believe there is only one true religion.... 477. My soul sometimes leaves my body.... 483. A minister can cure disease by praying and putting his hand on your head.... 486. Everything is turning out just like the prophets of the Bible said it would.... 505. I go to church almost every week.... 506. I believe in the second coming of Christ.... 516. I believe in a life hereafter.... 578. I am very religious (more than most people).... 580. I believe my sins are unpardonable.... 606. I believe there is a God.... 688. I believe there is a Devil and a Hell in afterlife."
>
> The test includes questions that might reveal an applicant's sexual orientation, such as: "137. I wish I were not bothered by thoughts about sex.... 290. I have never been in trouble because of my sex behavior.... 339. I have been in trouble one or more times because of my sex behavior.... 466. My sex life is satisfactory.... 492. I am very strongly attracted by members of my own sex.... 496. I have often wished I were a girl. (Or if you are a girl) I have never been sorry that I am a girl.... 525. I have never indulged in any unusual sex practices.... 558. I am worried about sex matters.... 592. I like to talk about sex.... 640. Many of my dreams are about sex matters."

The California appellate court found the test was a violation of the applicants' privacy under the California constitution:

While Target unquestionably has an interest in employing emotionally stable persons to be SSO's, testing applicants about their
religious beliefs and sexual orientation does not further this interest. To justify the invasion of privacy resulting from use of the
Psychscreen, Target must demonstrate a compelling interest and
must establish that the test serves a job-related purpose. In its
opposition to Soroka's motion for preliminary injunction, Target
made no showing that a person's religious beliefs or sexual orientation have any bearing on the emotional stability or on the
ability to perform an SSO's job responsibilities. It did no more
than to make generalized claims about the Psychscreen's relationship to emotional fitness and to assert that it has seen an
overall improvement in SSO quality and performance since it implemented the Psychscreen. This is not sufficient to constitute a
compelling interest, nor does it satisfy the nexus requirement.
Therefore, Target's inquiry into the religious beliefs and sexual
orientation of SSO applicants unjustifiably violates the state constitutional right to privacy. [1 Cal.Rptr.2d 77, 86 (1991)]

Confidentiality and Privacy in Employee Assistance Programs (EAPs)

With the rapid growth of employee assistance programs across the public
and private sectors, there has been a corresponding increased interest in
confidentiality and privacy in these programs. Nye observes: "confidentiality is a sine qua non in employee assistance; an EAP simply cannot function
if its clients cannot be assured that information about their personal affairs
will not be divulged" [Nye, 1990:21].

As an outgrowth of occupational alcohol programs, EAPs have become
widespread following federal drug-free workplace legislation [Nye,
1990:2–5]. While substance abuse remains a major focus, EAPs today may
address a diverse set of employee problems ranging from mental and emotional problems, including stress at home or on the job, to eating disorders,
nicotine addiction, and a range of other health problems.

EAPs may be internal, constituting a program or unit within the agency or business, or may be external, either free-standing or part of another entity such as a social service agency or a hospital. This organizational auspice may have ramifications for EAP confidentiality, with greater access to information—or sometimes pressure for access to information—in internal programs.[19]

Workers seeking services or treatment in an EAP may come of their own volition, may be referred by their business or agency, or may come on a court referral. While the employee need not participate in an EAP program, continued employment or court action may be dependent upon successful participation. "Sometimes, an employee who has broken work rules and is thus subject to firing or other discipline may be offered a reprieve or reinstatement if he or she participates in a treatment program. Although an employee cannot be forced to accept EAP services, an employer may not be forced to keep a rule-breaker in its employ. But the employee would be fired for breach of the work rules, not for refusing help from the EAP" [Nye, 1990:38].

When the employee comes to an EAP program as a referral, the referral source may be entitled to know that the client has applied to the program, is attending, or has successfully completed the program, depending on the company policies, agreements with the client, and an informed consent to release information. However, unless otherwise authorized—or compelled by law—what has been disclosed or discussed remains confidential and private.[20]

STATUTORY PROTECTIONS: PRIVILEGED COMMUNICATIONS; FEDERALLY FUNDED SUBSTANCE ABUSE PROGRAMS

The confidentiality of communications made to the EAP professional may be protected by privilege, depending upon state laws. The EAP counselor as counselor may not be extended privilege, but through a professional status, privilege may attach. Thus if the EAP counselor is a licensed social worker, psychologist, therapist, psychotherapist, or licensed substance abuse counselor, communications may be privileged, depending upon state law. (See generally Chapter 2.) Additionally, communications made to another professional not covered by state privilege laws may be privileged if that person was gathering the information for diagnosis or treatment by a professional—such as a social worker, psychologist, psychiatrist, or physician—who has privilege. Conversely, communications made to a professional not protected by privilege and who is not working and consulting with a covered professional are probably not privileged. As discussed in Chapter 2, the employee is the holder of the privilege and can waive the privilege.

If the EAP is part of a federally funded substance abuse program, then the extensive protections outlined in Chapter 10 apply, and any disclosures—with a very few exceptions, such as child abuse—including the identity of the participant, can only be made pursuant to a court order or with the informed consent of the employee.

LIMITATIONS ON CONFIDENTIALITY; DISCLOSURES OF CONFIDENTIAL INFORMATION

As with any confidential information shared with a social worker, disclosures made to the EAP professional are subject to the various limitations discussed throughout the text: disclosures about suspected child abuse; in some jurisdictions, disclosures of elder abuse, domestic violence, or past, present, or future criminal acts; disclosures on an intent to harm oneself or another (see Chapters 2 and 7). Additional problems may arise in the EAP setting, including past crimes in the workplace, and mental, physical, or emotional difficulties that might impair the employee's work performance and might result in injury to others or damage to property. These disclosures might be protected by state confidentiality statutes, but could be vital to an employer. Company and EAP provider policies should address these and related issues.

Disclosures about health conditions that do not impair performance should remain confidential unless there is law to the contrary. Disclosures about HIV/AIDS conditions are generally confidential and protected by state law, although there a growing number of exceptions, depending upon the jurisdiction (see Chapter 9). If the EAP program engages in joint or group counseling with the employee and others, confidentiality can be urged, but not promised (see Chapter 10).

It is clear from the foregoing that the confidentiality of communications in the EAP setting depends on a variety of factors, among them whether the EAP professional has a statutory privilege, whether the EAP is a federally funded substance abuse program, the nature of the confidential information disclosed, whether the disclosure takes place in an individual or multi-person context, informed consent by the employee, and company and EAP provider policies and regulations. This calls for clearly stated employer and EAP provider policies on confidentiality and its limitations in the EAP setting. Moreover, these policies should be carefully explained to the employee at the beginning of his or her contact with the EAP, and throughout the time of participation.

CONFIDENTIALITY AND LIABILITY IN THE EAP

The various liability actions that can be brought for breaches of confidentiality and invasions of privacy apply to the EAP setting. (See generally, Nye, 1990: chaps. 6–7.) Unauthorized intentional disclosure of confidential information from a federally funded substance abuse program carries significant penalties (see Chapter 10). Failure to warn or protect another can subject the social worker to liability, depending upon the range of factors discussed in Chapter 7. Conversely, a wrongful breach of confidentiality may also subject the social worker to liability. Violations of AIDS confidentiality statutes may be accompanied by liability actions (see Chapter 9). As stressed throughout the text, consultation, documentation, and legal advice are crucial in this context.

Sexual Harassment in the Workplace

Workplace sexual harassment involves privacy issues across several dimensions. Primarily, pressures for sexual favor impinge on an individual's privacy as does a hostile workplace environment, where there may be touching, advances, comments, and pictures of a sexual nature which the individual finds offensive. Related to this, the employer's efforts to address workplace sexual harassment may also involve privacy issues, as the employer attempts to impose limits on employee speech and action, both on and off the job. A social worker, patient, or client may be the subject of sexual harassment, may be accused of harassment, or may be an administrator or human relations officer trying to respond to the harassment charges.

While various state and federal statutes govern workplace sexual harassment actions, within federal law the primary vehicle for workplace sexual harassment actions is Title VII of the Civil Rights Act, which provides: "It shall be an unlawful employment practice for an employer—(1) to fail or refuse to hire or to discharge any individual, or otherwise to discriminate against any individual with respect to his compensation, terms, conditions, or privileges of employment, because of such individual's race, color, religion, sex, or national origin" [Title VII of the Civil Rights Act, 42 U.S.C. §2000e-2(a)(1)].

Title VII was originally enacted to address workplace discrimination on the basis of race, religion, gender, and national origin. With enforcement by the Equal Employment Opportunities Commission (EEOC), it was designed to address discrimination issues at a broad level, encouraging compliance through negotiation and conciliation as opposed to fines and penalties. In this, the focus was to address company- or industry-wide patterns of discrimination, rather than specific actions of particular individuals.

Early sexual harassment cases brought under Title VII were generally unsuccessful because courts held that sexual harassment did not equate to gender-based discrimination and the sexual harassment complained of was the action of specific individuals, rather than reflecting broad company policies. By the 1970s courts began to extend Title VII sex discrimination to sexual harassment situations. These early cases involved quid pro quo (literally, "this for that") harassment, in which sexual favors were linked to employment benefits such as promotion, compensation, or other work-related benefits. Typically, quid pro quo harassment involved supervisor-supervisee situations. In quid pro quo harassment, courts held that under agency principles, the employer could be liable for the actions of its supervisors.

Until the 1991 amendments to the Civil Rights Act of 1964, the remedies available to a successful plaintiff under Title VII were limited to reinstatement in the case of job loss, back pay if any was owing, reasonable attorney fees, and injunctive and equitable relief, those used to address company-wide discriminatory behaviors. In 1991, the act was amended to allow for punitive and compensatory damages if "the respondent engaged in a discriminatory practice . . . with malice or with reckless indifference." If this stringent standard is met, damage awards are limited by the size of the organization, ranging from $50,000 for organizations with 15 to 100 employees to a maximum of $300,000 for organizations with over 500 employees. Governments, governmental agencies, and political subdivisions are excluded [42 U.S.C. §1981a(b)].

HOSTILE ENVIRONMENT SEXUAL HARASSMENT

Quid pro quo sexual harassment litigation began to address the problem of a supervisor bargaining job benefits for employee sexual favors, but did not reach the broader problem of workplace sexual harassment between equals and sexual harassment that did not involve physical contact but rather words, gestures, pictures, and the like. This changed with a court decision, *Henson v. City of Dundee*, 682 F.2d 897 (11th Cir. 1982). In *Henson,* the court drew upon a prior decision, *Rogers v. EEOC*, 454 F.2d 234 (5th Cir. 1971), which held that a workplace environment filled with racial hostility could constitute racial discrimination under Title VII even if there was no actual discrimination in hiring, firing, and promotions.

The *Rogers* court wrote: "One can readily envision working environments so heavily polluted with discrimination as to destroy completely the emotional and physical stability of minority group workers, and I think Section 703 of Title VII was aimed at the eradication of such noxious practices" [454 F.2d 234, 238 (1971)]. In *Henson,* the court adopted the *Rogers* approach, finding Title VII applicable to hostile environment sexual harassment:

> Sexual harassment which creates a hostile or offensive environment for members of one sex is every bit the arbitrary barrier to sexual equality at the workplace that racial harassment is to racial equality. Surely, a requirement that a man or woman run a gauntlet of sexual abuse in return for the privilege of being allowed to work and make a living can be as demeaning and disconcerting as the harshest of racial epithets. A pattern of sexual harassment inflicted upon an employee because of her sex is a pattern of behavior that inflicts disparate treatment upon a member of one sex with respect to terms, conditions, or privileges of employment. There is no requirement that an employee subjected to such disparate treatment prove in addition that she has suffered tangible job detriment. [682 F.2d 897, 902 (1982)]

The *Henson* court listed four factors that must be proved in a successful hostile environment sexual harassment suit. These factors were cited by the U.S. Supreme Court in *Meritor Savings Bank v. Vinson,* 477 U.S. 57 (1986), and are now widely accepted as criteria for deciding if hostile environment sexual harassment is actionable under Title VII.[21] In *Meritor,* the plaintiff alleged a prolonged period during which her supervisor demanded that she have sexual intercourse with him, sometimes during business hours, sometimes afterwards, fondled her in front of other employees, exposed himself to her, and made other sexual advances. While Vinson was promoted during this period, she alleged that those promotions were based on merit, so the issue was not quid pro quo harassment. The supervisor denied the charges, and the employer bank argued that whether the charges were true or false, the bank was not responsible and could not be held liable. The issues the Court addressed were whether or not Title VII could be used to support a claim of hostile environment sexual harassment and whether the employer could be liable.

The Supreme Court, drawing upon EEOC guidelines, *Rogers,* and *Henson,* held that "a plaintiff may establish a violation of Title VII by proving that discrimination based on sex has created a hostile or abusive work environment" [477 U.S. 57, 66 (1986)]. The Court made several other important points in *Meritor.* It said that not all workplace conduct which might be termed harassment would fall within Title VII prohibitions: "Of course, as the courts in both Rogers and Henson recognized, not all workplace conduct that may be described as 'harassment' affects a 'term, condition, or privilege' of employment within the meaning of Title VII. ('Mere utterance of an ethnic or racial epithet which engenders offensive feelings in an employee' would not affect the conditions of employment to a sufficiently significant degree to violate Title VII); for sexual harassment to be actionable, it must be sufficiently severe or pervasive 'to alter the conditions of [the victim's] employment and create an abusive working environment'" [477 U.S. 57, 67 (1986)].

In addition, the Court emphasized that the issue in deciding whether or not sexual harassment occurred was not whether Vinson's sexual relationship with Taylor was "voluntary." The question the Court said should be addressed at the trial level was whether the alleged sexual advances were "unwelcome":

> But the fact that sex-related conduct was "voluntary," in the sense that the complainant was not forced to participate against her will, is not a defense to a sexual harassment suit brought under Title VII. The gravamen of any sexual harassment claim is

that the alleged sexual advances were "unwelcome." While the question whether particular conduct was indeed unwelcome presents difficult problems of proof and turns largely on credibility determinations committed to the trier of fact, the District Court in this case erroneously focused on the "voluntariness" of respondent's participation in the claimed sexual episodes. The correct inquiry is whether respondent by her conduct indicated that the alleged sexual advances were unwelcome, not whether her actual participation in sexual intercourse was voluntary. [477 U.S. 57, 68 (1986)]

Thus, although Vinson might have voluntarily engaged in sexual activities with Taylor, that is, she was not physically forced, she may not have wanted to. The latter issue, whether the sexual advances of Taylor were unwelcome, becomes determinative of whether Taylor's conduct was sexual harassment. This, the court said, would have to be established by evidence at trial.

Two other important issues were addressed by the *Meritor* Court. First, the Court did not decide whether the employer automatically should be held liable for its employee's, Taylor's, conduct. However, the Court did note that although Meritor did have a general nondiscrimination policy, it did not have a policy specifically addressing sexual harassment. Also, although there was an employee grievance procedure in effect, it required that the employee first lodge a complaint with her or his supervisor, thus requiring Vinson to first complain of Taylor's conduct to Taylor himself.

Second, the Court cited favorably the EEOC guidelines that specified that in deciding whether or not sexual harassment did occur, the plaintiff's behavior, dress, and demeanor could be considered:

It does not follow that a complainant's sexually provocative speech or dress is irrelevant as a matter of law in determining whether he or she found particular sexual advances unwelcome. To the contrary, such evidence is obviously relevant. The EEOC Guidelines emphasize that the trier of fact must determine the existence of sexual harassment in light of "the record as a whole" and "the totality of circumstances, such as the nature of the sexual advances and the context in which the alleged inci-

dents occurred." Respondent's claim that any marginal relevance
of the evidence in question was outweighed by the potential for
unfair prejudice is the sort of argument properly addressed to the
District Court. [477 U.S. 57, 69 (1986)]

With the *Meritor* decision, some issues were clarified, others were not. Title VII does include hostile environment sexual harassment as part of discrimination based on sex and it is actionable. Unlike quid pro quo
harassment where a supervisor has offered job benefits in return for sex—
and employer liability is automatic—in hostile environment situations, employer liability will depend upon existing sexual harassment policies and
procedures and how these are implemented. Moreover, the fact that an employee participated in sexual activities does not invalidate the sexual harassment claim. The issue is not whether the participation was voluntary,
but whether the advances were unwelcome. Finally, in litigating a sexual harassment claim, the plaintiff's conduct, including dress, demeanor, actions,
and speech, can be subject to examination by a defendant in the action.

Left undecided by *Meritor* were other issues, among them what constitutes a "hostile environment"; by what standard the impact of the environment on the worker should be judged; when employers are liable for
employee behavior and when they are not; and how far the workplace extends. Some of these questions have been addressed in more recent court decisions; others remain unresolved today. And some of these issues extend
into other areas of workplace privacy, such as to what extent an employer
can monitor employee speech and behavior in the workplace, and whether
an employer can—or must—also regulate off-duty conduct and speech.

THE "REASONABLE PERSON" STANDARD

Where one person might find another's actions and speech highly offensive,
a second person in the same situation might take no offense. Thus the standard by which to judge whether or not a person was, or should have been,
offended by sexually oriented speech or conduct becomes crucial. In one decision, *Rabidue v. Osceola Refining Co.*, 805 F.2d 611 (6th Cir. 1986), a female plaintiff complained about constant sexual insults, nude posters, and
attempts at sexual contact. The court dismissed the complaint, holding that
in a predominately male environment, the standard for determining whether
the environment was a hostile one should be that of a reasonable person

working within that context, and there it should be a reasonable male, who would not be offended by the speech and conduct.

In *Ellison v. Brady*, 924 F.2d 872 (9th Cir. 1991), a different circuit court addressed the reasonable person standard, with a different conclusion. In that case, the female plaintiff alleged that after having lunch with her on one occasion, the defendant, Gray, a co-worker, "started to pester her with unnecessary questions and hang around her desk." Although accepting another luncheon invitation, she tried to avoid him. He then sent her a note which read: "I cried over you last night and I'm totally drained today. I have never been in such constant term oil [sic]. Thank you for talking with me. I could not stand to feel your hatred for another day."

Ellison, the plaintiff, showed the note to her supervisor and said, "This is sexual harassment." Ellison instructed the supervisor not to do anything at that time, and asked a co-worker to talk with Gray. During an out-of-town training session, Ellison received a long letter from Gray, who wrote in part: "I know that you are worth knowing with or without sex. . . . Leaving aside the hassles and disasters of recent weeks. I have enjoyed you so much over these past few months. Watching you. Experiencing you from O so far away. Admiring your style and elan. . . . Don't you think it odd that two people who have never even talked together, alone, are striking off such intense sparks . . . I will [write] another letter in the near future" [924 F.2d 872, 874 (1991)].

Addressing whether or not Gray's conduct constituted actionable sexual harassment, the court held that the standard to be used would be that of a reasonable victim, in this case a reasonable woman in that situation:

> Next, we believe that in evaluating the severity and persuasiveness of sexual harassment, we should focus on the perspective of the victim. . . . If we only examined whether a reasonable person would engage in allegedly harassing conduct, we would run the risk of reinforcing the prevailing level of discrimination. Harassers could continue to harass merely because a particular discriminatory practice was common, and victims of harassment would have no remedy.
>
> We therefore prefer to analyze harassment from the victim's perspective. A complete understanding of the victim's view requires, among other things, an analysis of the different perspec-

tives of men and women. Conduct that many men consider un-
objectionable may offend many women. . . .

We realize that there is a broad range of viewpoints among
women as a group, but we believe that many women share common concerns which men do not necessarily share. For example,
because women are disproportionately victims of rape and sexual assault, women have a stronger incentive to be concerned
with sexual behavior. Women who are victims of mild forms of
sexual harassment may understandably worry whether a ha-
rasser's conduct is merely a prelude to violent sexual assault.
Men, who are rarely victims of sexual assault, may view sexual
conduct in a vacuum without a full appreciation of the social setting or the underlying threat of violence that a woman may perceive.

In order to shield employers from having to accommodate the
idiosyncratic concerns of the rare hyper-sensitive employee, we
hold that a female plaintiff states a prima facie case of hostile environment sexual harassment when she alleges conduct which a
reasonable woman would consider sufficiently severe or pervasive to alter the conditions of employment and create an abusive
working environment. [924 F.2d 872, 878 (1991)][22]

The case was returned to the trial court to determine whether under the
reasonable woman standard Gray's conduct constituted sexual harassment.

What constitutes a hostile environment? In a recent Supreme Court case,
Harris v. Forklift Systems, 126 L.Ed.2d 295 (1993), the Court described the
situation:

The Magistrate found that, throughout Harris' time at Forklift,
Hardy often insulted her because of her gender and often made
her the target of unwanted sexual innuendos. Hardy told Harris
on several occasions, in the presence of other employees, "You're
a woman, what do you know" and "We need a man as the rental
manager"; at least once, he told her she was "a dumb ass
woman." Again in front of others, he suggested that the two of
them "go to the Holiday Inn to negotiate [Harris'] raise." Hardy
occasionally asked Harris and other female employees to get

coins from his front pants pocket. He threw objects on the ground in front of Harris and other women, and asked them to pick the objects up. He made sexual innuendos about Harris' and other women's clothing.

In mid-August 1987, Harris complained to Hardy about his conduct. Hardy said he was surprised that Harris was offended, claimed he was only joking, and apologized. He also promised he would stop, and based on this assurance Harris stayed on the job. But in early September, Hardy began anew: While Harris was arranging a deal with one of Forklift's customers, he asked her, again in front of other employees, "What did you do, promise the guy . . . some [sex] Saturday night?" On October 1, Harris collected her paycheck and quit. [126 L.Ed.2d 295, 301 (1993)]

The Court then enunciated the standard for a hostile environment:

This standard, which we reaffirm today, takes a middle path between making actionable any conduct that is merely offensive and requiring the conduct to cause a tangible psychological injury. As we pointed out in Meritor, "mere utterance of an . . . epithet which engenders offensive feelings in an employee," does not sufficiently affect the conditions of employment to implicate Title VII. Conduct that is not severe or pervasive enough to create an objectively hostile or abusive work environment—an environment that a reasonable person would find hostile or abusive—is beyond Title VII's purview. Likewise, if the victim does not subjectively perceive the environment to be abusive, the conduct has not actually altered the conditions of the victim's employment, and there is no Title VII violation.

But Title VII comes into play before the harassing conduct leads to a nervous breakdown. A discriminatorily abusive work environment, even one that does not seriously affect employees' psychological well-being, can and often will detract from employees' job performance, discourage employees from remaining on the job, or keep them from advancing in their careers. Moreover, even without regard to these tangible effects, the very fact that the discriminatory conduct was so severe or pervasive that it created a work environment abusive to employees because of their race, gender, religion, or national origin offends Title VII's broad rule of workplace equality. The appalling conduct alleged in Meritor, and the reference in that case to environments "so heavily polluted with discrimination as to destroy completely the emotional and psychological stability of minority group workers," merely present some especially egregious examples of harassment. They do not mark the boundary of what is actionable. [126 L.Ed.2d 295, 302 (1993)]

EMPLOYER LIABILITY

As we have seen, *Meritor* left open whether or not the employer could be held liable for its supervisor's action. Where liability has been found, the awards to plaintiffs have escalated, sometimes reaching into the millions of dollars. Even if the employer is found not liable, there are attorneys' fees and administrative costs for time and effort in preparation for the action, not to mention real, but less obvious, costs in terms of morale, productivity, and publicity.

The easiest way to minimize these costs is for the employer to take steps to prevent sexual harassment, and if it is alleged to occur, to immediately investigate and resolve the allegations. EEOC guidelines suggest: "Prevention is the best tool for the elimination of sexual harassment. An employer should take all steps necessary to prevent harassment such as affirmatively raising the subject, expressing strong disapproval, developing appropriate sanctions, informing employees of their rights to raise and how to raise the issue of harassment under Title VII and developing methods to sensitize all concerned" [29 C.F.R. §.11(f)].

WORKPLACE PRIVACY LAW AND SOCIAL WORK PRACTICE

Privacy in the workplace encompasses many areas. These have relevance for both patients and clients and for social work professionals and students themselves, since they often work in an agency setting. As the chapter illustrates, the issues are complex. No one would advocate sexually harassing behavior or drug use in the workplace, and employee surveillance and monitoring can be a legitimate employer tool to insure performance and quality. But who should or should not be tested for drug use, when an office can or cannot be searched, when surveillance oversteps routine monitoring, and how much of an employee's on- and off-duty behavior can be regulated are only some of the difficult issues. Social work professionals, students, patients, and clients may legally and legitimately be tested for drug use in some employment contexts but not in others. Their e-mail may be read, their work monitored, they and their offices subjected to searches—at times. But under other conditions, any of these may constitute unwarranted and illegal invasions of privacy. It is important for social workers as practitioners or administrators to know what is permissible in this area for both themselves and their clients.

CHAPTER SIX

PRIVACY *and* CONFIDENTIALITY *in* FILES *and* RECORDS

Protecting the confidentiality of records and files in human service organizations is becoming more difficult as the volume and types of information gathered about patients and clients increase dramatically and the technology for receiving, storing, compiling, and transmitting information expands exponentially. With modern computer technology, vast amounts of data can be recorded, stored, and processed, often easily, quickly, and cheaply.

Client records have become more voluminous as more information is gathered, and more information is seen as important in decision making or necessary to provide protection from potential legal action. At one time, a patient's or client's record might have consisted of some basic information on a single file card, or a number of pages of personal data, process notes, and observations. Today, such a record might consist of hundreds of pages of text along with still or moving visual images and recorded sound, all stored on tape, disk, hard drive, or CD-ROM as electronic/magnetic impulses. The record might be copied into a central database of case records, and could be linked with or contain cross-references to other databases containing other records for the same individual, family, or condition. The records could be accessed, sorted, merged, compiled, and transmitted. They could be downloaded and printed, instantly copied, and transmitted by fax or computer modem to numerous other locations, anywhere in the country or internationally. And with the appropriate linkages, the record could be accessed by other computers or other data systems near and far. Along with all this, the expansion of federal and state government and private third-party insurers in monitoring and reimbursing service delivery has greatly increased the potential for broad access to and dispersion of recorded information.

Without appropriate legal and technical safeguards, a patient's or client's health, mental health, welfare, social service, juvenile court, and law enforcement records, among others, could be linked or combined. And given the technology for widespread transmission, a record may take on a life of its own: deleting, correcting, or updating a record in one data bank does not insure that the same will occur for the same record in other data banks. It may remain—and be further transmitted—in its previous form, even though inaccurate or dated, depicting the individual as he or she once, or perhaps never, was.

All this has drastically altered and expanded the problems of privacy and confidentiality. Where once a single person might overhear part of a conversation, now a breach of confidentiality might include entire faxed or computer-transmitted records that went awry or were intercepted by a third party. Where once a person overhearing a conversation might tell a few others, now the possibilities for transmitting the intercepted information are enormous. For example, a single item of information or an image now posted on the Internet can be seen, copied, and recopied by literally millions of people around the world.

Thus what information is collected about an individual or family, how it is stored, replicated, and transmitted, and who has access and for what purposes become crucial issues in social work.

Records and Record Keeping

Kagle identifies the following uses of social work records: client identification and specification of the need for service; documentation of service delivery; case continuity; facilitation of interprofessional collaboration; access by and discussion of information with the client; supervision, consultation, and peer review; service monitoring and evaluation; student education; and a source of data for social research [Kagle 1991:2–5].

Given such broad and disparate uses, the temptation for the social worker may be toward overinclusion, since the information may be of later use, and not to record information often means it will be lost forever. Here the NASW Code of Ethics provides some guidance. Standard 1.07(a) states in part: "Social workers should not solicit private information from clients unless it is essential to providing service or conducting social work evaluation or research" (see Chapter 4).

Certain information should be recorded for the purposes suggested by Kagle. In addition, proper documentation is very important to show why a particular action was taken or a decision reached, in case questions or legal challenges later arise. However, in recording information, the worker should keep in mind that along with the usual access by supervisors and others within the agency, individuals outside the agency, including the patient or client (or a legal representative or family member), a judge, prosecutor, plaintiff or defendant, and attorneys, may later access all or some of the record; and depending on the situation, it could be introduced in court. Thus great care should be taken in deciding what information must be recorded and what should not. As in other areas, one cannot assume the confidentiality or privacy of a record.

In the following sections, we will look at some of the laws that protect the privacy of records and limitations on those laws. Legal protection of some types of records are discussed elsewhere and reference will be made to those chapters.

ACCESS TO RECORDS

Patient and Client Access. There has been a trend toward greater patient and client access to their records. Under two federal statutes access is generally allowed for educational records and government agency records under the Family Educational Rights and Privacy Act (see Chapter 8) and the federal Privacy Act of 1974 (see below). State statutes and regulations provide for access by clients or their representatives to some health, medical, or service records. The NASW Code of Ethics standard 1.08(a) states that social workers should provide patients and clients "reasonable access" to their records, and also encourages the worker to provide assistance in interpreting the record. The standard recommends limiting client access only in "exceptional circumstances," where the access would cause the patient or client "serious harm." (See generally Chapter 4.)

For example, in Illinois inspection of mental health and developmental disabilities records is permitted by recipients of service if they are over twelve years of age, parents of recipients under twelve, and parents of recipients over twelve if the recipient concurs, among others:

> Sec. 4. (a) The following persons shall be entitled, upon request, to inspect and copy a recipient's record or any part thereof: (1) the parent or guardian of a recipient who is under 12 years of age; (2) the recipient if he is 12 years of age or older; (3) the parent or guardian of a recipient who is at least 12 but under 18 years, if the recipient is informed and does not object or if the therapist does not find that there are compelling reasons for denying the access. The parent or guardian who is denied access by either the recipient or the therapist may petition a court for access to the record. . . . (4) the guardian of a recipient who is 18 years or older; (5) attorney or guardian ad litem who represents a minor 12 years of age or older in any judicial or administrative proceeding, provided that the court or administrative hearing officer has entered an order granting the attorney this right; or (6) an agent appointed under a recipient's power of attorney for health care or for property, when the power of attorney authorizes the access. [740 ILCS 110/4]

The same act provides for the interpretation of the record to anyone under eighteen years of age: "(b) Assistance in interpreting the record may be provided without charge and shall be provided if the person inspecting the record is under 18 years of age. However, access may in no way be denied or limited if the person inspecting the record refuses the assistance. A reasonable fee may be charged for duplication of a record" [740 ILCS 110/4].

Also under the act, a person inspecting the record may add new information or challenge information in the record:

> (c) Any person entitled to access to a record under this Section may submit a written statement concerning any disputed or new information, which statement shall be entered into the record. Whenever any disputed part of a record is disclosed, any submitted statement relating thereto shall accompany the disclosed part. Additionally, any person entitled to access may request modification of any part of the record which he believes is incorrect or misleading. If the request is refused, the person may seek a court order to compel modification. (D) Whenever access or modification is requested, the request and any action taken thereon shall be noted in the recipient's record. [704 ILCS 110/4]

Whether or not a patient or client has a right of access to a record will depend on state or federal law, agency policy, and the content of the record. However, any client can subpoena a record for use in a judicial proceeding, and then a court may determine whether there should be total access, partial access, access to summaries of the record, or no access at all.

Confidential Records: Access by Defendants. While a record may be private and confidential, or even privileged, this does not mean that it cannot be viewed for some purposes. At times, a court may conduct a private *in camera* (in chambers) inspection of records, or may conduct an *in camera* inspection in the presence of attorneys for the plaintiff and defendant. In *Pennsylvania v. Ritchie*, 480 U.S. 39 (1987), the issue was whether a defendant could subpoena confidential child protective service records for use in his defense against sexual assault charges. Balancing the constitutional rights of the defendant with the confidentiality of the records, the U.S. Supreme Court held that the confidentiality of the records was not absolute, and the trial court could inspect the records *in camera* and decide what if anything was material to the defense or would serve to exculpate the defendant. (For a more detailed discussion see Chapter 10.)

In *People v. Stanaway*, 521 N.W.2d 557 (1994), the Michigan court quoted a legislative study supporting confidentiality of sexual assault victim records: "[Sexual assault] counselors feel obliged to warn their clients beforehand that communications between them may be used as evidence in court, and they report that this knowledge often has an important chilling effect on the client's willingness to be forthcoming. Crisis intervention centers often make it a practice to keep minimal records in order to protect privacy as much as possible, but this practice makes resumption of counseling after a lapse of time or by another counselor much more difficult" [521 N.W.2d 557, 566 (1994)].

As with the child abuse records, the conflict is between the legitimate need of a defense counsel to have access to information necessary for a client's defense, and the expectation—and need—of the individual alleging a sexual assault to maintain the confidentiality of the disclosures. States vary in their response to these difficult issues, and important factors are state privilege statutes, state constitutional provisions, and related statutory protections.

Many states permit judicial *in camera* inspection of the confidential material, permitting disclosure of material necessary to the defense. In deciding *Commonwealth v. Bishop,* the Massachusetts Supreme Court has developed procedures for judicial *in camera* inspection of confidential sexual assault victims' records.[1] Along with *Bishop,* two other cases raising questions of access to sexual assault victim counselor records were brought before the Massachusetts Supreme Court at about the same time. In those cases rape crisis centers in two cities were appealing contempt of court citations for refusing to disclose confidential client records pursuant to a court order. In each case, the trial court had held that the crisis centers would have to pay a find of $100 per day until the contempt was purged by release of the records. The Massachusetts Supreme Court held that one case was moot, since during the appeal the defendant had pled guilty, and the other case was returned to the trial court for additional findings. See *Commonwealth v. Rape Crisis Servs. of Greater Lowell,* 617 N.E.2d 635 (Mass. 1993); *Commonwealth v. Rape Crisis Program of Worcester,* 617 N.E.2d 637 (Mass. 1993).

DUAL RECORD SYSTEMS

The potential for access to records by a patient, client, family member, legal representative, judge, or even counsel for a defendant who is alleged to have harmed the patient or client is always present and should be considered by the social worker when recording confidential information. To deal with this problem, various commentators have argued that social workers and other therapists should keep dual sets of records, a very limited single set, or no records at all [Wilson, 1978]. Simon describes dual record keeping: "Therapists sometimes keep two separate sets of records: one set for diagnosis, prognosis, and treatment decisions and the other set for the therapist's speculations . . . and intimate details of the patient's life" [Simon, 1992: 87].

Wilson observes: "In reality, many social workers, especially those in private practice, do keep highly personal notes which are brief, often rather disorganized, and not part of any formal case record . . . Such a practice can effectively prevent unauthorized disclosures . . . However, there is no guarantee that such notes could not be subpoenaed by a court, along with any formal records" [Wilson, 1978:52].

While dual record keeping may have a practice rationale, the legal status is less clear. A few jurisdictions legally permit dual record keeping—both a permanent record and a second collection of informal notes, thoughts, guesses, and so forth. Two examples are the District of Columbia Mental Health Information Code and the Illinois Mental Health and Developmental Disabilities Confidentiality Act. The District of Columbia statute provides: "If a mental health professional makes personal notes regarding a client, such personal notes shall not be maintained as a part of the client's record of mental health information. Notwithstanding any other provision of this chapter, access to such personal notes shall be strictly and absolutely limited to the mental health professional and shall not be disclosed except to the degree that the personal notes or the information contained therein are needed in litigation brought by the client against the mental health professional on the grounds of professional malpractice or disclosure in violation of this section" [D.C. Code §6-2003].

In Illinois, the statute applies to all therapists, including social workers. Personal notes are defined as: "(i) information disclosed to the therapist in confidence by other persons on condition that such information would never be disclosed to the recipient or other persons; (ii) information disclosed to the therapist by the recipient which would be injurious to the recipient's relationships to other persons, and (iii) the therapist's speculations, impressions, hunches, and reminders" [740 ILCS 110/2 (1996)].

Personal notes are not part of the record as long as they are used only as provided in the statute and not otherwise disclosed. If they are disclosed, they become part of the record: "'Record' means any record kept by a therapist or by an agency in the course of providing mental health or developmental disabilities service to a recipient concerning the recipient and the services provided. . . . Record does not include the therapist's personal notes, if such notes are kept in the therapist's sole possession for his own personal use and are not disclosed to any other person, except the therapist's supervisor, consulting therapist, or attorney. If at any time such notes are disclosed, they shall be considered part of the recipient's record for purposes of this Act" [740 ILCS 110/2 (1996)].

Such personal notes, if not otherwise disclosed, are confidential and not subject to discovery: "Sec. 3. (a) All records and communications shall be confidential and shall not be disclosed except as provided in this Act. (b) A therapist is not required to but may, to the extent he determines it necessary and appropriate, keep personal notes regarding a recipient. Such personal notes are the work product and personal property of the therapist and shall not be subject to discovery in any judicial, administrative or legislative proceeding or any proceeding preliminary thereto" [740 ILCS 110/3].

Where there is no such statutory protection for a dual record system, social workers should be cautious: personal notes might or might not be protected, and could be subject to a subpoena.

DISCLOSURE OF RECORDS: INFORMED CONSENT

Disclosure of records to a third party is at times required and at times necessary for treatment, monitoring, or other purposes. Here the social worker should consult relevant statutes, regulations, and policies for guidance. Wrongful disclosure may result in significant penalties. Where possible and appropriate, an informed consent signed by the patient, client, or legal guardian is good practice. The Illinois Mental Health and Developmental Disabilities Confidentiality Act, for example, contains a number of consent and disclosure provisions. After specifying who may access the records, the act provides:

> Sec 5. (a) Except as provided in Sections 6 through 12.2 of this Act, records and communications may be disclosed to someone other than those persons listed in Section 4 of this Act only with the written consent of those persons who are entitled to inspect and copy a recipient's record pursuant to Section 4 of this Act.

(b) Every consent form shall be in writing and shall specify the following: (1) the person or agency to whom disclosure is to be made; (2) the purpose for which disclosure is to be made; (3) the nature of the information to be disclosed; (4) the right to inspect and copy the information to be disclosed; (5) the consequences of a refusal to consent, if any; and (6) the calendar date on which the consent expires, provided that if no calendar date is stated, information may be released only on the day the consent form is received by the therapist; and (7) the right to revoke the consent at any time.

The consent form shall be signed by the person entitled to give consent and the signature shall be witnessed by a person who can attest to the identity of the person so entitled. A copy of the consent and a notation as to any action taken thereon shall be entered in the recipient's record. Any revocation of consent shall be in writing, signed by the person who gave the consent and the signature shall be witnessed by a person who can attest to the identity of the person so entitled. No written revocation of consent shall be effective to prevent disclosure of records and communications until it is received by the person otherwise authorized to disclose records and communications.

(c) Only information relevant to the purpose for which disclosure is sought may be disclosed. Blanket consent to the disclosure of unspecified information shall not be valid. Advance consent may be valid only if the nature of the information to be disclosed is specified in detail and the duration of the consent is indicated. Consent may be revoked in writing at any time; any such revocation shall have no effect on disclosures made prior thereto.

(d) No person or agency to whom any information is disclosed under this Section may redisclose such information unless the person who consented to the disclosure specifically consents to such redisclosure.

(e) Except as otherwise provided in this Act, records and communications shall remain confidential after the death of a recipient and shall not be disclosed unless the recipient's representative, as defined in the Probate Act of 1975 and the therapist consent to such disclosure or unless disclosure is authorized by court order after in camera examination and upon good cause shown. [740 ILCS 110/5]

Sections 6 through 12 specify when disclosures may be made without informed consent, including disclosures to receive benefits; disclosure for record review, research, reimbursement, or monitoring of services; certain interagency disclosures; disclosures for investigations of abuse; disclosures to supervisors, consultants, treatment teams, and those conducting a peer review; and disclosures for various civil and criminal proceedings.

However, all disclosures are specifically limited to essential information, and redisclosure of any information not permitted by the statute is forbidden: "Information may be disclosed under this Section only to the extent that knowledge of the record or communications is essential to the purpose for which disclosure is made and only after the recipient is informed that such disclosure may be made. A person to whom disclosure is made under this Section shall not redisclose any information except as provided in this Act" [740 ILCS 110/9(4)].

Wrongful disclosure of information is a Class A misdemeanor and "Any person aggrieved by a violation of this Act may sue for damages, an injunction, or other appropriate relief" including attorney's fees and costs [740 ILCS 110/15, 110/16].

DISCLOSURE OF RECORDS: SUBPOENAS[2]

"A subpoena is a command to appear at a certain time and place to give testimony upon a certain matter" [*Black's Law Dictionary*, 1991]. A subpoena may require testimony (subpoena ad testificandum) or may require that certain documents be produced (subpoena duces tecum).[3] In civil proceedings, an individual may be subpoenaed to appear or provide documents as part of a deposition or a trial.[4] Because it is an order of the court, a subpoena cannot be ignored: failure to comply can result in a contempt citation, with a fine or even incarceration until the contempt is purged by compliance.[5] However, until a court orders the testimony given or the documents produced, the social worker and agency can contest the subpoena and with adequate grounds can refuse to provide the testimony or documents.

Under the federal rules, and the rules in many states, a clerk of the court provides blank subpoenas signed by the court to attorneys who request them, or the attorney as officer of the court may issue a subpoena on be-half of the court.[6] Consequently, there may be no court supervision over what material is subpoenaed or whether it is even legally obtainable. While the tendency of social workers and many professionals may be to comply with the terms of the subpoena duces tecum and release the requested ma-terial, this material may be protected by statutory confidentiality or privi-lege and should not be released without a court order or the patient's or client's consent. It is important to keep in mind that the decision to disclose confidential records rightfully rests with the court, and not the attorney is-suing the subpoena or the social worker or other professional who has re-ceived it.

Legal guidance is called for in these situations, and if the subpoena re-quests disclosure of patient or client records, the patient or client should be informed. As with any confidential or privileged information, if the client gives an informed consent for release, disclosure can be made. Social work-ers have an ethical obligation to protect client confidentiality in these mat-ters. (See Chapter 4.) Moreover, where a court orders a disclosure of confidential or privileged material, the social worker has an ethical obliga-tion to request that the court "withdraw or limit the order as narrowly as possible and/or maintain the records under seal, unavailable for public in-spection" [NASW Code of Ethics standard 1.07(j)]. When discussing the subpoena with a patient or client, the social worker should be sure that he or she is aware what material is being subpoenaed and how it might be used, and cannot assume the client knows or remembers what has been included in records. Under the Federal Rules, when complying with a subpoena the social worker should produce the records "as they are kept in the usual course of business or shall organize and label them to correspond with the categories in the demand," and, if the worker or client is objecting to the subpoena, "the claim shall be made expressly and shall be supported by a description of the nature of the documents, communications, or things not produced that is sufficient to enable the demanding party to contest the claim" [Federal Rule 45(d)].

Technical grounds for contesting a subpoena might include an invalid service of process, lack of jurisdiction, or subpoenaing the wrong docu-ments or the wrong people or agencies. Substantive grounds for contesting a subpoena include the confidential or privileged nature of the material and the harm that might result from its disclosure. The Federal Rules specify the time limits for objection to a subpoena and grounds upon which a subpoena may be quashed (voided) or modified by a court. Among these are unreasonable time for compliance, requiring extensive travel, other undue burdens, and that the material is confidential or privileged.[7]

Polowy and Gilbertson list some important considerations for the social worker:

Receiving a subpoena can be intimidating, but the social worker should remember that the court has not made a decision about the validity of the subpoena. Although an attorney has broad power in issuing a subpoena, the social worker must not be misled into mistakenly producing privileged materials. When considering how to respond to a subpoena, the social worker must always remember the rights of the client and the authority of the court. The failure to respond correctly can lead to disclosure of privileged information without the client's consent or the imposition of contempt sanctions by the court.

The social worker should thoroughly read a subpoena, noting the date for response, action required, and the court and attorney issuing it. The social worker should contact the client and provide him or her with a copy. . . . Records should never be released before thoroughly verifying and documenting the legal and ethical mandates for doing so, and, if possible, advising the client.

The social worker should obtain the client's written consent to discuss the subpoena with the client's attorney and to provide the attorney with a complete set of the subpoenaed documents or the documents the client wants the attorney to review. . . .

The social worker should generally not provide any information if contacted by the issuing attorney and the client has not consented to a release of information. . . . If the material requested is privileged or the subpoena is procedurally improper, the social worker has the right to object by filing written objections, requesting a protective order, or filing a motion to quash or modify the subpoena. The issuing party then cannot gain access to the information without first receiving a court order. [Polowy and Gilbertson, 1997:4–5]

RETENTION AND DESTRUCTION OF RECORDS

An often troublesome issue for the social worker or agency is how long and in what form records should be retained; and to protect confidentiality, how records should be destroyed. There are no easy guidelines for record retention. State laws, regulations, guidelines from professional associations, licensing requirements, and agency policies are all important here. Some records may need to be retained indefinitely, others may be destroyed within a specified period of years. Kagle describes a survey of records:

> The survey revealed about 35 percent of agencies never destroy their records. Child welfare agencies, which are influenced both by the legal responsibility to retain certain documents and by the widespread use of computer technology, are especially likely to retain all portions of their records. . . .
>
> Those agencies that do destroy portions of the record do so differentially; they are likely to retain client identification and legal documents. They are likely to destroy documentation of service delivery, communications within the agency (such as interprofessional reports), communications with other agencies and progress notes. [Kagle, 1991:158]

An important consideration in record retention is the statute of limitations for legal actions that might arise from improper diagnosis, service, or treatment, breaches of confidentiality, termination, and related areas. Usually actions must be brought within two or three years of the injury or the discovery of it, but the statute may be extended for minors, incompetents, or those with other disabilities. Depending on state law, a minor has several years after attaining majority to sue for injuries sustained during childhood. Recent lawsuits for civil damages for past child abuse where the victim remembers—often as a result of therapy—abuse that has been long forgotten or suppressed, have relied upon the "recovered memory syndrome." Here, some courts have permitted actions to go forward long after the statute of limitations has expired, on the theory that the delayed memories of the abuse had tolled (that is, suspended) the statute of limitations.[8] In light of this trend, agencies and social workers should be cautious when deciding what records need not be retained.

Destruction of records is no longer as simple as it once was. Records can be torn up, thrown out, shredded, or erased from a computer file, but with modern technology for reproduction and transmission of information, a record that was assumed to be destroyed may exist in another location, in a central database, or under another name or identification number. Here it is important that the agency keep a log of what information has been transmitted, when, to where, and in what form.

The Federal Privacy Act

The Federal Privacy Act of 1974 as amended by the Computer Matching and Privacy Protection Act of 1988, 5 U.S.C. §552a, remains the most important federal statutory law protecting the privacy of an individual's records maintained by federal agencies. As such, it applies directly to social workers who are employees of the federal government and their patients and clients, and to federal records kept on social workers, patients, and clients who are outside the federal system. In combination with the Freedom of Information Act (FOIA), 5 U.S.C. §552b, the statute limits access to or transmission of an individual's records without notice and consent, allows an individual to access and correct the records, and permits public access to other governmental information. In some states, similar statutes have been enacted which apply to a number of state agencies' records.

While the Privacy Act of 1974 provides for the protection of federal agency records and includes significant penalties for violations of its provisions, it also contains a number of exceptions that severely limit its overall effectiveness. Enacted in the post-Watergate era in a spirit of governmental openness and citizen protection, over time its protections have been eroded to the point where some have argued that it has become a bureaucrat's tool for avoiding privacy protection and for obstructing legitimate access to records.

COVERAGE

When dealing with any statute, terminology and definitions are important; with legislation as complex as the Privacy Act, they are crucial. In general, the act pertains to an individual's records that are part of a system of records maintained in a federal agency. The statutory definitions of these terms have to be examined to understand what is—and just as importantly, what is not—included within the protection of the act. The coverage of the act is restricted to an "individual" defined as "a citizen of the United States or an alien lawfully admitted for permanent residence" [§552a(a)(2)]. Excluded from the protection of the act would be a business, a noncitizen, and an unlawful alien.

The act applies to a "record" that is part of a "systems of records." Records are "any item, collection, or grouping of information about an individual that is maintained by an agency, including, but not limited to, his education, financial transactions, medical history, and criminal or employment history and that contains his name, or the identifying number, symbol, or other identifying particular assigned to the individual, such as a finger or voice print or a photograph" [§552a(a)(4)]. With this definition, personal notes or memoranda that are not part of the official agency record are probably excluded from coverage. See 40 Fed. Reg. 28,952 (1975).

A system of records is "a group of any records under the control of any agency from which information is retrieved by the name of the individual or by some identifying number, symbol, or other identifying particular assigned to the individual" [§552a(a)(5)].

An agency is "any executive department, military department, Government corporation, Government controlled corporation, or other establishment in the executive branch of the Government (including the Executive Office of the President), or any independent regulatory agency" [§552a(f)].

Thus to fall within the coverage of the act, the record of the individual must contain identifiable information, must be part of a system of records, and that system must be under control of a covered agency. A record that is not part of a system of records, information that is not identifiable as defined, and identifiable information that does not constitute a record are excluded. Covered agencies are primarily limited to federal agencies within the executive branch and independent regulatory agencies. Congressional and judiciary agencies are excluded [§552a(e)].

DISCLOSURE

A main thrust of the legislation is to prevent disclosure of information in government records about an individual without his or her prior request or informed consent. The general privacy rule is: "No agency shall disclose any record which is contained in a system of records by any means of communication to any person, or to another agency, except pursuant to a written request by, or with the prior written consent of, the individual to whom the record pertains" [5 U.S.C. §552a(b)].

Along with the general disclosure rule, there are twelve exceptions. The most relevant for our purposes are:

(1) to those officers and employees of the agency which maintains the record who have a need for the record in the performance of their duties;

(2) required under section 522 of this title;[9]

(3) for a routine use as defined in subsection (a)(7) of this section and described under section (e)(4)(D) of this section;

. . . .

(7) to another agency or to an instrumentality of any governmental jurisdiction with or under the control of the United States for a civil or criminal law enforcement activity if the activity is authorized by law, and if the head of the agency or instrumentality has made a written request to the agency which maintains the record specifying the particular portion desired and the law enforcement activity for which the record is sought;

(8) to a person pursuant to a showing of compelling circumstances affecting the health or safety of an individual if upon such disclosure notification is transmitted to the last known address to such individual;

. . . .

(11) pursuant to the order of a court of competent jurisdiction. [§552a(b)]

Perhaps the biggest loophole in these statutory exceptions is exception 3, the "routine use" exception. "Routine use" means "with respect to the disclosure of a record, the use of such record for a purpose which is compatible with the purpose for which it was collected" [§552a(7)]. Thus under the broad routine use exception, a disclosure of information that is compatible with the purpose for which it was collected—a broad standard not otherwise clarified in the statute—is permissible. Coupled with this is another provision in the act that gives the agency making the disclosure the authority to determine and publish what constitutes a routine use of the records. Under §552(e)(4)(D) each agency covered by the act must publish at least annually in the Federal Register "a notice of the existence and character of the system of records, which notice shall include . . . each routine use of the records contained in the system, including the categories of users and the purpose of such use." Thus the agency that discloses the records is also the agency empowered to make the rules that determine whether that disclosure is legally acceptable under the statute. These factors combine to severely limit the effectiveness of the statute.

Other provisions of the act include an accounting of disclosures, inspection of the record by the individual, and mechanisms for correcting or challenging the accuracy of the information in the record. The act

1. requires an agency to maintain an accurate accounting of disclosures (except for within agency or FOIA disclosures) and make this record available to the individual (except for law enforcement disclosures) [5 U.S.C. §552a(c)];

2. allows individuals to inspect their records and, if there is disagreement about the accuracy of the records, either permits an amendment by the individual or if the agency refuses to permit the change, provides for a procedure for individuals to challenge that refusal [§552a(d)];

3. limits the information kept, requires that the information be collected directly from individuals if it may have an adverse impact, and specifies that when collecting information from individuals they be informed of the authority, purpose, routine use, and adverse effects of refusing to supply the information [§552a(e)(1)-(3)]; and

4. requires that the information kept by the agency in making any determination about individuals be accurate, relevant, timely, and complete "as is reasonably necessary" to assure a fair determination [§552a(e)(5)].

The act also provides for a civil action where there is a refusal to amend a record or a failure to follow the amendment procedures, a failure to maintain accurate, relevant, timely, and complete information under §522a(e)(5), or any other failure under the act that results in an adverse effect, and permits the court to amend the record and assess reasonable attorney's fees and costs. If there has been an adverse effect and the court determines that the agency acted in an intentional or willful manner—a higher standard than negligence—actual damages (with a minimum of $1,000) plus costs and attorney's fees can be assessed [§522a(g)(1)]. The act specifies that it is a criminal offense, a misdemeanor with a $5,000 maximum fine, when any officer or employee of the agency knowingly discloses prohibited information to any person or agency not entitled to receive it or willfully maintains a system of records without meeting the annual notice requirements [§522a(i)(1)]. Finally, some records such as law enforcement are generally exempt from the act, and others may be specifically exempted [§522a(j),(k)].

In 1988, the Privacy Act was amended by the Computer Matching and Privacy Protection Act to include protection from computerized matching of some data sets. "Matching programs" are defined as computerized comparisons of "two or more automated systems of records or a system of records with non-Federal records." Computer matching is not allowed without safeguards if the purpose of the match is "establishing or verifying the eligibility or continuing compliance" of applicants, recipients, beneficiaries, or participants of federal benefits programs, or for recouping payments or delinquencies in federal benefit programs. Excepted are matches for statistical, law enforcement, or tax purposes or if the computer match is used for routine administrative purposes. Otherwise, the act requires a prior written agreement between agencies before a computer match can be made, including procedures for initial and periodic notice to individuals whose records are within the computer programs, procedures around verification, retention, and destruction of the records, and a prohibition to take any action against an individual until there is some independent verification of the material and the individual affected has an opportunity to challenge the material [§552a(f)(p)]. The act also calls for the creation of a Data Integrity Board to oversee and review the systems and agreements [§522a(f)(u)].

Privacy and Health Records

UNIQUE IDENTIFIERS

The demand for accurate, complete, current, and accessible electronic data is emerging in an environment in which the existing automated systems are already undergoing significant change.

Although many health records have long existed in automated form, they have traditionally supported only specific functions, such as those of the laboratory, pharmacy, or finance department. A shift to patient-based longitudinal health records, now visualized as part of longer-term efforts toward building national health information networks, would fundamentally change the nature of existing record systems. Patient-based longitudinal health records are not merely automated versions of current records. They are patient-specific records in automated form containing all data relevant to the health of an individual (e.g., clinical, financial, and research-oriented information, including diagnostic images) collected over a lifetime. What is foreseen, then, is a single record for every person in the United States, continually expanded from prebirth to death and accessible to a wide range of individuals and institutions for a variety of purposes. [Gostin, 1995:458]

A key issue in the growth of computerized data banks is the development of systems of unique personal identifiers, through which various patient or client health and treatment records could be matched and combined. Along with clear advantages of efficiency and more effective service delivery are linked serious questions of confidentiality and privacy. One proposal is to draw upon the existing system of social security numbers (SSN), now in wide use across the health and human services. However, given its broad usage—and multiple access points—legitimate privacy concerns have been raised [Gostin, 1995; Minor, 1995].[10]

RECORDS, MANAGED CARE, AND DATA BANKS

With or without a system of unique identifiers, the computerization of health and treatment records has proceeded at a rapid pace. Gostin describes the growth of health database organizations (HDOs):

HDOs operate under the authority of government, private, or not-for-profit organizations. They have access to databases of health information and have as their chief mission the public release of data and of analyses performed on the data. HDOs serve specific geographic areas and hold comprehensive health status data on all persons in a defined population. HDOs acquire data from individual health records currently kept by physicians and hospitals. They also collect information from a wide variety of secondary sources: financial transactions from private insurance companies and government programs; public health surveillance and tracking systems; epidemiological, clinical, behavioral, and health services research; surveys conducted by government, academics, and private foundations; and numerous other data sources. The data collected include patient identified and patient identifiable data, as well as aggregate (nonidentifiable) data. They also include data on the performance of physicians and other health care providers. [Gostin, 1995:463]

Along with Medicare and Medicaid databases are those maintained by other federal agencies, by state governments and agencies, and by public and private health and treatment organizations.[11] The result is a massive amount of sometimes very personal, sometimes identifiable data, ranging from clinical diagnosis and treatment to HIV status to various physical and mental disabilities.

The laws protecting the privacy of this information are developing in response to specific needs, but remain varied and inconsistent, sometimes effective and sometimes not. Along with the federal Privacy Act, state privacy acts, and specific federal and state legislation, there are probably broad constitutional protections on informational privacy as discussed in Chapter 3, but these, of course, are limited to situations involving governmental action.

MANAGED CARE

The widespread growth of managed care organizations increases privacy concerns as pressures mount on social workers and other human service professionals to document in detail patient need and treatment to third parties for review and reimbursement. Here the privacy and confidentiality issues center around protection of the confidentiality of the material accessed by the managed care organization, limiting the amount of information shared to the minimum necessary for the review, masking identities where possible, and probably most important, educating the patient or client about the third party access: what information will be reviewed, what confidentiality protections are in place. Release of information should be based on a specific informed consent from the patient or client for the release of the records and information.

Through a review of service delivery (utilization review), confidential records may be accessed:

> Generally a utilization review documents the need for services, diagnoses and treatment plan including short- and long-term goals which are attainable within the time limits of the insurance coverage. The reviewer of this information works directly for the third party payor. And yet, at the time when the patients are concerned with the need for treatment, they probably do not know much at all about this influential third party. Most likely, patients have little awareness that a utilization reviewer may be privy to the private matters of needing treatment, may determine if the treatment is warranted, may determine the course of the confidential relationship, and even decide to whom one may confide. The managed care reviewer may even be informed about the content of treatment and a patient's progress. [Corcoran and Winslade, 1994:353]

DNA DATA BANKS

Almost one-half of the states have established data banks storing DNA (deoxyribonucleic acid) records, and Congress has authorized federal funding to assist in the establishment of data banks in more states. Currently, a DNA data bank is being developed for all those in the armed forces to aid in the identification of casualties in a time of war. Parents are being urged to enroll their children in DNA data banks for identification purposes. And, in a number of states, there are now statutes requiring that certain convicted criminal offenders undergo DNA testing, with the results stored in data banks which can be used in the future to determine if the offender was at the scene of a crime.

Among privacy issues here are the contents of data banks, whose DNA information is stored, who will have access and for what purposes, to what extent an individual whose DNA records are kept in the data bank will have control over that information, and whether that person's informed consent will be required for disclosure. The area is evolving, and though there is little law, some of the picture is emerging.

Advocates of DNA data storage argue that DNA is just another identifying mechanism, akin to fingerprinting but far superior. Human material left at a crime scene—for example, blood, hair strands, fingernails, flecks of skin, and semen—can be analyzed for its DNA composition and matched with known offenders in a data bank to identify a suspect. From this perspective, the storage of DNA is just another weapon to be used in the war against crime. Advocates of expanded DNA data banks argue that with more individuals recorded, the information can be used to identify lost children, victims of mass disaster, persons who cannot remember their identity, and so forth.

Opponents of DNA collection and storage argue that the information now collected and readily available can have far wider uses, constituting a significant invasion of privacy. Much more information than an identity can be abstracted from the DNA samples, including one's ancestry, genetic makeup, and the presence of various genetically based diseases. Opponents argue that the release of this information to governmental agencies, insurance companies, and others could be used to discriminate against the individual through refusals to provide services, employment, or insurance.

Somewhere between these two groups is a third perspective, which argues that the information currently being collected is of very limited use beyond identification purposes, and although the genetic material could be subjected to further analysis and further information abstracted, this is currently a complex and costly process. However, insofar as the DNA data banks retain the tissue or blood after their analysis, this group concedes that far more genetic information could be obtained at a later date, perhaps when the cost of the procedures decreases [De Gorgey, 1990; Burk, 1992; Krent, 1995].

A number of states have enacted statutes requiring mandatory blood testing and DNA analysis of various criminal offenders. Most require the testing of those who have committed sex offenses, and depending on the statute these can range from rape to indecent exposure. Some statutes are broader, including other criminal offenses such as crimes of violence.

Where legal challenges have been raised, to date the statutes have been upheld. Among the decisions upholding involuntary DNA testing are *Vanderlinden v. Kansas,* 874 F.Supp. 1210 (D. Kan. 1995); *Rise v. Oregon,* 59 F.3d 1556 (9th Cir. 1995); *Sanders v. Coman,* 864 F.Supp. 496 (E.D. N.C. 1994); and *Washington v. Olivas,* 856 P.2d 1076 (Wash. 1993). In *Vander-*

linden, the court dismissed a challenge to the Kansas sex offender statute that included mandatory DNA testing for all Kansas prisoners who were convicted of a sex offense. At the time of the suit, approximately 2,700 Kansas prisoners had been tested. In *Rise,* the court upheld the constitutionality of an Oregon statute requiring persons convicted of murder or sex offenses, ranging from rape to public indecency, to submit a blood sample to be used by the state to create the DNA data bank. In *Sanders,* a North Carolina district court upheld a broader convicted felon DNA testing statute, under which over 8,000 inmates had been tested. In *Olivas,* among those challenging the mandatory testing and creation of DNA data banks were individuals who had pled guilty to crimes of assault, robbery, and sexual relations with an underage girlfriend. Most challenges have invoked Fourth Amendment illegal search and Fourteenth Amendment due process privacy protections. Among the grounds for upholding the laws are the minimal intrusiveness of a blood test, a diminished privacy right for incarcerated criminals, and a special need, such as solving crimes and identifying recidivists.

CHAPTER SEVEN

THE DUTY *to* BREACH CONFIDENTIALITY *to* WARN *or* PROTECT *a* POTENTIAL VICTIM

The obligation of social workers, psychologists, psychiatrists, and therapists to breach a confidential relationship and take steps to protect an individual from intended harm remains one of the most discussed and debated topics in the professions. The well-known *Tarasoff* decision in California [*Tarasoff v. Regents of University of California,* 17 Cal.3d 425, 551 P.2d 334 (1976)] held that therapists have a legal duty to breach a confidential relationship and take steps to protect an identifiable third party from foreseeable harm threatened by a patient or client, and in failing to do this, could be liable for damages. Since then, there have been numerous cases decided and statutes enacted that have adopted, modified, or extended that ruling, depending on the jurisdiction.

The professional's obligation to protect another from intended harm has been discussed extensively in the legal, psychiatric, psychological, and social work literature.[1] Here we will first examine the duty to breach confidentiality and protect a third party as presented in the *Tarasoff* case, then analyze later case decisions in California and other jurisdictions, and finally address some state statutes that have been enacted to limit therapists' liability. While there has long been an obligation for physicians to protect others or the community from harmful disease, only relatively recently has a parallel duty to protect been imposed on social workers and other human service professionals.

The *Tarasoff* Case

The factual situation in *Tarasoff* is well known: Prosenjit Poddar, a graduate student at the University of California, had been receiving counseling from professionals at a campus clinic on a voluntary outpatient basis. During one of the counseling sessions with his therapist, he disclosed that he intended to kill an unnamed girl—readily identifiable as his girlfriend, Tatiana Tarasoff—when she returned from a vacation. The therapist, a psychologist, with the concurrence of two other therapists at the clinic, determined that Poddar should be committed to a mental hospital for observation. The campus police were called and notified in writing. Poddar was briefly detained by the police, who determined that he was rational and, upon his promise to stay away from Tatiana Tarasoff, released him. Following this, the campus clinic's director, a psychiatrist, requested that all clinic correspondence and notes be destroyed and no further action be taken. Poddar met Tarasoff upon her return and killed her.

In their wrongful death action, Tarasoff's parents sued the therapists, the campus police, and the Regents of the University of California as their employer for a failure to warn and a failure to confine Poddar. The case twice reached the California Supreme Court on appeal, and the second decision of that court will be discussed here. The California Supreme Court ruled that the suits against the police should be dismissed because of governmental immunity, but the action against the therapists for damages could go forward. In its opinion, the court held that when a therapist determines a third party is endangered by a patient or client, the therapist incurs a duty to disclose confidential communications to protect an intended victim:

> We shall explain that defendant therapists cannot escape liability
> merely because Tatiana herself was not their patient. When a

therapist determines, or pursuant to the standards of his profession should determine, that his patient presents a serious danger of violence to another, he incurs an obligation to use reasonable care to protect the intended victim against such danger. The discharge of this duty may require the therapist to take one or more of various steps, depending upon the nature of the case. Thus it may call for him to warn the intended victim or others likely to apprise the victim of the danger, to notify the police, or to take whatever other steps are reasonably necessary under the circumstances. [17 Ca.3d 425, 431 (1976)]

CONFIDENTIALITY CONSIDERATIONS

Taking steps to protect Tarasoff necessarily would have required revealing confidential communications between Poddar and his therapist, a licensed psychologist. Under California law, these were privileged communications. The defendants argued this would constitute a breach of confidentiality and would have severe consequences for therapeutic practice, which relies on the free flow of confidential information between patient and therapist: "Defendants further argue that free and open communication is essential to psychotherapy, that 'Unless a patient . . . is assured that . . . information [revealed by him] can and will be held in utmost confidence, he will be reluctant to make the full disclosure upon which diagnosis and treatment . . . depends.' The giving of a warning, defendants contend, constitutes a breach of trust which entails the revelation of confidential communications."

Similarly, Justice Clark, in his dissent, warned that such a breach of confidentiality would deter patients and clients from seeking treatment, would limit the effectiveness of treatment because less would be disclosed in the therapeutic relationship, and would result in a distrust of therapists, thereby limiting their effectiveness.

The *Tarasoff* majority disagreed with these conclusions and balanced confidentiality considerations with the potential harm that could occur if there was no disclosure:

We cannot accept without question counsels' implicit assumption that effective therapy for potentially violent patients depends upon either the patient's lack of awareness that a therapist can disclose confidential communications to avert impending danger, or upon the therapist's advance promise never to reveal nonprivileged threats of violence.

We recognize the public interest in supporting effective treatment of mental illness and in protecting the rights of patients to privacy, and the consequent public importance of safeguarding the confidential character of psychotherapeutic communication. Against this interest, however, we must weigh the public interest in safety from violent assault. . . .

We realize that the open and confidential character of psychotherapeutic dialogue encourages patients to express threats of violence, few of which are ever executed. Certainly a therapist should not be encouraged routinely to reveal such threats; such disclosures could seriously disrupt the patient's relationship with his therapist and with the persons threatened. To the contrary, the therapist's obligations to his patient require that he not disclose a confidence unless such disclosure is necessary to avert danger to others, and even then that he do so discreetly, and in a fashion that would preserve the privacy of his patient to the fullest extent compatible with this prevention of the threatened danger. . . .

We conclude that the public policy favoring protection of the confidential character of patient-psychotherapist communications must yield to the extent to which disclosure is essential to avert danger to others. The protective privilege ends where the public peril begins. [17 Cal.3d 425, 441 (1976)]

ESTABLISHING A DUTY TO THIRD PERSONS

A major obstacle for the California court in establishing that the therapists had a duty to protect Tarasoff was that the therapists had no relationship to her, and at common law there was no duty. The court avoided this barrier by drawing upon an exception to the rule of "no relationship therefore no duty" which occurs in special situations such as the relationship of doctors, their patients, and a duty to others in the community. The court said:

Although, as we have stated above, under the common law, as a general rule, one person owed no duty to control the conduct of another,[2] nor to warn those endangered by such conduct, the courts have carved out an exception to this rule in cases in which the defendant stands in some special relationship to either the person whose conduct needs to be controlled or in a relationship to the foreseeable victim of that conduct. Applying this exception to the present case, we noted that a relationship of defendant therapists to either Tatiana or Poddar will suffice to establish a duty of care. . . . Thus, for example, a hospital must exercise reasonable care to control the behavior of a patient which may endanger other persons. A doctor must also warn a patient if the patient's condition or medication renders certain conduct, such as driving a car, dangerous to others. [17 Cal.3d 425, 435 (1976)]

FORESEEABILITY OF HARM

If a special relationship exists between the therapist and patient that creates a duty to third parties to disclose confidential information, then the issue is when this duty is incurred. The key concept for the *Tarasoff* court is "foreseeability," that is, the conditions under which the therapist should have predicted that harm would occur and therefore had a duty to breach confidentiality, disclose information, and protect the third party. The California court rejected the defendants' argument that the violence of a patient or client is essentially unpredictable:

Defendants contend, however, that imposition of a duty to exercise reasonable care to protect third persons is unworkable because therapists cannot accurately predict whether or not a patient will resort to violence. In support of this argument amicus representing the American Psychiatric Association and other professional societies cites numerous articles which indicate that therapists, in the present state of the art, are unable reliably to predict violent acts; their forecasts, amicus claims, tend consistently to overpredict violence, and indeed are more often wrong than right. Since predictions of violence are often erroneous, amicus concludes, the courts should not render rulings that predicate the liability of therapists upon the validity of such predictions.

The role of the psychiatrist, who is indeed a practitioner of medicine, and that of the psychologist who performs an allied function, are like that of the physician who must conform to the standards of the profession and who must often make diagnoses and predictions based upon such evaluations. Thus the judgment of the therapist in diagnosing emotional disorders and in predicting whether a patient presents a serious danger of violence is comparable to the judgment which doctors and professionals must regularly render under accepted rules of responsibility.

We recognize the difficulty that a therapist encounters in attempting to forecast whether a patient presents a serious danger of violence. Obviously, we do not require that the therapist, in making that determination, render a perfect performance; the therapist need only exercise "that reasonable degree of skill, knowledge, and care ordinarily possessed and exercised by members of [that professional specialty] under similar circumstances." Within the broad range of reasonable practice and treatment in which professional opinion and judgment may differ, the therapist is free to exercise his or her own best judgment without liability; proof, aided by hindsight, that he or she judged wrongly is insufficient to establish negligence. [17 Cal.3d 425, 437 (1976)]

STEPS TO PROTECT A THIRD PARTY

Once the therapist has determined that the patient or client does present a potentially serious, imminent danger to another, then the duty of care extends to the third party and the therapist must take steps to protect that person:

> In our view, however, once a therapist does in fact determine, or under applicable professional standards reasonably should have determined, that a patient poses a serious danger of violence to others, he bears a duty to exercise reasonable care to protect the foreseeable victim of that danger. While the discharge of this duty of due care will necessarily vary with the facts of each case, in each instance the adequacy of the therapist's conduct must be measured against the traditional negligence standard of the rendition of reasonable care under the circumstances. . . .
>
> The risk that unnecessary warnings may be given is a reasonable price to pay for lives of possible victims that may be saved.

> We would hesitate to hold that the therapist who is aware that his patient expects to attempt to assassinate the President of the United States would not be obligated to warn the authorities because the therapist cannot predict with accuracy that his patient will commit the crime. [17 Cal.3d 425, 439–440 (1976)]

Under *Tarasoff*, then, the requirements are an identifiable victim and foreseeable serious violence to another; if these are present, the therapist must take steps to protect the victim.

Patient Confidentiality after *Tarasoff*

Following the *Tarasoff* decision, courts, legislatures, and various professionals and their organizations have attempted to deal with the many issues raised in that case. Here we will limit the discussion to those pertinent to confidentiality: who has a duty to breach confidentiality and to protect others, who is an intended victim requiring protection or a warning, when is harm foreseeable thus necessitating the breach of confidentiality, how is the duty discharged, and what are the implications for social worker liability. Since *Tarasoff* is precedent only in California courts, other states have been free to adopt it, modify it, or develop their own approaches and policies. At present, there are a number of different formulations, often depending on how these questions are answered.

WHO HAS A DUTY TO BREACH CONFIDENTIALITY?

The duty to breach a confidential relationship to protect an individual—and potential liability for failure to protect—may apply to a limited number of professions, or may be extended to a broad range of health and mental health professionals depending upon state statutes and decisions. In states that have adopted or extended the *Tarasoff* rule, the duty has most often been applied to psychiatrists, psychotherapists, and therapists. While the profession of psychiatry is well established, "psychotherapists" could include psychologists, social workers, and others as licensed psychotherapists, and "therapists" is an even less precise category since licensed and unlicensed individuals from the fields of psychology, social work, religion, and education, among others, may at times present themselves as therapists or perform therapy. (See, for example, the California statute defining "psychotherapist," Cal. Evid. Code §1010, on page 36.)

The *Tarasoff* decision specifically applies to therapists who are psychiatrists and psychologists, since those were the professional defendants in the case. While many decisions in other jurisdictions are similar in this respect, a number of duty-to-protect court decisions have involved social workers, psychiatric nurses, or other human service professionals. A Vermont Supreme Court decision, *Peck v. Counseling Service of Addison County,* 449 A.2d 422 (Vt. 1985), extended the duty to protect third persons to "mental health professionals," defined in the statute as persons "with professional training, experience and demonstrated competence in the treatment of mental illness, who shall be a physician, psychologist, social worker, nurse or other qualified person designated by the commissioner" [V.S.A. §7101(13)]. In a number of states there are now statutes designed to limit professional liability in these situations (discussed on page 165), including mental health professionals, psychologists, social workers, and others within their coverage. Since these statutes detail steps to be taken to avoid liability when a duty to protect has been incurred by these professionals, by implication, those groups also may be seen as having a duty to protect or warn.

Several decisions have held that nonprofessionals do not have the same obligation. In *Kaminski v. Town of Fairfield,* 578 A.2d 1048 (Conn., 1990), the Connecticut court refused to hold the town liable for the failure of its police officer to warn parents of their son's dangerousness since there was no professional relationship. Similarly, in *Nally v. Grace Community Church of the Valley,* 763 P.2d 948 (Cal. 1988), the California Supreme Court refused to extend a duty to protect a potentially suicidal individual to nonprofessional religious and lay therapists who were working with him. In one case, *Vu v. Singer Co.,* 706 F.2d 1027 (9th Cir. 1983), there was an unsuccessful attempt to hold a Job Corps center liable for the failure to take steps to protect neighbors from actions of its residents.

WHO IS A VICTIM AND WHEN IS A DUTY INCURRED?

In many states that have adopted the *Tarasoff* formulation, the victim must be readily identifiable before the therapist is required to breach confidentiality. However, some decisions have extended the range of potential victims, and correspondingly the duty to protect. The cases appear to fall into three categories:

1. decisions that essentially follow *Tarasoff*, requiring that the victim be identified or readily identifiable—finding that liability could be imposed in situations where the readily identifiable victim is not warned or protected, and refusing to impose liability where there is no readily identifiable victim;

2. decisions that extend *Tarasoff* to include victims who, although not specifically identified, could have been identified by the therapist from observations or past records—holding that a therapist should have concluded that the individuals were in danger, and finding liability if confidentiality was not breached and these individuals were not warned or protected; and

3. decisions that extend *Tarasoff* even further—holding that potential victims include anyone who could be harmed by the acts of the dangerous person, and finding liability could be imposed if there was not a general protection from these acts.

It is important to note that the following discussion of these categories is illustrative, and does not attempt to include all court decisions or the law in all jurisdictions.[3]

Identifiable Victims: Court decisions requiring release of confidential information and taking steps to protect when the victim is identified or readily identifiable.

In *Tarasoff*, the court said that the victim, Tatiana Tarasoff, although not named by Poddar, was "readily identifiable" by the therapist. Several subsequent California decisions addressed this issue. In *Mavroudis v. The Superior Court of San Mateo County*, 162 Cal.Rptr. 724 (1980), the case involved an action by parents who had been injured by their son, who was a psychiatric patient. The California appellate court noted:

> In addition, the intended victim need not be specifically named by the patient. In Tarasoff, the patient did not name his intended victim but she was "readily identifiable." The court indicated what it meant by "readily identifiable" in a footnote in which it recognized that it would be unreasonable to require the therapist to interrogate the patient or to conduct an independent investi-

gation to discover the patient's intended victim's identity. On the other hand, it stated that there are cases in which a "moment's reflection" will reveal the victim's identity. In such cases, the court indicated that the therapist had a duty to protect that person from the danger presented by his patient. [162 Cal.Rptr. 724, 729 (1980)]

In a subsequent decision, *Thompson v. County of Alameda,* 614 P.2d 728 (Cal. 1980), the California court was faced with a situation where the victim was not "readily identifiable." The court found no liability, in part because no specific victim had been identified. Similarly, in *Brady v. Hopper,* 570 F.Supp. 1333 (D.C. Colo. 1983), the court held there was no liability when John Hinckley in his attempt to assassinate President Reagan injured those nearby. The court found that Hinckley had never during his counseling sessions with Dr. Hopper, his therapist, made threats to injure the president or his aides.[4]

Several decisions have also extended liability for injuries to individuals— such as children or relatives—who were in close proximity to the victim and also were injured, reasoning that the therapist should have known they were at risk.[5]

Past Records: Court decisions holding that although no specific threats were made, a review of records would have revealed a third party in danger and warnings should have been given.

In *Jablonski by Pahls v. U.S.,* 712 F.2d 391 (9th Cir. 1983), the patient had volunteered to undergo a psychiatric evaluation at a veterans' hospital. In their evaluation, the therapists concluded there was no emergency and no need for involuntary hospitalization. Subsequent to this he killed his girlfriend. It later turned out that he had a past history of violence toward women who were close to him, which was well documented in his medical records. However, the therapists never requested these records. The court found the therapists and hospital liable for a failure to warn the victim, whom they should have concluded from past records was in danger.[6]

Expanded Class of Victims: Court decisions extending the class of potential victims who should be warned to include all those who could be harmed by the acts of a dangerous person.

Several court decisions outside of California have substantially extended the concept of victims owed a duty of protection to include all those who might be harmed by a dangerous person. Although some of these have been criticized in the literature and in other decisions, they remain authority in their jurisdictions and indicate how far the duty to protect can be extended.

In the earliest of these cases, *Lipari v. Sears Roebuck & Co.*, 497 F.Supp. 185 (1980), a Veterans Administration psychiatric outpatient, who had been an inpatient and had stopped treatment against the advice of his doctors, fired a shotgun purchased from the company into a nightclub, killing Lipari and wounding his wife. In the lawsuit, the company argued that the V.A. should be a defendant in the suit because they knew or should have known that their former outpatient was dangerous. The Nebraska district court agreed, basing their decision not on the readily identifiable victim approach of *Tarasoff*, but on the broader duty that a physician owes to third parties or manufacturers owe to consumers. Although the court said liability was limited to those for whom the V.A. employees "could have reasonably foreseen an unreasonable risk of harm," this included the "Liparis or a class of persons of which the Liparis were members." "To satisfy this standard, the plaintiff need not prove that the V.A.'s employees knew the identity of the plaintiff or her decedent" [497 F.Supp. at 195].

Perhaps the broadest expansion of the duty to protect is *Schuster v. Altenburg*, 424 N.W.2d 159 (Wis. 1988). In that case, an outpatient psychiatric patient was involved in an automobile accident, in which she was injured and her mother killed. Among the claims were that the psychiatrist had not instituted commitment proceedings or warned the family of the patient's "condition or its dangerous implications." Using Wisconsin tort law and precedents rather than *Tarasoff*, the court said in Wisconsin, "a 'duty' exists when it is established that it was foreseeable that an act or omission to act may cause harm to someone. Consequently, the duty to warn or to institute commitment proceedings is not limited by a requirement that threats made be directed to an identifiable target" [424 N.W.2d at 165].

DETERMINING FORESEEABLE DANGER

Perhaps the most hotly debated issue in the duty to warn or protect cases is the ability to determine when danger is foreseeable, requiring a breach of confidentiality and taking steps to protect. In *Tarasoff*, as quoted earlier, the court acknowledged the difficulty of predicting whether a patient will become violent, but said that the therapist must "exercise 'that reasonable degree of skill, knowledge, and care ordinarily possessed and exercised by members of [that professional specialty] under similar circumstances.'" Here we will examine some cases where the courts held that based on what was or could have been known, the therapist should have concluded that harm was foreseeable, breached confidentiality, and warned or protected the potential victim; and several with the opposite result, where the court concluded that harm was not foreseeable. Although many of these cases involve psychiatrists, this does not in any way reduce their importance for social workers and other human service professionals. The purpose of the discussion is to illustrate factors the courts focus upon as determinative in deciding whether harm was or was not foreseeable—a threshold issue in breaching confidentiality to protect a possible victim.

In *Bardoni v. Kim,* 390 N.W.2d 218 (Mich.App. 1986), the court held there was sufficient evidence to go to trial to determine whether the therapist should be held liable for a failure to determine that his patient was a foreseeable danger to his brother, whom he had later killed. The *Bardoni* court said:

> Thus, the next question is whether plaintiff established or could have established that Dr. Kim, according to the standards of his profession, should have known that his patient was dangerous specifically to his brother, Robert Bardoni. Dr. Kim stated in his affidavit and deposition that his patient's paranoia was directed at the school system, that his patient never exhibited any hostility toward or threatened decedents and that he was never informed of any such hostility or threats. Based on these facts, Dr. Kim's position was that he was under no duty to protect the decedents (i.e., he should not have known that decedents were targets of his patient's violence). However, plaintiff's psychiatric expert stated in a second affidavit that, had Dr. Kim performed in accordance with the standard care of his profession, he would have determined that Robert Bardoni was a specific individual who was in danger from Richard Bardoni. The expert supported this conclusion by stating that Dr. Kim, although recognizing the danger posed by his patient, improperly relied on Evelyn Bardoni's statements that she felt her husband was not dangerous and so failed to specifically inquire into the nature of his patient's

delusions. According to plaintiff's expert, Dr. Kim, who diagnosed Richard Bardoni as a paranoid schizophrenic, failed to more specifically inquire as to the nature of his patient's paranoia and, had he done so, his inquiry would have revealed who the patient thought was attacking him (i.e., his brother), and that the patient was laying the groundwork to attack those persons. [390 N.W.2d 218, 225 (1986)]

In *Peck v. The Counseling Service of Addison County, Inc.* 499 A.2d 422 (Vt. 1985), the issue was whether the therapist, a social worker, should have known that the defendant was a foreseeable danger to his father. After a fight with his father, who called him "sick and mentally ill" and told him he should be hospitalized, Peck left home. He told his therapist about the fight and expressed a desire to get back at his father.

"In response to a question by the therapist about how he would get back at his father, John stated, 'I don't know, I could burn down his barn.' After the therapist and John discussed the possible consequences of such an act, John, at the request of the therapist, made a verbal promise not to burn down his father's barn. Believing that John would keep his promise, the therapist did not disclose John's threats to any other staff member of the Counseling Service or to the plaintiffs."

Subsequently, Peck set fire to the barn, which was destroyed. The court held that the harm was foreseeable based on the therapist's current knowledge and Peck's past history, which the therapist had failed to obtain:

> The evidence also revealed that at the time of John's threat the therapist was not in possession of John's most recent medical history. The Counseling Service did not have a cross-reference system between its therapists and outside physicians who were treating the medical problems of its patients. Nor did the Counseling Service have any written policy concerning formal intrastaff consultation procedures when a patient presented a serious risk of harm to another. The defendant's own expert testified that a therapist cannot make a reasonable determination of a patient's propensity for carrying out a threatened act of violence without knowledge of the patient's complete medical history. [499 A.2d 422, 425 (1985)]

Finally, in an Ohio decision, *Littleton v. Good Samaritan Hospital,* 529 N.E.2d 449 (Ohio 1988), the court held that the jury could have found that the danger was foreseeable:

> Dr. Litvak testified that Dr. Murray did not conduct a thorough evaluation of Theresa's homicidal potential. Basing his opinion on his review of the hospital records and the depositions of Dr. Murray and Dr. Wales, Dr. Litvak concluded that Dr. Murray should have talked with Theresa and asked her what her thoughts were, trying to ascertain whether those thoughts were rational or not, what her reasons were for wanting to hurt the baby, what means she had thought of for hurting the baby, if she had a specific date, time and place that she might be doing it, and whether or not she had actually attempted to do anything like that in the past; that Dr. Murray should have ascertained in general how impulsive a person Theresa might be, and then whether her illness might make her more impulsive, unpredictable and unreliable; that Dr. Murray should have determined whether Theresa had previously acted aggressively toward anyone else and under what circumstances; and that Dr. Murray should have determined whether family members had seen Theresa acting in such a way as to indicate she would hurt the baby or heard her talking about hurting the baby. Dr. Litvak found no indication that Dr. Murray went into that amount of detail in the records Dr. Litvak reviewed. [529 N.E.2d 449, 460 (1988)]

In the three decisions, the courts—and the plaintiff's experts—indicate that the therapists' failure to predict the future harm occurred because they did not gather enough available information. In *Bardoni,* the therapist failed to inquire about an intention to harm the brother, relying instead on the assessment of the patient's wife that he presented no danger. In *Peck,* the therapist relied on John's promise, without considering his past behavior and without requesting his past medical records, which were available. In *Littleton,* the therapist concluded there was no plan to injure the baby although harm had been threatened, and did not adequately gather information from the patient or her family.[7]

In other decisions, courts have held that adequate assessments were made, danger was not foreseeable; and warnings were not necessary. In *Doyle v. United States,* 530 F.Supp. 1278 (C.D. Cal. 1982), the patient was discharged from the army after psychiatric treatment and two days later killed a college security guard near his home. It was later learned that the patient had told a high school friend about his fantasies of killing his parents and then going to the college and killing a security guard to obtain his magnum pistol so he could go into the woods and start a revolution. Relatives of the guard argued that had the army psychiatrist asked specific questions, he would have found this out, and so the danger was foreseeable. The court disagreed:

> Plaintiffs attempt to overcome the fact that Mr. Doyle was not an identifiable and foreseeable victim by arguing that specific inquiries would have revealed that Carson's intended victim was a security guard at Ventura College. As to this, plaintiffs presented testimony by psychiatrists which attempted to reconstruct his mental state when he was in the Army. On this basis, plaintiffs argue that had Dr. Johansen conducted his interview differently, Carson's threatening thoughts regarding Ventura College security guards would have been discovered. The court concludes, however, that the evidence offered in support of this theory is too speculative to support recovery under California law.
>
> Of course, the duty to warn victims is dependent upon a determination that the patient is dangerous. But plaintiffs have not proven that Dr. Johansen should have determined that Carson was dangerous. . . . That a person makes threatening statements is not enough. Such statements are commonly expressed to psychiatrists and merely pose but do not answer the difficult question of whether or not danger is actually present. And that question, which is generally difficult for psychiatrists to answer, is even more difficult to answer if the subject has never committed an assaultive act. Here, Carson had no history of violence and was not violent during the five days he was observed in the Fort Polk Hospital or during the four weeks preceding his discharge. . . . That after his discharge Carson killed Mr. Doyle does not constitute proof that Dr. Johansen should have discovered his dangerousness. As the Tarasoff court stated: "Proof,

aided by hindsight that . . . (the therapist) judged wrongly is insufficient. [530 F.Supp. 1278, 1288 (1982)][8]

FORESEEABILITY BASED ON PAST VIOLENT BEHAVIOR

If a patient or client communicates in confidence that he or she has committed a past act of violence, does that indicate that the individual may be a future threat, and therefore that confidentiality must be breached? This would seem to be a judgment call, requiring consultation and careful documentation. In *In re Kevin F.,* 261 Cal.Rptr. 413 (Cal.App. 1989), Kevin F., a minor, was committed to a state institution for committing a delinquent offense. While there, he confided in his psychotherapist that in the past he had set fire to a trailer and people in it at the time were seriously burned. The therapist later informed Kevin's probation officer of the disclosure. Kevin was prosecuted and convicted for the prior offense, and given an additional maximum term of nine years. Kevin challenged that conviction—based only on his confidential disclosure to his therapist—because his communication was privileged and inadmissible. The California court upheld the conviction, relying on Cal. Evid. Code §1024, which states: "There is no privilege under this article if the psychotherapist has reasonable cause to believe that the patient is in such mental or emotional condition as to be dangerous to himself or to the person or property of another and that disclosure of the communication is necessary to prevent the threatened danger." The court found that due to his past actions, Kevin constituted a potential future danger and so fell within the "dangerous person" exception of the statute:

> Kevin admitted to Hobbs [his psychotherapist] that he had set fire to Ames's residence and was fascinated with fire. Kevin was suspected of setting a fire in a trashcan in the bathroom at Our Family. Based on this information, Hobbs believed Kevin presented a danger to the property and residents at Our Family. Her written account of June 10, disclosing Kevin's confession to setting the Ames fire, was included in a report to Kevin's probation officer. The purpose of the report was to explain the reasons for Kevin's discharge from Our Family and inform the probation officer of his dangerous propensities. . . . The residents of Our Family and the institution to which Kevin might be transferred were persons within the contemplation of section 1024

potentially threatened by Kevin's mental and emotional condition as revealed by his confession. [261 Cal.Rptr. 413, 415 (1989)]

DISCHARGING A DUTY TO PROTECT; LIABILITY IMPLICATIONS

In *Tarasoff* the court identified several possible steps to take to protect potential victims: a warning, notification of police, or "whatever other steps are reasonably necessary under the circumstances."

Some states, including California, now list specific steps that certain professionals can take to satisfy their duty to protect a third party from foreseeable harm. These steps are part of broader immunity statutes discussed below. Usually, when a duty to protect is incurred, taking any one of the steps will discharge the duty in terms of liability. Those whose professions are not enumerated in the immunity statutes probably can satisfy any duty they have incurred by taking the same steps, although this is not clear. The theory would be that the enumerated professionals are being held to an even higher standard of performance than others, and by meeting this higher standard no liability should be incurred.

Some states have expanded on the steps suggested in *Tarasoff*. In *Schuster v. Altenberg,* 424 N.W.2d 159 (Wis. 1989), the Wisconsin Supreme Court wrote:

> Certainly, if a patient announces an intention to, for example, leave the psychotherapist's office and commit random acts of violence, the psychotherapist would be unable to warn victims of potential danger and would arguably unjustifiably impinge upon the patient's privacy interests by attempting generalized public warnings. Nevertheless, notwithstanding the absence of a readily identifiable victim, warnings could, in certain instances, effectively be made to, perhaps, the patient's family or police. However, the query as to who might be the appropriate party to warn in light of a general threat to the public is, for the most part, a misdirected question. Specifically, where a patient's dangerous tendencies are imminent yet generalized, the only effective recourse for the psychiatrist or psychologist, in most instances, would be to contact the police in order to institute emergency detention proceedings. . . .

In some circumstances, when the potential victim is an un-identified individual or group, . . . the only responsible inter-vention may be clinical—for example, hospitalization. . . . Specifically, when a psychiatrist is genuinely concerned about a patient's propensity for immediate violence, he or she should ini-tiate civil commitment of the patient at once. . . .

"[W]arning the police and third parties . . . is not necessarily the best way to protect third parties or to help patients. This is not to say that warning cannot be useful. Warning third parties has been shown to be a therapeutic option that can contribute to the patient's progress in therapy. However, warning alone does not always protect third parties. Clearly, use of both warn-ing and clinical remedies such as reassessment, consultation, changes in medication, or civil commitment offers more protec-tion for third parties as well as help for potentially violent pa-tients." [424 N.W.2d 159, 172 (1988)]

Notice to Patients or Clients. Need the social worker or therapist inform the client at the point he or she has concluded there is a foreseeable danger that a disclosure is going to be made? The answer probably depends on the situation and the patient or client. Where the social worker or thera-pist is concerned that such information will increase the possibility of harm to the intended victim—or the professional—it would seem that no notice need be given. The social work code of ethics does state that social workers should inform clients—to the extent possible—about the disclosure of con-fidential information [NASW Code of Ethics standard 1.07(d)]. (See Chap-ter 6.)

Liability for Breach of Confidentiality. Social workers and other human service professionals often express a legitimate concern that in de-ciding whether or not to breach confidentiality and protect another they are in a no-win situation. If they maintain the confidential relationship, they face liability under *Tarasoff* and its progeny, but if they breach confidential-ity, they may face liability for any harm stemming from that breach. There is some case law in this area, and more importantly, for certain profession-als in some states, there now is statutory protection. When there is no statu-tory protection, consultation combined with careful documentation should minimize the chances of successful litigation.

In *Oringer v. Harold G., 556 N.Y.S. 2d 67 (1990)*, a plaintiff sued his therapist for a breach of confidentiality when the therapist revealed a privileged conversation in which the plaintiff had threatened the life of a child. The court held the action could not prevail when there was a reasonable, properly documented decision to take steps to protect someone potentially at risk:

> In his complaint, plaintiff alleged that during a therapy session with defendant, his psychologist for five years, he communicated certain privileged information which defendant thereafter revealed, without plaintiff's authorization. After plaintiff allegedly threatened the life of his son's schoolmate during this session, defendant informed the police that plaintiff was dangerous and told plaintiff's wife that plaintiff would be arrested unless she told him "the names and addresses of certain individuals." Defendant also called the family of a boy named by plaintiff's wife and warned them that plaintiff was violent. Plaintiff claimed that defendant's actions were a breach of CPLR 4507 and caused him physical and emotional harm. . . . Here, defendant established that there is no triable issue of fact as to whether he was justified in disclosing the confidence. Defendant was an employee of the Rockland Psychiatric Institute, a State facility, at the time of his session with plaintiff. His allegation that plaintiff threatened the life of his son's schoolmate during this session was unrefuted. The contemporaneous clinical records kept by defendant document his finding that plaintiff presented a serious and imminent danger and authorized him to disclose the threat to the authorities and to the family of the boy. Moreover, his initial disclosure to plaintiff's spouse, which was made for the purpose of identifying the threatened boy, was also justified. [556 N.Y.S. 2d 67, 68 (1990)]

Statutory Limitations on Liability. A number of states have enacted statutes to limit liability when the professional determines that confidentiality needs to be breached to protect another from harm. Some of these statutes also clarify when the duty to protect another is incurred and how that duty is satisfied. Among the states that have adopted such statutes are

California, Colorado, Indiana, Kentucky, Louisiana, Massachusetts, Minnesota, Montana, New Hampshire, New Jersey, Utah, and Washington. In addition, Ohio has enacted a statute that appears to preclude liability for organizations and individuals in all situations, whether a duty to protect is incurred or not [Ohio Rev. Code §5122.34].

All twelve of the statutes surveyed apply to licensed psychologists and psychiatrists or physicians, while social workers are specifically covered in eight states: California, Colorado, Indiana, Kentucky, Minnesota, Montana, New Jersey, and Utah. Social workers working under the supervision of a psychiatrist or psychologist are likely to be covered in all states.[9] Some statutes also include a much broader range of professionals, including nurses, marriage counselors, mental health professionals, and school psychologists. The Indiana statute also applies to mental health organizations, including some hospitals, private institutions, university or college counseling centers, some mental health partnerships, community health centers, drug/alcohol abuse programs, and state institutions [Ind. Code Ann. §34-4-12.4-1]. Along with named professionals, the Colorado statute specifies: "no mental health hospital, community mental health center or clinic, institution, or their staff" shall be liable [Colo Rev. Stat. §13-21-117].

Some statutes are limited to licensed social workers or licensed clinical social workers—for example, New Jersey and Minnesota; others, such as Colorado and Indiana, appear to include all social workers. Several include social workers as part of a larger professional population—psychotherapists in California, mental health professionals in Kentucky—and in other states such as New Hampshire social workers are included when they are providing treatment under the supervision of a physician. While the statutes differ in some respects, in general:

1. they provide protection for the professional from civil liability for injuries caused by a patient's or client's violent behavior except in situations where the professional has incurred a duty to protect another;

2. where the professional has incurred a duty to protect another, they grant immunity from civil liability if the professional discharges that duty; and

3. they specify that the duty is discharged when the professional takes one or more of the steps enumerated in the statute to protect the victim.

Within these broad similarities, there is variation. New Hampshire, for example, includes threats to property. New Jersey specifies that the duty is incurred when "The patient has communicated to that practitioner a threat of imminent, serious physical violence." Perhaps the greatest variation is in what steps should be taken to protect another when the duty is incurred. Some states, such as California and Utah, specify that certain steps must be taken. The California statute states that the duty is discharged by the professional "making reasonable efforts to communicate the threat to the victim or victims and to a law enforcement agency" [Cal. Civ. Code §43.92]. Other statutes are broader. The Colorado statute, for example, provides: "When there is a duty to warn and protect under the circumstances specified above, the duty shall be discharged by the mental health care provider making reasonable and timely efforts to notify any person or persons specifically threatened, as well as notifying an appropriate law enforcement agency or by taking other appropriate action including, but not limited to, hospitalizing the patient" [Colo. Rev. Stat. §13-21-117].

New Jersey and Indiana list a number of options and absolve the professional of liability if any one is taken. The New Jersey statute provides:

> c. A licensed practitioner of psychology, psychiatry, medicine, nursing, clinical social work or marriage counseling shall discharge the duty to warn and protect as set forth in subsection b. of this section by doing any one or more of the following:
>
> (1) Arranging for the patient to be admitted voluntarily to a psychiatric unit of a general hospital, a short-term care facility, a special psychiatric hospital or a psychiatric facility. . . .
>
> (2) Initiating procedures for involuntary commitment of the patient to a short-term care facility, a special psychiatric hospital or a psychiatric facility. . . .
>
> (3) Advising a local law enforcement authority of the patient's threat and the identity of the intended victim;
>
> (4) Warning the intended victim of the threat, or, in the case of an intended victim who is under the age of 18, warning the parent or guardian of the intended victim; or
>
> (5) If the patient is under the age of 18 and threatens to commit suicide or bodily injury upon himself, warning the parent or guardian of the patient. [N.J.S.A. §2A:62A-16c]

For social workers and other professionals included in these statutes, the advantages are clear. Liability is limited, and many of the ambiguities of the *Tarasoff* decision and its progeny, such as who is an identifiable victim, when there is harm, and what steps must be taken to avoid liability, are clarified. On the other hand, for the intended victims there are disadvantages. Their recovery for harm incurred is limited, and it appears that in one state, Ohio, liability is removed entirely by statute in all situations. Perhaps more important, by specifying that only one—or in some states, two—actions will satisfy the duty and avoid liability, there is no guarantee that the steps opted for are the most effective. The only guarantee is that they will avoid liability. For example, a strong case can be made that depending on the situation and professional judgment, some or all of the possible steps described in the above New Jersey statute might be necessary to protect an individual, but any one will satisfy the liability statute. Note that the therapists in the *Tarasoff* case would have satisfied the New Jersey requirements by notifying the police, but the victim died.

THE DUTY TO PROTECT AND THE SUICIDAL PATIENT OR CLIENT

Most of the liability statutes deal only with violent harm to another individual. The above New Jersey statute differs in that it includes "a patient's violent act . . . against himself" [§2A:62A-16a] and addresses steps to be taken to protect a patient under eighteen from threatened self-harm or suicide. Threatened suicides may implicate ethical questions of self-determination, particularly where the patient or client makes a reasoned, rational decision to end his or her life. Where there are substantial burdens to continuing life or where the individual is in a terminal condition, a professional might make an ethical decision not to intervene. In terms of liability, however, there are risks.

Citing several sources, Bongar notes:

> Failure to prevent suicide is now one of the leading reasons for malpractice suits against mental health professionals. Indeed, the most common legal action involving psychiatric care is the failure to "reasonably" protect patients from harming themselves. . . .
>
> The clinician must take adequate precautions against patient suicide, consistent with accepted psychotherapeutic practices

and on the basis of his or her knowledge and assessment of the patient.[10] [Bongar, 1991:39]

Since the *Tarasoff* decision dealt only with the issue of foreseeable harm to another, it does not directly apply to this issue. In *Bellah v. Greenson*, 147 Cal.Rptr. 535 (1978), the California appellate court refused to extend the *Tarasoff* duty-to-protect requirements to obligate a therapist to warn the parents of an adult child that she might be suicidal. However, the court left open the malpractice question of whether the defendant therapist had taken appropriate measures to prevent the suicide.[11]

In the case of a minor who is a potential suicide, some courts have stated there is an obligation to take steps to protect the child, and the standard for foreseeable harm appears to be much lower. In *Eisel v. School Board of Montgomery County*, 597 A.2d 447 (Md. 1991), the court held that there could be liability where a school guidance counselor heard secondhand that one of his students was planning suicide and, relying on the student's denial of any suicidal intention, did nothing further. Citing the national problem of teenage suicides as well as school policy, the court said that in the case of adolescents, "even a remote possibility of suicide may be enough to establish a duty" [597 A.2d 447, 454 (1991)]. (See generally, Chapter 8.)

THE DUTY TO PROTECT AND SOCIAL WORK PRACTICE

While the *Tarasoff* decision established a duty to protect in California, it was originally limited to psychologists and psychiatrists as therapists, and applied to a limited range of situations. It has since then been extended to different professionals, including social workers, in many states and at times has broadened to cover many more situations. While it is generally conceded that those in danger should be protected, the duty remains troublesome for professionals and students for all the reasons addressed in this chapter. While the law has many variations, there are strong reasons based in practice and ethics for taking steps to protect others. Where statutory immunity laws have been enacted, they often clarify what minimum standards are required. Particular vigilance is called for when dealing with children, especially when self-harm is indicated.

CHAPTER EIGHT

MINORS *and* PRIVACY

At common law, children possessed few rights. They were once regarded as property and later (and to some extent even now) as incompetents who, unless married, apprenticed, or otherwise emancipated, were incapable of exercising most civil rights—such as owning property, making contracts, getting married, or filing lawsuits—available to adults.[1] While many of these restrictions still exist in America today, there are important exceptions, particularly in the area of privacy law. In general, unless a minor is legally emancipated, the parents are legal guardians. If there are no living parents, or where parental rights have been terminated, another adult—often a relative—or the state can be appointed guardian. In any case, most decision-making powers are vested in the adult, not the child. Included here are decisions to consent to treatment or therapy, and the right to access medical records, school records, or treatment records kept by professionals such as therapists, counselors, or psychologists.

"Traditionally at common law, and still today, unemancipated minors lack some of the most fundamental rights of self-determination—including even the right to liberty in its narrow sense, i.e., the right to come and go at will. They are subject, even as to their physical freedom, to the control of their parents or guardians" [*Vernonia School District 47J v. Acton,* 132 L.Ed.2d 564, 575 (1995)]. Yet minors do possess legal rights, under both federal and state law. Although the federal constitution never mentions minors, children, or families, a number of recent Supreme Court decisions have addressed the constitutional rights of minors. In *Planned Parenthood of Central Missouri v. Danforth,* 428 U.S. 52 (1976), the Court observed: "Minors, as well as adults, are protected by the Constitution and possess constitutional rights" [428 U.S. 52, 74 (1976)].[2]

Among the constitutionally protected rights the Supreme Court has held apply to minors include a right of privacy to make decisions about abortion, *Planned Parenthood of Central Missouri v. Danforth* (above); the right to purchase contraceptives, *Carey v. Population Services International,* 431 U.S. 678 (1977); the right of free expression and peaceful protest in public schools, *Tinker v. Des Moines School Dist.,* 393 U.S. 503 (1969); the right not to salute the American flag, *West Virginia Bd. of Education v. Barnette,* 319 U.S. 624 (1943); the right of equal protection against racial discrimination, *Brown v. Board of Education,* 347 U.S. 483 (1954); the right of due process in school suspensions, *Goss v. Lopez,* 419 U.S., 565 (1975); and a variety of rights as defendants in delinquency or criminal proceedings.[3]

At the same time, the Supreme Court has made it clear minors do not possess all the constitutional rights that adults have, nor do they necessarily possess them to the same degree. For example, certain constitutional protections to which adults are entitled as defendants in criminal courts are not available to minors, such as a trial by jury.[4] The state may legally limit what minors may view or read, and how late they can stay out at night.[5] Public schools, in particular, are an area in which the Court has ruled that minors are entitled to less constitutional protection than adults in similar situations. Thus minors and adults are entitled to First Amendment free speech protection and Fourth Amendment prohibitions against illegal searches and seizures, but in schools minors legally can be subjected to searches with less than probable cause; can be restricted in their speech, publications, and dress; and can be tested for drug use without suspicion. Nor are minors protected from corporal punishment in schools by the Eighth Ammendment's prohibition against cruel and unusual punishment.[6] In sum, although minors are entitled to a number of constitutional protections, the reality is that they possess many of them to a lesser degree than adults.

Autonomy and Paternalism

At times, minors are legally regarded as autonomous actors, capable of making decisions for themselves, and this decision making is protected by various constitutional provisions including due process and a right to privacy implicit in the Fourteenth Amendment. At other times, minors are viewed as incapable of making their own decisions, and require another— either an adult or the state—to make decisions for them. This tension in the law can be seen as a conflict between two behavioral perspectives: autonomy, viewing minors as independent actors, and paternalism, viewing minors as incapable of acting independently and needing someone older and wiser to make decisions for them in their own best interests.

Two examples suffice. In *Planned Parenthood of Central Missouri v. Danforth* (above), the Supreme Court held that certain minor females— known as "mature minors"—have a privacy right that includes a right to decide with their physician to have an abortion without parental approval. Yet in another case decided only a few years later, *Parham v. J.R.,* 442 U.S. 584 (1979), the Court held that parents should decide, along with a mental health professional, when to voluntarily place a minor in a state mental hospital—even against the minor's wishes—and when the minor should be released.

In the *Planned Parenthood* case the court said: "Constitutional rights do not mature and come into being magically only when one attains the state-defined age of majority. Minors, as well as adults, are protected by the Constitution and possess constitutional rights. . . . Any independent interest the parent may have in the termination of the minor daughter's pregnancy is no more weighty than the right of privacy of the competent minor mature enough to have become pregnant" [428 U.S. 52, 79 (1976)].

However, in *Parham,* the Court said: "Simply because the decision of a parent is not agreeable to a child or because it involves risks does not automatically transfer the power to make that decision from the parents to some agency or officer of the state. The same characterizations can be made for a tonsillectomy, appendectomy, or other medical procedure. Most children, even in adolescence, simply are not able to make sound judgments concerning many decisions, including their need for medical care or treatment. Parents can and must make those judgments" [442 U.S. 584, 604 (1979)].

The difference in these perspectives may to some extent reflect differences in the types of decisions being made and changes in the composition of the Court (for example, Justice Blackmun, who wrote the *Planned Parenthood v. Danforth* decision, dissented from *Parham*); nonetheless the two sometimes contradictory perspectives remain today. For example, there are laws that allow eighteen-year-olds to vote but not to purchase alcoholic beverages, allow sixteen-year-olds to purchase contraceptives but not to view sexually explicit materials, and provide separate judicial and correctional systems for delinquents but allow waiver to adult courts for some crimes by the age of twelve or fourteen. The Supreme Court has upheld capital punishment for minors, while various other statutes limit confinement for minors and regard it as rehabilitation rather than punishment.[7]

EMANCIPATED MINORS

In many states, some minors are recognized as emancipated—free of parental control and able to assume many of the rights and obligations of adults. Emancipation may occur through parental permission, by court order, or by certain actions of the minor such as marriage, childbirth, independent living, or enlisting in the armed forces, depending upon the state of residence. Through emancipation, these minors can assume many of the decision-making responsibilities formerly vested in their parents, including consent to health care and treatment. For example, in California a minor may become emancipated through military service, marriage, or court decree after a finding that the minor is at least fourteen years old, living apart from parents of guardian, and is managing his or her own financial affairs [Cal. Civ. Code §7002].

California has particularly detailed statutory provisions for emancipation and the rights of emancipated minors. Once emancipated, the minor in California is considered an adult for many purposes and may do any of the following:

(1) Consent to medical, dental, or psychiatric care, without parental consent, knowledge, or liability. (2) Enter into a binding

contract or give a delegation of power. (3) Buy, sell, lease, en-
cumber, exchange, or transfer an interest in real or personal
property, including, but not limited to, shares of stock in a domestic or foreign corporation or a membership in a nonprofit
corporation. (4) Sue or be sued in the minor's own name. (5)
Compromise, settle, arbitrate, or otherwise adjust a claim, action, or proceeding by or against the minor. (6) Make or revoke
a will. (7) Make a gift, outright or in trust. . . . (15) Establish the
minor's own residence. (16) Apply for a work permit pursuant to
Section 49110 of the Education Code without the request of the
minor's parents. (17) Enroll in a school or college. [Cal. Civil
Code §7050]

As evidence of emancipation, the minor may apply to have the information
recorded on his or her driver's license [Cal. Civil Code §7140].

Minors and Decisional Privacy

Minors possess several types of decisional privacy rights. For the most part,
minors' decisions are protected from interference by the state through their
parents' privacy rights or perhaps through a broader familial privacy. For
example, the state cannot interfere with basic family decisions around education, nutrition, medical treatment, religion, clothing, and so forth barring
a violation of child abuse statutes, compulsory education laws, and the like,
in which case the state may step in, assume the role of the parent (in loco
parentis), and give permission for the needed care, treatment, or education.

A minor's decision making, though protected by parental or familial privacy, occurs mainly where the interests of parent and child are reasonably
congruent and there is agreement on the decision being made. In most areas,
parents are legally empowered to make decisions for their children, and minors themselves are not empowered to make their own decisions independent of their parents. Legally, parents select schools, make choices about
religious upbringing, and decide on needed medical treatment, involving the
minor as they—and the minor—wish.[8]

There are important exceptions, however, such as a minor's consent for needed emergency medical treatment when a parent is not available to give consent, or a minor's consent for treatment for drug or alcohol abuse, treatment for sexually transmitted diseases, or, in some instances, procuring an abortion or obtaining contraceptives.

MINORS AND ABORTION

In *Planned Parenthood v. Danforth,* the Supreme Court struck down a Missouri statute that, among other provisions, required parental consent before a minor female could have an abortion. The Court wrote:

> We agree with appellants and with the courts whose decisions have just been cited that the State may not impose a blanket provision, such as §3(4), requiring the consent of a parent or person in loco parentis as a condition for abortion of an unmarried minor during the first 12 weeks of her pregnancy. Just as with the requirement of consent from the spouse, so here, the State does not have the constitutional authority to give a third party an absolute, and possibly arbitrary, veto over the decision of the physician and his patient to terminate the patient's pregnancy, regardless of the reason for withholding the consent. . . . Any independent interest the parent may have in the termination of the minor daughter's pregnancy is no more weighty than the right of privacy of the competent minor mature enough to have become pregnant. [428 U.S. 52, 73, 75 (1976)]

However, the Court qualified this, stating that not all minors are able to give an informed consent for an abortion: "We emphasize that our holding that §3(4) is invalid does not suggest that every minor, regardless of age or maturity, may give effective consent for termination of her pregnancy. The fault with §3(4) is that it imposes a special-consent provision, exercisable by a person other than the woman and her physician, as a prerequisite to a minor's termination of her pregnancy and does so without a sufficient justification for the restriction" [428 U.S. 52, 75 (1976)].

Later Supreme Court cases have addressed various aspects of a minor's decision making in abortion and the role of parents, including parental consent, parental notification, and mandatory waiting periods for minors who wish to have an abortion. In *Bellotti v. Baird,* 443 U.S. 622 (1979), the

Court held that a Massachusetts statute requiring an unmarried minor under eighteen to have the consent of both her parents before she could undergo an abortion was unconstitutional. In its decision the Court indicated approval of a plan where as an alternative to parental consent the state provided a "judicial bypass": a minor not wishing to obtain parental consent could go directly to a court to request judicial consent for the abortion. If the court found she was a "mature minor" capable of making an informed abortion decision, the court would approve the procedure. If the court found that she was not mature, the abortion procedure could still be approved by the court if it found it was in her best interests.[9]

The issue of parental notification was raised in *H.L. v. Matheson,* 450 U.S. 398 (1981), where the Court upheld the constitutionality of a Utah statute mandating prior notification of the parents of a minor who wanted to have an abortion when she was not a "mature" minor. According to the Court, the minor who brought the action was not a mature minor because she was "unmarried, fifteen years of age, resides at home and is a dependent of her parents."

In *Hodgson v. Minnesota,* 497 U.S. 417 (1990), the Court voided that part of a state statute that required two-parent prior notification of their minor daughter's decision to have an abortion, but upheld that part of the statute that required two-parent notification as long as a judicial bypass was provided so that minors who did not wish to have their parents notified could apply to the court for consent for the abortion. Exceptions were allowed in cases of child abuse or incest. The Court was particularly concerned with the required notice of both parents, pointing to the prevalence of single-parent households and questioning the involvement of an absent parent in the decision. The Court held that if the trial court found that the minor was a mature minor or that parental notification would not be in her best interests, the court could consent to the abortion.[10]

According to the Court in *Hodgson,* at least thirty-eight states have enacted statutes that mandate the involvement of one or both parents in a minor's abortion decision, either requiring prior parental notification or consent. To meet the requirements of *Bellotti* and *Hodgson,* however, such statutes would have to provide for a judicial bypass for those minors who do not want parental involvement in their decisions.

MINORS AND CONTRACEPTION

Following the *Planned Parenthood v. Danforth* decision, in *Population Services International v. Carey*, 431 U.S. 678 (1977), the Court found unconstitutional a New York statute that, among other provisions, criminalized the distribution of contraceptives to minors under sixteen. The state's rationale for preventing the distribution of contraceptives to minors was that it served as "a regulation of the morality of minors, in furtherance of the State's policy against promiscuous sexual intercourse among the young" [431 U.S. 678, 691 (1977)]. In its decision, the Court wrote:

> Of particular significance to the decision of this case, the right to privacy in connection with decisions affecting procreation extends to minors as well as to adults. Planned Parenthood of Central Missouri v. Danforth held that a State "may not impose a blanket provision . . . requiring the consent of a parent or person in loco parentis as a condition for abortion of an unmarried minor during the first 12 weeks of her pregnancy. . . . State restrictions inhibiting privacy rights of minors are valid only if they serve "any significant state interest . . . that is not present in the case of an adult. . . ." Since the State may not impose a blanket prohibition, or even a blanket requirement of parental consent, on the choice of a minor to terminate her pregnancy, the constitutionality of a blanket prohibition of the distribution of contraceptives to minors is a fortiori foreclosed. The State's interests in protection of the mental and physical health of the pregnant minor, and in protection of potential life are clearly more implicated by the abortion decision than by the decision to use a nonhazardous contraceptive. [431 U.S. 678, 693 (1977)]

A MINOR'S CONSENT TO TREATMENT

Some states allow minors who have reached a certain age—anywhere from twelve to sixteen years old—to consent to emergency or routine medical treatment or counseling services without parental consent. In some states, this consent is limited to treatment for drug or alcohol abuse or contagious or sexually transmitted diseases; in others the range of treatment is broader. Typical of the statutes permitting consent for emergency medical treatment is the Rhode Island statute, which provides: "Any person of the age of sixteen (16) or over or married may consent to routine emergency medical or surgical care. A minor parent may consent to treatment of his or her child" [R.I. Gen. Laws §23-4.6-1].

In Kansas, if no parent or guardian is immediately available, a minor over sixteen can give consent,[11] while in Oregon, minors fifteen and older can consent to medical treatment.[12] However, coupled with this provision is the Oregon statutory authority for parental notification of any treatment, which can be given without the minor's consent.[13]

In California, minors fifteen years of age and older, living apart from their parents and not dependent upon them for financial support, may consent to their own medical and dental care. As in the Oregon statute, parental notification of such care is permitted without a minor's consent [Cal. Civ. Code §6922].

Also in California, a minor twelve years or older may consent to mental health treatment, counseling, or residential shelter services if two conditions are satisfied: "(1) The minor, in the opinion of the attending professional person, is mature enough to participate intelligently in the outpatient services or residential shelter services. (2) The minor (A) would present a danger of serious physical or mental harm to self or to others without the mental health treatment or counseling or residential shelter services, or (B) is the alleged victim of incest or child abuse" [Cal. Civ. Code §6924(b)]. Notification of the minor's parent or guardian is required if residential services are provided, and participation of the minor's parent or guardian in the mental health treatment or counseling is required unless the professional finds that the involvement would be "inappropriate" [Cal. Civ. Code §6924(c), §6924(d)].

Other states vary significantly in terms of parental notification of a minor's treatment, ranging from permitting notification to prohibiting it in most situations. For example, Minnesota permits parental notification for any treatment where a failure to notify would seriously jeopardize the health of the minor.[14] In North Carolina, on the other hand, most parental notification is prohibited.[15]

Privacy and the Minor's Treatment for Substance Abuse and Sexually Transmitted Diseases. Many states have enacted statutes permitting the confidential treatment of minors for drug or alcohol abuse or sexually transmitted diseases without parental consent. The rationale is to encourage minors with substance abuse problems or contagious venereal diseases to obtain needed treatment. With a minor's consent, his or her parents may be involved in the treatment process, but if the minor does not want the parents to know of the problem, treatment can proceed on a confidential basis. In addition, federally funded drug and alcohol treatment programs are governed by strict federal confidentiality laws. (For a more detailed discussion of substance abuse program confidentiality, see Chapter 10.)

For example, in California minors twelve and older may consent to medical treatment or counseling services for substance abuse provided by professionals including clinical social workers, marriage and family counselors, and psychologists:

> (b) A minor who is 12 years of age or older may consent to medical care and counseling relating to the diagnosis and treatment of a drug or alcohol related problem.
>
> (c) The treatment plan of a minor authorized by this section shall include the involvement of the minor's parent or guardian, if appropriate, as determined by the professional person or treatment facility treating the minor. The professional person providing medical care or counseling to a minor shall state in the minor's treatment record whether and when the professional person attempted to contact the minor's parent or guardian, and whether the attempt to contact the parent or guardian was successful or unsuccessful, or the reason why, in the opinion of the professional person, it would not be appropriate to contact the minor's parent or guardian.
>
> (d) The minor's parents or guardian are not liable for payment for any care provided to a minor pursuant to this section, except that if the minor's parent or guardian participates in a counseling program pursuant to this section, the parent or guardian is liable for the cost of the services provided to the minor and the parent or guardian. [Cal. Civ. Code. §6929]

Recent revisions in the California statute permit a parent to seek medical care and counseling services for a minor child with a drug- or alcohol-related problem even if the child does not consent to the treatment, and, where such treatment has been requested, permit the parent access to medical information about the treatment even if the minor does not consent to disclosure [Cal. Civ. Code. §6929(f),(g)].

Age limits for a minor's consent to treatment in these situations vary across the states, with some setting twelve years of age as the minimum age for consent (e.g., Vermont, Wisconsin, Massachusetts), others with older minimum age requirements, and some specifying no minimum age at all (e.g., Oregon, Minnesota, Colorado).

In light of this wide variation in state laws in terms of treatments covered, minimum ages for a minor's consent, and whether parental notification is necessary, permitted, or forbidden, it is incumbent on social workers to consult their current state statutes and to keep abreast of changes. It also should be noted that while treatment for sexually transmitted diseases is on a confidential basis, state statutes do require reporting cases to public health agencies, who are empowered to investigate on a confidential basis, and if necessary may attempt to trace sexual partners for disease control purposes.

A Minor's Privacy in the Public Schools

No area better illustrates the competing interests of paternalism and autonomy than the public schools. While the courts have held that school administrators acting in the role of parents do not have unfettered control over their students, the courts have made it clear that they will defer to school administrators who are trying to educate children and impose discipline. In a 1968 decision, *Ferrell v. Dallas Independent School District,* 392 F.2d 697 (5th Cir. 1968), the circuit court upheld a high school principal's decision to deny enrollment to four male students with long hair as necessary to maintain order. In *Goss v. Lopez,* 419 U.S. 565 (1975), the Supreme Court required minimal procedural due process protections for high school students facing suspensions—however, the protections were designed not to intrude upon the administration of the school. Not infrequently parents side with the schools and their policies that limit their children's rights.[16]

Yet minors in the public schools are not without rights. In a frequently quoted passage, the Supreme Court observed: "It can hardly be argued that either students or teachers shed their constitutional rights to freedom of speech or expression at the schoolhouse gate. This has been the unmistak-able holding of this Court for almost 50 years" [*Tinker v. Des Moines Independent Community School District*, 393 U.S. 503, 506 (1969)].

In *Tinker,* the Court upheld students' First Amendment constitutional right of free expression—to wear black armbands in school to protest the Vietnam war, when there was no showing that the action was disruptive or interfered with the educational process. However, in two later decisions, the Court upheld the public schools' right to limit free speech. In one decision the Court upheld the punishment of a high school student who made a nom-inating speech for a class officer, which while not obscene, was viewed as unacceptable by the school [*Bethel School District No. 403 v. Fraser,* 478 U.S. 675 (1986)]. In another, *Hazelwood School District v. Kuhlmeier,* 484 U.S. 260 (1988), the Court upheld the censorship of a high school newspa-per by the school principal because it discussed pregnancy, birth control, and divorce. The Court wrote:

> Educators are entitled to exercise greater control over this sec-ond form of student expression to assure that participants learn whatever lessons the activity is designed to teach, that readers or listeners are not exposed to material that may be inappropriate for their level of maturity, and that the views of the individual speaker are not erroneously attributed to the school. . . .
>
> In addition, a school must be able to take into account the emotional maturity of the intended audience in determining whether to disseminate student speech on potentially sensitive topics, which might range from the existence of Santa Claus in an elementary school setting to the particulars of teenage sexual activity in a high school setting. [484 U.S. 260, 272 (1988)]

PUBLIC SCHOOL SEARCHES

In Highland, Indiana, in May 1979, approximately 2,800 junior and senior high school students were locked in their school building and confined to their classroom desks while, at the request of the school administrators, fourteen teams of police and canine units searched the classrooms. The dogs, trained in drug detection, sniffed every student and his or her belong-ings. The dogs alerted their handlers to fifty students, whose pockets were searched. After the pocket search, the dogs continued to identify twelve students. Body searches were conducted of these students, including Jane Doe, a junior high school student who, along with others, was required to undress totally. She was visually examined and her clothing was checked. No drugs were found. (She later reported that she had been playing with her dog, which was in heat, earlier that morning.) The trial court upheld the legality of the search conducted with the dogs and the subsequent pocket search. While holding the strip searches unconstitutional, the court held there could be no financial damages awarded because the school officials were protected by a qualified immunity when acting in good faith [*Doe v. Renfrow,* 475 F.Supp. 1012 (N.D.Ind. 1979)].[17]

On appeal, the federal circuit court upheld the constitutionality of all searches except the strip search, where the school administrators and school board could be held liable for monetary damages.[18]

In *New Jersey v. T.L.O.,* 469 U.S. 325 (1985), the Supreme Court upheld a warrantless search of a high school student's purse by a school administrator. A teacher discovered T.L.O. and another girl smoking in a school restroom, in violation of school rules. Taken to the administrative offices, T.L.O. denied she had been smoking. An assistant principal took her into his private office and requested permission to inspect her purse. The search revealed a package of cigarettes and cigarette rolling papers, which he associated with marijuana use. Searching further, he found "a small amount of marijuana, a pipe, a number of empty plastic bags, a substantial quantity of money in one-dollar bills, an index card that appeared to be a list of students who owed T.L.O. money, and two letters that implicated T.L.O. in marijuana dealing."

The Court held that the Fourth Amendment applied but a search warrant requirement was an unnecessary burden for school administrators. Balancing the Fourth Amendment requirement for probable cause against the needs of the school administrators to maintain discipline and order in the schools, the Court further held that the probable cause standard was too stringent, and that a search of a student could be conducted in the schools as long as it was based on a more relaxed standard, a reasonable cause:

> The school setting also requires some modification of the level of
> suspicion of illicit activity needed to justify a search. Ordinarily,
> a search—even one that may permissibly be carried out without

a warrant—must be based upon "probable cause" to believe that a violation of the law has occurred. However, "probable cause" is not an irreducible requirement of a valid search. The fundamental command of the Fourth Amendment is that searches and seizures be reasonable, and although "both the concept of probable cause and the requirement of a warrant bear on the reasonableness of a search, . . . in certain limited circumstances neither is required." . . . We join the majority of courts that have examined this issue in concluding that the accommodation of the privacy interests of schoolchildren with the substantial need of teachers and administrators for freedom to maintain order in the schools does not require strict adherence to the requirement that searches be based on probable cause to believe that the subject of the search has violated or is violating the law. Rather, the legality of a search of a student should depend simply on the reasonableness, under all the circumstances, of the search. . . . Under ordinary circumstances, a search of a student by a teacher or other school official will be "justified at its inception" when there are reasonable grounds for suspecting that the search will turn up evidence that the student has violated or is violating either the law or the rules of the school. Such a search will be permissible in its scope when the measures adopted are reasonably related to the objectives of the search and not excessively intrusive in light of the age and sex of the student and the nature of the infraction. [469 U.S. 325, 339 (1985)]

There has been some litigation around the related issue of privacy of student lockers in the school. In general, courts have upheld student locker searches.[19]

DRUG TESTING IN PUBLIC SCHOOLS

In *Vernonia School District 47J v. Acton,* 132 L.Ed.2d 564 (1995), the U.S. Supreme Court upheld the mandatory drug testing of grade and high school athletes. In that case, the school district adopted a policy authorizing random urinalysis drug testing of all students participating in interscholastic athletic programs. The parents of a twelve-year-old seventh grade student who wished to play football refused to sign the mandatory consent form and brought suit claiming that the mandatory drug testing was unconstitutional.[20]

Justice Scalia, writing for the majority, reaffirmed that students in school have fewer rights because of the school setting:

> T.L.O. did not deny, but indeed emphasized, that the nature of [the school's] power is custodial and tutelary, permitting a degree of supervision and control that could not be exercised over free adults. "[A] proper educational environment requires close supervision of schoolchildren, as well as the enforcement of rules against conduct that would be perfectly permissible if undertaken by an adult." . . . For their own good and that of their classmates, public school children are routinely required to submit to various physical examinations, and to be vaccinated against various diseases. Particularly with regard to medical examinations and procedures, therefore, "students within the school environment have a lesser expectation of privacy than members of the population generally." [132 L.Ed.2d 564, 575 (1995)]

Of particular importance to the Court was a reduced expectation of privacy in the school which has justified other searches. (See generally Chapter 3.) Here the Court addressed the privacy expectations of student athletes:

> Legitimate privacy expectations are even less with regard to student athletes. School sports are not for the bashful. They require "suiting up" before each practice or event, and showering and changing afterwards. Public school locker rooms, the usual sites for these activities, are not notable for the privacy they afford. The locker rooms in Vernonia are typical: no individual dressing rooms are provided; shower heads are lined up along a wall, unseparated by any sort of partition or curtain; not even all the toilet stalls have doors. As the United States Court of Appeals for the Seventh Circuit has noted, there is "an element of 'communal undress' inherent in athletic participation." [132 L.Ed.2d 564, 577 (1995)]

Along with a reduced privacy expectation, the Court agreed that the concern of school administrators and parents over student drug use was sufficient to justify the search. It found neither the requirement for a reasonable suspicion nor that the administration have a "compelling interest" in the search necessary:

> That the nature of the concern is important—indeed, perhaps compelling—can hardly be doubted. Deterring drug use by our Nation's schoolchildren is at least as important as enhancing efficient enforcement of the Nation's laws against the importation of drugs, which was the governmental concern in Von Raab, or deterring drug use by engineers and trainmen, which was the governmental concern in Skinner. School years are the time when the physical, psychological, and addictive effects of drugs are most severe. . . . And of course the effects of a drug-infested school are visited not just upon the users, but upon the entire student body and faculty, as the educational process is disrupted. In the present case, moreover, the necessity for the State to act is magnified by the fact that this evil is being visited not just upon individuals at large, but upon children for whom it has undertaken a special responsibility of care and direction. Finally, it must not be lost sight of that this program is directed more narrowly to drug use by school athletes, where the risk of immediate physical harm to the drug user or those with whom he is playing his sport is particularly high. Apart from psychological effects, which include impairment of judgment, slow reaction time, and a lessening of the perception of pain, the particular drugs screened by the District's Policy have been demonstrated to pose substantial physical risks to athletes. [132 L.Ed.2d 564, 579 (1995)]

In her dissent to the mandatory suspicionless drug testing in Vernonia, Justice O'Connor wrote:

> The population of our Nation's public schools, grades 7 through 12, numbers around 18 million. By the reasoning of today's decision, the millions of these students who participate in inter-

scholastic sports, an overwhelming majority of whom have given school officials no reason whatsoever to suspect they use drugs at school, are open to intrusive bodily search.

In justifying this result, the Court dispenses with a requirement of individualized suspicion on considered policy grounds. First, it explains that precisely because every student athlete is being tested, there is no concern that school officials might act arbitrarily in choosing who to test. Second, a broad-based search regime, the Court reasons, dilutes the accusatory nature of the search. In making these policy arguments, of course, the Court sidesteps powerful, countervailing privacy concerns. Blanket searches, because they can involve "thousands or millions" of searches, "pose a greater threat to liberty" than do suspicion-based ones, which "affect one person at a time" . . .

I recognize that a suspicion-based scheme, even where reasonably effective in controlling in-school drug use, may not be as effective as a mass, suspicionless testing regime. In one sense, that is obviously true—just as it is obviously true that suspicion-based law enforcement is not as effective as mass, suspicionless enforcement might be. "But there is nothing new in the realization" that Fourth Amendment protections come with a price. . . .

The instant case, however, asks whether the Fourth Amendment is even more lenient . . . i.e., whether it is so lenient that students may be deprived of the Fourth Amendment's only remaining, and most basic, categorical protection: its strong preference for an individualized suspicion requirement, with its accompanying antipathy toward personally intrusive, blanket searches of mostly innocent people. It is not at all clear that people in prison lack this categorical protection, and we have said "we are not yet ready to hold that the schools and the prisons need be equated for purposes of the Fourth Amendment." Thus, if we are to mean what we often proclaim—that students do not "shed their constitutional rights . . . at the schoolhouse gate,"—the answer must plainly be no. [132 L.Ed.2d 564, 583 (1995)]

SCHOOL RECORDS

The single most important law governing school records is the federal Family Educational Rights and Privacy Act (FERPA) (also known as the Buckley/Pell Amendment), 20 U.S.C. §1232g. The act conditions federal funding to educational agencies and institutions on compliance with its terms. In general, the act specifies the conditions for student and parent access to educational records; the procedures for challenging and correcting inaccurate educational records; and the requisites for the release of educational records or identifying student information to other individuals, agencies, or organizations. For students who are eighteen years old or older, or who attend post-secondary institutions, the access to records and the consent required before access by others resides with them rather than their parents.

The act covers educational institutions and agencies, public or private, that receive federal funds [20 U.S.C. §1232g(a)(3)]. Education records are defined as "those records, files, documents, and other materials which—(i) contain information directly related to a student; and (ii) are maintained by an educational agency or institution or by a person acting for such agency or institution" [20 U.S.C. §1232g(a)(4)(A)], and specifically exclude

> 1. records of instructional, supervisory, and administrative personnel among others where the records are in the sole possession of the person making the record and which are not accessible by anyone else except a substitute. 2. records maintained by a law enforcement unit of the educational institution or agency that were created by the unit for law enforcement purposes. 3. records of employees who are not attending the educational institutions or agencies when the records are made in the "normal course of business" and relate exclusively to that employee as an employee. 4. those records of students eighteen and older, or attending post secondary schools, which are made or maintained by a "physician, psychiatrist, psychologist, or other recognized professional or paraprofessional acting in his professional or paraprofessional capacity, or assisting in that capacity," where the records are made and used "only in connection with the provision of treatment" and are not available to anyone not providing treatment, with the exception that they can be reviewed by

professionals chosen by the student. [20 U.S.C. §1232g(a) (4)(B)(i–iv)]

Under the act, parents have the right to inspect and review the education records of their minor children, and each covered agency and institution is mandated to establish procedures for parental access [20 U.S.C. §1232g(a)(1)]. Students eighteen and older or in attendance at a postsecondary school have the right to access their own records, excluding their parents' financial records, and where the student has not waived the right to access, confidential recommendations [20 U.S.C. §1232g(a)(1)(C)]. Access by parents of these students would require student consent. Provisions for student waiver of access to confidential recommendations are detailed in 20 U.S.C. §1232g(a)(1)(D). Parents and students eighteen and older must be given the opportunity for a hearing to challenge information in the education records and must be provided an opportunity "for the correction or deletion of any such inaccurate, misleading, or otherwise inappropriate data contained therein and to insert into such records a written explanation of the parents respecting the content of such records" [20 U.S.C. §1232g(a)(2)].

An educational institution or agency can release "directory information" as long as it has given public notice of the categories of information to be released about each student and has given parents reasonable time to notify the institution of information not to be released without parental consent [20 U.S.C. §1232g(a)(5)(B)].[21]

Any agency with a policy or practice of releasing educational records or identifiable information other than directory information without written consent of a parent is denied funding under 20 U.S.C. §1232g(b)(1). Exceptions to this written consent provision include other school officials including teachers who have legitimate educational interest, and for other limited purposes such as receipt of financial aid, audits, research, and in emergencies "if the knowledge of such information is necessary to protect the health or safety of students or other persons" [20 U.S.C. §1232g(b)(1)]. Release based upon a court order, subpoena, state statute, or to a juvenile justice system is also allowed in the same section.

Release of personally identifiable information in education records— other than directory information or the exceptions covered above—must be consented to in writing by the student's parents—or by those students age eighteen or older—and the consent must specify what will be released, to whom, and for what reasons [20 U.S.C. §1232g(b)(2)].

Under 20 U.S.C.§1232g(b)(4)(A), each agency or institution must maintain a record of individuals, agencies, and institutions who have requested or obtained access to a student's educational record and what their "legitimate interest" is in obtaining the information. When information is made available to a third party, it must be conditioned on their agreement not to allow any other access without the consent of parents or students eighteen years and older [20 U.S.C. §1232g(b)(4)(B)]. Finally, institutions of postsecondary education are permitted to disclose to alleged victims of crimes of violence the results of any disciplinary proceeding conducted by the institution against an alleged perpetrator of the crime which pertain to the crime [20 U.S.C. §1232g(b)(6)].

The accompanying federal regulations outline steps for students and their parents who wish to challenge the information in a record and make corrections.[22] There are several important points to note about the statute. First, the remedy for a violation of the statute is a denial of federal funding rather than a private action by an aggrieved party. Such a denial appears to be a lengthy and cumbersome process.[23] However, case law indicates that injunctive relief may be available to a party successfully claiming a violation of the act.[24] In addition, it may be possible to successfully bring an action under 42 U.S.C. §1983 for a violation of constitutional or civil rights and still obtain monetary damages, although such a suit would have to address sovereign immunity and qualified immunity issues.[25] Finally, case law and federal regulations are clear that a noncustodial parent has the same access to a minor child's records as does a custodial parent.

Minors and Their Confidences: Privacy and Disclosure

PARENT-CHILD AND GUIDANCE COUNSELOR–STUDENT PRIVILEGE

Several states have enacted parent-child privilege statutes, which protect the confidentiality of those communications. The Minnesota statute, Minn. Rev. Stat. §595.02, extends privilege to all communications made within the family if no outsiders are present. Either parent or child can waive the privilege. There are exceptions for criminal acts, litigation between spouses, child abuse, and termination of parental rights proceedings.[26]

In the school setting, at least eighteen states have privilege protections for school guidance counselors and students. Oregon extends privilege to communications between school employees and students: "A certificated staff member of an elementary or secondary school shall not be examined in any civil action or proceeding, as to any conversation between the certificated staff member and a student which relates to the personal affairs of the student or family of the student, and which if disclosed would tend to damage or incriminate the student or family. Any violation of the privilege provided by this subsection may result in the suspension of certification of the professional staff member as provided in ORS 342.175, 342.177 and 342.180" [Ore. Rev. Stat. §40.245(1)]. In addition, the Oregon statute forbids disclosure of communications with students concerning past substance abuse.[27]

LIMITATIONS ON CONFIDENTIALITY OF DISCLOSURES BY MINORS: CHILD ABUSE AND SUICIDAL INTENT

A minor's disclosure of abuse or neglect is not confidential and must be reported in all states. What constitutes a disclosure of abuse or neglect is less clear, depending on state statutes and child welfare agency policies. Some state statutory definitions of child abuse and neglect are complex and confusing, raising questions for the social worker as to whether a given situation does or does not fall within the scope of the state child protective services agency. Moreover, the statutes may call for reporting if there is a reasonable cause to believe, a reasonable suspicion, or a suspicion of abuse, without further clarification of these terms. Thus whether or not to report abuse or neglect is not always an easy decision. However, it should be reemphasized that many states provide statutory immunity from liability for good faith reporting and some specify criminal penalties for a failure to report.[28]

Disclosures by minors of possible suicidal intentions must be treated with care and taken seriously: "The Centers for Disease Control (CDC) in Atlanta has reported on a new survey of high school students, which revealed that twenty-seven percent 'thought seriously' about suicide in the preceding year, and 'one in 12 said they had actually tried.' The CDC report noted that suicide rates among teenagers between fifteen and nineteen years old had quadruped between 1950 and 1988" [*Eisel v. Board of Education of Montgomery County,* 597 A.2d 447, 456 (Md. 1991)].

Because suicide is a major cause of death among teenagers, many states and school districts have policies on how social workers, psychologists, and others should treat communications about any suicidal intentions of a minor. In *Eisel,* the Maryland court upheld a wrongful death action against the school board and two guidance counselors brought by the father of a girl who had committed suicide. The facts of the case were set forth by the court:

> During the week prior to the suicide, Nicole told several friends and fellow students that she intended to kill herself. Some of these friends reported Nicole's intentions to their school counselor, Morgan, who relayed the information to Nicole's school counselor, Jones. Morgan and Jones then questioned Nicole about the statements, but Nicole denied making them. Neither Morgan nor Jones notified Nicole's parents or the school administration about Nicole's alleged statements of intent. Information in the record suggests that the other party to the suicide pact shot Nicole before shooting herself. The murder-suicide took place on a school holiday in a public park at some distance from Sligo Middle School. The other party to the pact attended another school. [597 A.2d 447, 448 (1991)]

The counselors and the school board cited a number of cases where it was held that there was no duty to prevent a suicide when there was no custody or control over the individual. The court found these cases inapplicable. The counselors and the board also argued that there could be no liability because the harm was not foreseeable since Nicole had denied suicidal intentions. The court disagreed.

> Nor would reasonable persons necessarily conclude that the harm ceased to be foreseeable because Nicole denied any intent to commit suicide when the counselors undertook to draw out her feelings, particularly in light of the alleged declarations of intent to commit suicide made by Nicole to her classmates. "An

adolescent who is thinking of suicide is more likely to share these feelings with a friend than with a teacher or parent or school guidance counselor. But, we all—parents, teachers, administrators, service providers and friends—can learn what the warning signs are and what to do." 3 Maryland Office for Children and Youth, Monthly Memo, at 3 (Apr. 1986). [597 A.2d 447, 453 (1991)]

The court took note of the school's suicide prevention policy, which clearly stated that the confidential nature of the disclosure should not prevent action: "Nicole's school had a suicide prevention program prior to her death. The superintendent produced . . . a memorandum . . . from the principal to the staff of Sligo Middle School on the subject of 'Suicide Prevention. . . .' Part IX lists ten answers to the question, 'How Can You Help In A Suicidal Crisis?' Answer D is: 'Tell others—As quickly as possible, share your knowledge with parents, friends, teachers or other people who might be able to help. Don't worry about breaking a confidence if someone reveals suicidal plans to you. You may have to betray a secret to save a life.'" [597 A.2d 447, 453 (1991)].

The court concluded that the problem of adolescent suicide required the counselors to act even if the risk appeared slight: "The harm that may result from a school counselor's failure to intervene appropriately when a child threatens suicide is total and irreversible for the child, and severe for the child's family. It may be that the risk of any particular suicide is remote if statistically quantified in relation to all of the reports of suicidal talk that are received by school counselors. We do not know. But the consequence of the risk is so great that even a relatively remote possibility of a suicide may be enough to establish duty" [597 A.2d 447, 455 (1991)].

SOCIAL WORK PRACTICE, PRIVACY, AND MINORS

Minors present some unique issues in privacy law. The legal tension between the perspectives of the minor as an autonomous actor and as someone to be protected and for whom decisions must be made of course reflects in part adolescence in American society. Some minors sometimes are capable of making decisions, even difficult and weighty ones; others are not. Some need more protection than others. The law begins with a universalistic premise: minors are incompetent to make decisions—and then scales back to allow certain minors to make certain decisions. The public school systems present particular problems at law, where the courts have held that the legitimate rights of minors must be protected, but within the context of school discipline and order. The social worker, often dealing with not only the minor but also parents, guardians, schools, and perhaps the state, has to balance these pressures, protecting the legal privacy and confidentiality rights of the minor, yet doing so within the context of the legal rights of the other parties.

CONFIDENTIALITY, PRIVACY, *and* PERSONS WITH AIDS

The rapid growth of HIV and AIDS[1] since the first cases were reported in the early 1980s has presented numerous social, medical, and legal and ethical challenges. Some of the most significant of these come within confidentiality and privacy. Here problematic issues include the autonomy of an individual to decide voluntarily whether or not to undergo a blood test for HIV and the authority of the state, employer, or insurance company to mandate such tests; the clash between one individual's right of privacy concerning his or her medical condition and another's wish or need to know about that individual's HIV/AIDS status; an individual's desire to keep his or her HIV condition totally confidential and laws mandating or permitting the release of that information to data banks or specific individuals, to name only a few that have arisen.

In this area—as is true of all parts of AIDS law—the issues are complex, and the law remains conflicting, confusing, and rapidly changing. While the following discussion draws upon existing court decisions and statutory law, it must be emphasized that the law in this area is in flux. Statutes are enacted and then may—or may not—be implemented or may be repealed. Rules and guidelines are proposed, revised, sometimes adopted and sometimes withdrawn. Court decisions may be reversed, or may stand but at times the underlying laws may have changed. While this can be true in all areas of law, it seems particularly true in the rapidly evolving law related to AIDS. Thus while the issues will remain, it is incumbent upon professionals and students reading this material to check carefully into their own state laws and regulations to ascertain the current law and recent changes.

The chapter is divided into four parts. First, we will look at data on AIDS and HIV in the United States, tests for AIDS and their reliability, and the transmission of HIV and AIDS. Then we will look at AIDS and public health from a broad legal perspective. In the third part of the chapter, we will examine confidentiality and privacy issues in voluntary and mandatory HIV/AIDS testing. In the final section, we will address the laws on HIV/AIDS confidentiality, voluntary and mandatory disclosure of an individual's HIV/AIDS condition, and liability issues for violations of confidentiality and wrongful disclosures of a person's HIV/AIDS status.

An AIDS Overview: Incidence, Testing, and Transmission

INCIDENCE AND PREVALENCE OF AIDS AND HIV

As of June 1996, there were 548,000 reported cases of AIDS in the United States, resulting in 343,000 deaths. The incidence of AIDS, and its precursor, HIV, although cutting across all economic, social, racial, and ethnic groupings, remains concentrated primarily in three groups: males who have sex with other males, intravenous drug users, and those who have heterosexual relations with individuals in high-risk groups. Together these groups comprise at least 89 percent of all AIDS cases. Adolescent AIDS cases, thirteen to nineteen years old, and pediatric AIDS, children under thirteen, total respectively 2,500 and 7,000 cases. However, the most rapid recent growth of AIDS cases has been among women and children. Of 72,000 new AIDS cases reported between July 1995 and June 1996, 58,000 were males and 14,000 females. Of the total new cases, 700 were pediatric AIDS cases.[2]

The number of individuals infected with HIV is less well known, but estimates are that there are at least one million cases in the United States. These cases sooner or later may result in full-blown AIDS. Also, a redefinition of HIV by the Centers for Disease Control (CDC) in 1993 resulted in the addition of a significant number of cases to those classified as HIV-positive.[3]

TESTING FOR THE HIV VIRUS

At present two tests are most frequently used to determine HIV status, the enzyme-linked immunosorbent assay (ELISA) test and the Western Blot test. The ELISA test is cheaper but less accurate because it produces a high rate of false positives—individuals who test as having HIV but who do not. The Western Blot, because of its cost, is often used in conjunction with the first, to determine if an individual testing positive on the ELISA test is actually infected with HIV. Important in both tests is that they do not directly measure the presence of HIV in the body, but rather are a measure of the body's reaction to the virus. Since it takes time for the body to react to the presence of the HIV virus, there is a period—often called a window—where a person may have contracted HIV but, because his or her body has not reacted to the presence of the virus, will test HIV-negative. This period is estimated to last from six weeks to as long as six months. And, of course, accurate results are dependent on error-free transmission of the samples, accurate laboratory work, and error-free transmission and interpretation of the results.

The resulting situation is one where, even if there is no lab error, a positive ELISA test is only an indication that HIV may be present. A positive Western Blot, or with greater accuracy, several positive test results, means that HIV is very likely to be present, but a negative test result only confirms that HIV was not present in the individual up to six months prior to the administration of the test [Burris, 1993:117–118].

AIDS testing of newborn infants seems to be particularly problematic in that an HIV-positive result, although indicative that the mother is HIV-positive, does not necessarily mean that the virus has been transmitted to the newborn child. Studies have shown that a significant number of HIV-positive newborn children will within the next twelve months retest as HIV-negative as their own immune systems develop. (See discussion on page 201.)

TRANSMISSION OF AIDS AND HIV

HIV is a communicable but not contagious disease. It is not airborne, nor is it transmitted through casual contact such as touching, sharing eating utensils, and drinking from the same water glass. The known means of transmission of the virus are relatively few, and all involve the exchange of bodily fluids. In *Nolley v. County of Erie,* 776 F.Supp. 715 (W.D.N.Y. 1991), the HIV-positive plaintiff inmate had been required to wear rubber gloves when using a typewriter and could not handle books in the prison library due to fear of transmission of HIV. The *Nolley* court succinctly described HIV/AIDS transmission:

> There are only five known ways of transmitting the HIV virus:
> (1) sharing needles with an infected person; (2) having intimate
> sexual contact with an infected person; (3) carrying a developing
> fetus or breast-feeding a newborn; (4) receiving a transfusion of
> tainted blood or blood products; and (5) in rare circumstances,
> by blood-to-blood contact initiated through percutaneous cuts.
> AIDS cannot be transmitted by books, casual contact, being
> present in the same room as an infected person, toilet seats, door
> knobs, air conditioning, coughing, sneezing, urine, feces, sputum, nasal secretions, saliva, sweat, tears, or vomit. It certainly
> cannot be transmitted by attending church with an infected person or by sharing books with him or her. [776 F.Supp 715, 718
> (1991)]

Moreover, the exchange of these bodily fluids need not mean that an HIV infection will occur. For reasons not well understood, it appears that some individuals are less likely to contract HIV than others, and the likelihood of infection will vary with the volume of fluid transmitted and the number of exchanges that have taken place.

While an HIV-positive individual may not convert to full-blown AIDS for many years—if ever—once the conversion has taken place, the AIDS condition often lowers the body's ability to fight off other infections and singularly or in combination these infections become fatal. Some medications appear to be effective in forestalling the conversion from HIV-positive to AIDS and in significantly lengthening the life span of a person with AIDS, and some seem effective in preventing prenatal transmission of HIV from mother to unborn child. But to date, there remains no vaccine to prevent infection nor any permanent cure for an infected person.

AIDS, Public Health, and the Law

AIDS AND THE LAW

The many evolving and expanding legal issues surrounding AIDS cannot be covered here.[4] Suffice it that among them are AIDS as a disability under the Americans with Disabilities Act and the Rehabilitation Act of 1973; discrimination against those with HIV or AIDS in the workplace, housing, health care, insurance, and education; immigration policies restricting the entrance of individuals who are HIV-positive or have AIDS; and criminal penalties or civil liability for transmitting or attempting to transmit the virus to others [Dickson, 1995: 444].

Within AIDS confidentiality and privacy, major issues include the rights of privacy and informed consent of an individual in voluntary or mandatory testing for HIV and, if HIV-positive, under what conditions and to whom may or must that information be disclosed. Related liability issues include wrongful release of confidential information, failure to inform others of one's own or another's HIV-positive/AIDS condition, incorrectly informing an individual of his/her test results, and discriminatory actions that have resulted from the disclosure of the confidential test results.

AIDS AND PUBLIC HEALTH LAW

As a communicable and often fatal disease, AIDS as a public health problem could be treated as other communicable or contagious diseases have been in the past: screening, identification of those infected, reporting, and registration—at times coupled with contact tracing—and depending upon the degree of communicability or contagion, isolation or quarantine. That such legally acceptable public health approaches have not been used with AIDS reflects a combination of factors, including their substantial cost and limited effectiveness, combined with an increasing concern for the infected individual's civil rights and real fears of discrimination once the positive HIV status becomes known.[5]

In that all scientific evidence indicates HIV/AIDS is not contagious, is communicated by limited and known means of transmission, cannot be transmitted to others through casual contact, and need not impair the work or functioning of the person infected, there are strong arguments for not restricting HIV/AIDS carriers. Moreover, following the U.S. Supreme Court decision in *School Board of Nassau County v. Arline*, 480 U.S. 273 (1987), which held that tuberculosis is a legally protected disability under Section 504 of the Rehabilitation Act of 1973, it is commonly accepted that AIDS is also a disabling condition under Section 504 and the Americans with Disabilities Act.[6] To restrict or deny access to any of the rights and privileges specified in those acts would constitute unlawful and actionable discrimination. Conversely, in that the disease is incurable, debilitating, and when conversion to full-blown AIDS occurs, often fatal, there are also strong arguments that certain classes of individuals to whom the disease may be transmitted—such as sexual partners—should be informed about a person's HIV-positive condition either by the infected individual or, failing that, by someone else.

AIDS Testing and the Law

Testing for AIDS may be voluntary or mandatory.[7] If an individual voluntarily chooses to be tested, the test can by anonymous or identifiable. In anonymous testing, the results are never linked with the individual's name and there is no way to trace the results to the individual tested. In identifiable testing, although the results are recorded by name, they constitute confidential medical information. However, this does not mean that they cannot be accessed or released for certain purposes. For example, AIDS- or HIV-positive results may be reported to federal and state public health agencies for statistical and monitoring purposes, and some states require that identifying information be included with the test results.[8]

VOLUNTARY AIDS TESTING

Any person may choose to have his or her blood tested for the presence of HIV, although in the case of children, parental consent may be required. (See the following discussion.) Some states provide for anonymous testing, and self-testing kits, which preserve anonymity, have recently come on the market.[9] All states have general laws that protect the confidentiality of medical information, and many have laws that specifically protect the confidentiality of HIV and AIDS information. However, the confidential voluntary test results may be accessed by or made available to others, depending on the circumstances and the applicable laws. Disclosure to health care professionals, patients, and sexual partners, among others, has been permitted in some states, often without revealing the identity of the HIV-infected individual.

As public concern over the transmission of HIV increases, the confidentiality of HIV health records may be at risk. For example, in 1991, Illinois enacted legislation that permitted the screening of the confidential public health registry of individuals who were infected with the HIV virus to identify all those who were employed in health care. The law would allow the state to notify former patients of possible exposure to HIV. Although enacted, the law was not implemented.[10]

Voluntary Testing of Minors. Testing minors for HIV presents a number of complex issues, including whether parents can give informed consent for the tests, whether the minor's informed consent is also necessary, whether minors can request tests without parental consent, whether test results must be released to parents, and whether minors under supervision of the state can be tested without parental permission. Some states establish an age limitation, such as twelve or fourteen years of age, below which consent for testing must be given by a parent or guardian.[11] Others have AIDS-specific informed consent statutes for testing minors[12] or, in some cases, more broadly for anyone being tested for AIDS.[13] In addition, many states have informed consent and confidentiality statutes for testing and treating minors for communicable, contagious, or sexually transmitted diseases. For those that classify HIV as one of the communicable or sexually transmitted diseases, presumably the provisions would apply to minors undergoing HIV testing. At least one state, Iowa, requires a minor's informed consent for HIV testing and mandates parental notification of HIV-positive results [Iowa Code Ann. §141.22]. An emancipated minor may give informed consent for testing or treatment. (See generally Chapter 8.)

MANDATORY AIDS TESTING

Mandatory testing for HIV/AIDS may occur in a number of circumstances. For example, all persons enlisting in the armed forces are routinely screened for HIV, and an HIV-positive applicant is automatically rejected. (HIV-positive individuals already in the armed forces can remain and can reenlist as long as their health permits.)[14] Mandatory testing for others, including some federal employees and state and federal prisoners, has been legally upheld on a need-to-know basis.[15] The following discussion addresses some situations where mandatory testing has occurred. In particular, California statutes and case law are drawn upon since the state has enacted statutes that mandate AIDS/HIV testing in a variety of contexts.

Premarital HIV Testing. For a time Illinois mandated premarital HIV screening but then repealed the law, which appears to have been costly and ineffective. Similar laws have been proposed elsewhere.[16]

Biting, Scratching, or Spitting. California's Proposition 96, which passed in 1988, allows for mandatory HIV testing and disclosure of HIV results when saliva or other bodily fluids are transferred by biting, scratching, or spitting on police, firefighters, or emergency medical personnel. The statute, Cal. Health and Safety Code §199.97, was upheld in *Johnetta J. v. Municipal Court,* 267 Cal.Rptr. 666 (Cal. App. 1990), although there is scant evidence that any of these behaviors have infected others.

Prostitution and Sex Offenders. In some states, individuals arrested for prostitution are mandatorily tested for HIV. A California statute requires mandatory testing of arrested prostitutes, and if an HIV-positive individual is re-arrested for prostitution, the offense is elevated to a felony. See *Love v. California,* 276 Cal.Rptr. 660 (Cal. App. 1990). An increasing number of states, including California and New Jersey, permit mandatory HIV testing of sex offenders—adult or juvenile—with the results disclosed to the victim.[17]

Testing Newborns for HIV. Routine HIV testing of newborns, children, and even adults without informed consent appears to take place in some health care facilities, whether or not it is permitted by law. In these instances, neither the testing nor the results are revealed to the patient, and presumably they are used only for statistical reporting. More recently, some states have enacted legislation requiring mandatory screening of all newborn children for HIV and AIDS. In New York, mandatory screening has been in place for some time, and the mothers of newborn children have been informed of the testing and the availability of the results. Recent New York legislation requires that this information be disclosed to mothers of newborn children.[18] Since most newborn HIV-positive children will convert to HIV-negative status within the first year, it can be argued that the testing/mandatory disclosure law serves more to test and reveal the HIV status of the mother than of the child.[19]

Testing Children in State Child Welfare Systems. Children in state child welfare systems often undergo AIDS testing, particularly those who are in or are being placed into foster care. Consent for testing may be provided by a parent or guardian, the supervising child welfare agency, or a family court. Testing and disclosure of HIV information for children in child welfare systems appears in state child welfare policies rather than state statutory law [English, 1992]. Mandatory testing of children placed in foster care is now policy in a number of states.[20]

AIDS test results of children in child welfare systems may be disclosed to a number of persons regarded as needing to know the information. These often include foster parents, but could also include adoptive parents, child welfare workers, biological parents, residential and institutional staff, and the child himself or herself, depending on state statutes and agency policies. This potentially wide range of disclosures raises serious confidentiality questions and calls for education in confidentiality of the information and privacy rights of the child, as well as pre- and post-test counseling.

AIDS Testing in Corrections Facilities. AIDS testing of prisoners is standard policy in federal and many state prisons. Testing inmates in the Federal Bureau of Prisons system is permitted under federal law. Testing state prisoners is now permitted in a number of states and has been upheld in several lawsuits. However, knowing or having established that a prisoner is HIV-positive then raises problematic issues, including safeguarding that information, determining who should access it, and deciding what can be done with it. Several litigated cases are instructive.

In *Nolley v. County of Erie* (above), the plaintiff, a former inmate in a state corrections institution, prevailed in a suit against the state for damages from violations of state and constitutional law during her confinement. Having ascertained that she was HIV-positive, the institution invoked its "red sticker policy," affixing a red sticker to her inmate, medical, and transportation records, her clothing bag, and other records seen by noninstitutional personnel to indicate that she was infected with a contagious disease.

In addition, she was confined in a special unit housing mentally disturbed, suicidal, and dangerous inmates. She was often prevented from using libraries or taking part in religious services. When on rare occasions she was allowed to use the law library, she was required to wear plastic gloves when using its typewriter and could not handle the books.

Although HIV/AIDS training had been provided at the institution, including training on how the disease is transmitted, Dray, the acting superintendent, did not believe the medical evidence provided: "Nevertheless, Dray, in his testimony, said that he did not believe the information he had received about the limited way in which HIV could be transmitted. He believed that HIV could be transmitted through saliva, tears, spit, mucus, urine and feces, by casual contact, by plaintiff using the typewriter in the law library, and even by coming into contact with plaintiff's personal items but not plaintiff" [776 F.Supp. 715, 719]. The court found the institution and its administrators in violation of the provisions of the New York AIDS/HIV confidentiality statute 27F as well as Nolley's constitutional rights.

Similarly, a Wisconsin federal court found there could be liability where an inmate's HIV-positive status was disclosed to nonmedical personnel and other inmates.[21] However, other courts have upheld decisions to physically segregate HIV-infected inmates.[22]

Constitutional Restrictions on HIV Testing. In a few cases, courts have held that blanket mandatory testing of workers is unconstitutional. In *Glover v. Eastern Nebraska Community Office of Retardation*, 686 F.Supp. 243 (D.Neb. 1988), a state agency providing services to retarded citizens adopted a policy of mandatory testing for HIV and several other infectious diseases for all employees in certain positions on an annual or more frequent basis. The staff brought a legal challenge, and a federal district court found that the testing policy constituted an unreasonable Fourth Amendment search. In its analysis, the court balanced the reasonableness of the bodily invasion including limited or nonexistent pre- and post-test counseling and the ramifications for the individuals if HIV-positive results became known with the expected benefits of the tests, preventing the transmittal of HIV to patients, clients, or fellow workers. The court stated:

> Although the pursuit of a safe work environment for employees
> and a safe training and living environment for all clients is a wor-
> thy one, the policy does not reasonably serve that purpose. There

is simply no real basis to be concerned that clients are at risk of contracting the AIDS virus at the work place. These clients are not in danger of contracting the AIDS virus from staff members and such an unreasonable fear cannot justify a policy which intrudes on staff members' constitutionally protected rights.

There was testimony in this case that there can be no guarantee that the ENCOR clients could not possibly contract the AIDS virus, and thus the policy is necessary because of the devastating consequences of the disease. This overly cautious, "better to be safe than sorry" approach, however, is impermissible as it infringes on the constitutional rights of the staff members to be free from unreasonable searches and seizures.

In addition, the mandatory testing of staff members is not an effective way to prevent the spread of the disease. This policy simply ignores the current state of medical knowledge which establishes that the AIDS virus is not contracted by casual contact. . . . The Court is convinced that the evidence, considered in its entirety, leads to the conclusion that the policy was prompted by concerns about the AIDS virus, formulated with little or erroneous medical knowledge, and is a constitutionally impermissible reaction to a devastating disease with no known cure. [686 F.Supp. 243, 251 (D.Neb. 1988)]

Important in *Glover* was the court's balancing of the potential harm of the invasion of privacy against the possible benefits of the testing. The court found the potential for harm far exceeded the possible benefits. A different conclusion was reached in *Anonymous Fireman v. City of Willoughby,* 779 F.Supp. 402 (N.D.Ohio, 1991), where a federal district court upheld unannounced mass testing of firefighters as reasonable. In its decision, the court upheld the testing for "high risk" positions such as firefighters and paramedics. The court noted that a negative HIV test would bring "peace of mind" to the individual, while a person testing HIV-positive could then take increased precautions or could be transferred to lower risk positions [779 F.Supp. 402, 417 (1991)].

Mandatory HIV Testing for Health Care Professionals and Patients. Particularly controversial today is mandatory testing of health care professionals or patients. Following the publicity surrounding the case of Kimberly Bergalis and four other patients in Florida who apparently con-tracted HIV from an infected dentist, there has been increased demand for mandatory HIV testing of health care workers and disclosure of the HIV-positive condition to present, past, and future patients, and mandatory test-ing of patients with disclosure to health care workers.[23]

Even if the testing of employees or patients/clients is permissible, there are some strong reasons why an agency should be cautious. As in *Glover,* the benefits must be weighed against the potential costs, which can be broader than only legal considerations. If any agency finds out that a worker, patient, or client is HIV-positive, questions remain as to whether that information can be used either to protect others or to provide better services. If universal precautions are in use, there should be no reason for further protection of staff or patients/clients from the HIV-positive individ-ual. In the case of HIV-positive patients or clients, Gostin (1989) suggests that health care workers treating a known HIV-positive individual may, through their concern for their own safety, actually put themselves more at risk by being overly cautious and more prone to mistakes. He also argues that staff may take fewer precautions with those who are known to have tested HIV-negative—who might nevertheless be HIV-positive due to the testing window phenomenon—and thereby be more at risk.

Whatever benefits might accrue from knowing an individual's HIV-positive status, they must be balanced against the real costs. First, as many newspaper articles and much litigation has shown, keeping this information confidential is extremely difficult. If the information becomes known, a le-gal action for invasion of privacy is possible. Second, if an agency knows that a client is HIV-positive or if an employer or supervisor knows that a worker is HIV-positive, actions taken by the agency or employer may be-come suspect and scrutinized as potentially discriminatory. For known HIV-positive patients or clients, a denial of benefits or changes in or termination of service may be harder to defend or justify. For known HIV-positive em-ployees, changes in working conditions, a failure to promote or reward, transfers or firing all become suspect as being based on the medical condi-tion and not workplace performance.

Confidentiality and Disclosure
of AIDS/HIV Information

In a suit for damages stemming from the wrongful release of a person's confidential HIV-positive condition, the Second Circuit Court of Appeals said:

> Individuals who are infected with the HIV virus clearly posses a constitutional right to privacy regarding their condition. In Whalen v. Roe, the Supreme Court recognized that there exists in the United States Constitution a right to privacy protecting "the individual interest in avoiding disclosure of personal matters." . . . There is, therefore, a recognized constitutional right to privacy in personal information. . . .
>
> Extension of the right to confidentiality to personal medical information recognizes there are few matters that are quite so personal as the status of one's health, and few matters the dissemination of which one would prefer to maintain greater control over. Clearly, an individual's choice to inform others that she has contracted what is at this point invariably and sadly a fatal, incurable disease is one that she should normally be allowed to make for herself. This would be true for any serious medical condition, but is especially true with regard to those infected with HIV or living with AIDS, considering the unfortunately unfeeling attitude among many in this society toward those coping with the disease. An individual revealing that she is HIV seropositive potentially exposes herself not to understanding or compassion but to discrimination and intolerance, further necessitating the extension of the right to confidentiality over such information. We therefore hold that Doe possesses a constitutional right to confidentiality under Whalen in his HIV status. [*Doe v. New York Commission of Human Rights,* 15 F.3d 264, 267 (2d Cir. 1994)]

When information that an individual is HIV-positive or has AIDS is recorded as the result of a voluntary or mandatory blood test, issues then include who has access to that information, what can be done with the information, and what are the liability issues for wrongful release of the information. In addition to the usual protection of medical information found in confidentiality statutes or in social worker and psychotherapist privilege statutes, a number of states have enacted specific confidentiality statutes for AIDS/HIV information.

AIDS CONFIDENTIALITY STATUTES

Burris (1993), Gostin (1989), and others have noted the existence of two generations of AIDS confidentiality statutes. Early statutes primarily were concerned with protecting the privacy of the HIV-infected individual and maintaining confidentiality of records. An example is in the New Jersey AIDS statute, which permits disclosure of HIV information without an informed consent or pursuant to a court order in only a few situations [N.J.S.A. §26:5C-5-5C-16].

While second-generation statutes also protect confidentiality and often require a written, informed release by the patient or client—or representative—for disclosure, the statutes contain significant exceptions to the overall confidentiality of the information. The California statutes exemplify second-generation statutes, containing numerous exceptions to confidentiality of an individual's HIV/AIDS information.

DISCLOSURE OF CONFIDENTIAL HIV/AIDS INFORMATION

Disclosure of confidential HIV/AIDS information may be voluntary with informed consent, or in some states without informed consent under certain circumstances. However, in either instance, the social worker must remember that disclosure of an individual's HIV-positive condition may have disastrous consequences for that person, including loss of friends or family, loss or denial of work, denial of education, and social stigma, to name only a few. Where there is a wrongful disclosure, the HIV-positive person might be successful in litigation, but successful litigation cannot compensate for the injuries that may occur. Also, for the social worker who could be a defendant in the litigation, even if he or she prevails in the defense, the litigation is expensive, arduous, and time-consuming. Therefore, social workers should be very careful either to obtain written, informed consent from the individual or his/her legal guardian prior to release of AIDS/HIV information or, failing that, to obtain qualified legal advice before making disclosures without informed consent.

DISCLOSURE WITH INFORMED CONSENT

"By the end of 1991, thirty-six states had enacted legislation requiring informed consent for HIV testing, and virtually every state provided some degree of protection for the confidentiality of HIV information" [Burris, 1993:121]. Some statutes require that a patient's or client's consent to the release of HIV/AIDS information must be written, specific, and time-bound and must limit any further release of the information. The Arizona statutes contain the following informed consent provisions:

E. A release of confidential communicable disease related information shall be signed by the protected person, or, if the protected person lacks capacity to consent, a person authorized pursuant to law to consent to health care for the person. A release shall be dated and shall specify to whom disclosure is authorized, the purpose for disclosure and the time period during which the release is effective. A general authorization for the release of medical or other information, including confidential communicable disease related information, is not a release of confidential HIV-related information unless the authorization specifically indicates its purpose as a general authorization and an authorization for the release of confidential HIV-related information and complies with the requirements of this section.

F. A person to whom confidential communicable disease related information is disclosed pursuant to this section shall not disclose the information to another person except as authorized by this section. . . .

G. If a disclosure of confidential communicable disease related information is made pursuant to a release, the disclosure shall be accompanied by a statement in writing which warns that the information is from confidential records which are protected by state law that prohibits further disclosure of the information without the specific written consent of the person to whom it pertains or as otherwise permitted by law.

H. The person making a disclosure pursuant to a release of confidential communicable disease related information shall keep a record of all disclosures. On request, a protected person or his legal representative shall have access to the record. [Ariz. Rev. Stat §36-664][24]

Social workers should ascertain the relevant provisions for informed consent for the release of confidential HIV/AIDS information in their jurisdiction. If there are none, caution is advised, and following the steps listed in the above Arizona statute could aid in avoiding future litigation.

DISCLOSURE WITHOUT INFORMED CONSENT

Disclosure of confidential HIV/AIDS information is permissible without informed consent in a number of situations, depending on the jurisdiction and the law. For example, release of the information to federal, state, and local health departments may be permitted as an exception to the usual confidentiality restrictions. In addition, release to medical personnel for treatment purposes often is allowed.[25]

Disclosure to Patients or Clients. In *In re Application of Milton S. Hershey Medical Center*, 595 A.2d 1290 (Pa.Super. 1991), a surgeon, having sustained a cut during an operating procedure, voluntarily underwent testing for HIV. He then notified the hospital that he had tested HIV-positive and voluntarily agreed to withdraw from all invasive procedures. The preliminary ELISA test was confirmed by a Western Blot test. The hospitals where he had performed surgery applied to court for permission to notify about 450 former patients of Dr. Doe (a pseudonym) for whom he had either attended or directly performed surgery that they had been operated on in the presence of an HIV-positive physician and should be tested for HIV. Dr. Doe was not to be identified to these patients by name. In addition, the physicians of these patients were to be notified, identifying Dr. Doe by name. The appellate court upheld the trial court approval of notification, basing its decision on a provision of the Pennsylvania AIDS confidentiality statute allowing the release of the confidential information if there is "compelling need." In balancing Dr. Doe's privacy with the need for notification, the court said:

> Dr. Doe presented a health risk to his patients and to the patients of others. It is admirable that he chose to withdraw from his residency program voluntarily. Indeed, he must have recognized the

jeopardy involved, however slight. This Court does not deny Dr. Doe's right to privacy. Without question, one's health problems are a private matter to be dealt with by the individual in the way that s/he feels most comfortable and sees fit. However, Dr. Doe's medical problem was not merely his. It became a public concern the moment he picked up a surgical instrument and became a part of a team involved in invasive procedures. . . .

AIDS is not a disease that is, or that should be taken lightly by our society. Rather, many view it as a problem of epidemic proportion that knows no bounds and discriminates against no one. . . . We conclude, given the nature of Dr. Doe's profession, the demands of his work, the facts of this case, the need for disclosure, the harm that could result from disclosure and importantly, Dr. Doe's privacy interest, that the trial court acted properly. . . . We feel that this is a case in which Section 8(a)(2) was properly invoked and applied. Certainly, we do not wish to "punish" Dr. Doe or to encourage litigation. Privacy rights are of paramount importance in this Commonwealth. But the public's right to be informed in this sort of potential health catastrophe is compelling and far outweighs a practicing surgeon's right to keep information regarding his disease confidential. [595 A.2d 1290, 1298 (1991)]

Similarly, in *Scoles v. Mercy Health Corp.,* 887 F.Supp. 765 (E.D.Pa. 1994), a federal district court upheld the hospital's suspension of operating privileges and a court-ordered notification of over one thousand former patients of an orthopedic surgeon who had tested HIV-positive. The hospital had agreed to permit the surgeon to continue his practice only if he agreed to inform patients of his condition before performing surgery. Scoles, the surgeon, argued that the suspension of privileges and required disclosure to patients before invasive surgery was a violation of Section 504 of the Rehabilitation Act of 1973 and the Americans with Disabilities Act. The court disagreed, holding that Scoles presented a "significant risk" to patients under the provisions of Section 504 and constituted a "direct threat" to patients under the provisions of the Americans with Disabilities Act.

Disclosure When Health Care Providers or "First Responders" Are Exposed to Bodily Fluids. A recent California law allows for disclosure of a person's HIV status when health care or safety personnel are exposed to blood or bodily fluids. Included in the coverage of the statute are "exposed individuals," defined as "any individual health care provider, first provider, first responder, or any other person, including, but not limited to, any employee, volunteer, or contracted agent of any health care provider, who is exposed, within the scope of his or her employment, to the blood or other potentially infectious materials of a source patient."

When there has been a determination of a "significant exposure" to bodily fluids, the physician certifying the exposure can request that the physician of the patient disclose the HIV status of that individual. The physician first attempts to obtain voluntary informed consent from the patient for a disclosure, but must disclose the information with or without consent. If the HIV status is not known, any existing blood or tissue sample of the source patient may be tested and the results revealed to the exposed individual. The exposed individual is bound by confidentiality not to identify the HIV information. However, no blood may be drawn from the source patient without informed consent [Cal. Health & Safety Code §121130–121136].

Mandatory Disclosure to Employers. In *Leckelt v. Board of Commissioners*, 909 F.2d 820 (5th Cir. 1990), the court upheld a hospital's discharge of a nurse because he refused to reveal the results of an HIV test he had voluntarily undertaken. The worker was not discharged because of his possible HIV-positive condition but for insubordination in refusing what the court saw as a reasonable request:

> On a number of occasions, the Supreme Court has recognized the strong governmental interest in a safe, efficient workplace. Likewise, TGMC [the hospital] had a strong interest in protecting the health of its employees and patients by preventing the spread of infectious diseases, such as HIV. Under all the circumstances respecting Leckelt, including his apparent homosexuality, medical condition, and long-term relationship with a man who was hospitalized with and ultimately died from AIDS-related complications, Smith was justified in demanding the results of Leckelt's HIV antibody test. Leckelt's duties as a licensed practical nurse provided opportunities for HIV transmission, and if he were infected with HIV, he would need to be advised of the risks and be evaluated periodically as to whether he could

safely and adequately perform his duties. Thus, we conclude that TGMC's strong interests in maintaining a safe workplace through infection control outweighed the limited intrusion on any privacy interest of Leckelt in the results of his HIV antibody test. [909 F.2d 820, 833 (1990)]

Partner Notification and Contact Tracing. There are increasing pressures for notifying spouses or sexual partners—or needle sharers in the case of IV drug use—of an individual's HIV-positive status and for tracing previous contacts. Contact tracing, a longtime public health tool, has the limitation that it relies heavily on a voluntary, accurate response from the HIV-positive individual. To the extent that the individual fears the consequences of disclosure, or the system becomes punitive, disclosures of contacts will decrease. And to the extent that the individual cannot accurately report past sexual contacts or needle sharers, the contact tracing program is limited. Nonetheless, a number of contact tracing programs are now in place.

For social workers—and other professionals—disclosure of a patient's or client's HIV/AIDS status to others presents significant ethical and perhaps legal problems. Ethically, a strong argument can be made that if the patient or client refuses to tell a spouse, sexual partner, or other who is in danger of exposure, the social worker should take steps to protect that individual. Legally, the issue is frequently unclear. As seen in Chapter 7, there is now a substantial body of law around the duty to warn or protect. Although much of it focuses on the *Tarasoff* rationale and is limited to threatened serious physical injury, some court decisions go farther, suggesting that the duty to protect is also based on the physician's broad obligation to protect the health of the community. For these decisions, the inclusion of a duty to protect another from HIV/AIDS would seem to follow. However, there is often a conflicting state confidentiality statute, with penalties for unauthorized disclosure of HIV or AIDS. Until the case and statutory law are better harmonized, the best course for the social worker is to work with the patient or client to get him or her to notify those at risk or, failing that, to gain an informed consent for notification. If this is unsuccessful, a court-ordered release of the confidential information is possible. As always, consultation and careful documentation are called for.

A growing number of states—and the federal government—have enacted laws addressing partner notification. Two examples will be discussed here, the California statute and the federal government statutes for partner notification of patients within the Veterans Administration system. In the Veterans Administration, along with provisions for confidentiality of HIV records and court-ordered disclosures, the statute provides that physicians and counselors may disclose HIV information to a spouse or sexual partner if the disclosure is necessary to protect the health of the spouse or partner and they believe the patient will not provide the information himself or herself. (Note that the disclosure is permissive, not mandatory, and no mention is made of disclosure in the case of IV drug-using partners.)

(f)(1) Notwithstanding subsection (a) but subject to paragraph (2), a physician or a professional counselor may disclose information or records indicating that a patient or subject is infected with the human immunodeficiency virus if the disclosure is made to (A) the spouse of the patient or subject, or (B) to an individual whom the patient or subject has, during the process of professional counseling or of testing to determine whether the patient or subject is infected with such virus, identified as being a sexual partner of such patient or subject.

(2) (A) A disclosure under paragraph (1) may be made only if the physician or counselor, after making reasonable efforts to counsel and encourage the patient or subject to provide the information to the spouse or sexual partner, reasonably believes that the patient or subject will not provide the information to the spouse or sexual partner and that the disclosure is necessary to protect the health of the spouse or sexual partner. [38 U.S.C. §7332]

The California statute permits both physicians and county health officers to make disclosures to spouses, sexual partners, and IV drug-using partners:

(a) Notwithstanding Section 120980 or any other provision of law, no physician and surgeon who has the results of a confirmed positive test to detect infection by the probable causative agent of acquired immune deficiency syndrome of a patient under his or her care shall be held criminally or civilly liable for disclosing to a person reasonably believed to be the spouse, or to a person reasonably believed to be a sexual partner or a person with whom the patient has shared the use of hypodermic needles, or to the county health officer, that the patient has tested positive on a test to detect infection by the probable causative agent of acquired immune deficiency syndrome, except that no physician and surgeon shall disclose any identifying information about the individual believed to be infected.

(b) No physician and surgeon shall disclose the information described in subdivision (a) unless he or she has first discussed the test results with the patient and has offered the patient appropriate educational and psychological counseling, that shall include information on the risks of transmitting the human immunodeficiency virus to other people and methods of avoiding those risks, and has attempted to obtain the patient's voluntary consent for notification of his or her contacts. The physician and surgeon shall notify the patient of his or her intent to notify the patient's contacts prior to any notification. When the information is disclosed . . . the physician and surgeon shall refer that person for appropriate care, counseling, and followup. . . .

(c) This section is permissive on the part of the attending physician. . . . No physician has a duty to notify any person of the fact that a patient is reasonably believed to be infected by the probable causative agent of acquired immune deficiency syndrome. [Cal. Health & Safety Code §121025]

As in the VA statute, disclosure in California is permissive, not mandatory. Unlike the VA statute, counselors are not included among those who may make disclosures in California. There are several other important differences. The California statute includes both needle-sharing and sexual partners within the notification provisions; the VA statute only mentions sexual partners. The VA statute does not mention immunity from liability for disclosure, while the California statute specifically provides for immunity from civil or criminal liability. In addition, the California statute prohibits informing the person notified of the identity of the HIV-positive individual, while the VA statute is silent on this important point. Also, the

California statute has stronger provisions for counseling, care, and followup for patient and partner. Finally, unlike the VA statute, the physician in California is required to notify the HIV-infected patient of the disclosure before it takes place.

Liability for Unlawful Disclosure of HIV/AIDS Information. Releasing confidential HIV/AIDS information about a patient or client could subject a social worker to a number of penalties, both civil and criminal, depending upon the circumstances. Among these are an invasion of privacy under the federal or state constitutions, violation of the individual's civil rights under Section 1983 of Title 42 of the U.S. Code, malpractice actions for a breach of fiduciary duty or a violation of one's professional code of ethics, violation of the federal Privacy Act of 1974, and violation of confidentiality protections surrounding federally funded drug and alcohol programs, to list only a few. In addition, a number of state AIDS confidentiality statutes contain penalties for unlawful disclosure.[26]

In an action for damages the plaintiff must be able to show that he or she has been harmed by the disclosure. In the case of HIV/AIDS, with the widespread ramifications of disclosure, this indeed may be possible. In *Estate of Behringer v. The Medical Center at Princeton,* 592 A.2d 1251 (N.J.Super. 1991), a surgeon practicing at the Medical Center was briefly hospitalized and diagnosed as having AIDS. According to the court,

> Plaintiff's concern about public knowledge of the diagnosis was not misplaced. Upon his arrival home, plaintiff and his companion received a series of phone calls. Calls were received from various doctors who practiced at the Medical Center with plaintiff. All doctors, in addition to being professional colleagues, were social friends, but none were involved with the care and treatment of plaintiff. All indicated in various ways that they were aware of the diagnosis. Statements were made either directly to plaintiff's companion or by insinuation, such as an inquiry as to whether the companion was "tested. . . ." During the evening of June 18, she received a call from social non-medical friends who indicated their knowledge of the diagnosis and expressed support to her and plaintiff. She indicated that the relationships with various neighbors and friends changed as a result of the di-

agnosis. There was less social contact and communication and what she perceived as a significant diminution in the popularity of plaintiff.

Plaintiff's condition and the growing awareness of that condition in the community impacted upon not only plaintiff's social relationships but, more significantly, on his practice as well. In July, 1987, plaintiff returned to his office practice. During his short absence from his office and in the ensuing months, calls were received at his practice from doctors and patients alike who indicated an awareness of plaintiff's condition and in many cases, requested transfer of files or indicated no further interest in being treated by plaintiff. . . . Over an extended period of time, the practice diminished as more of plaintiff's patients became aware of his condition. [592 A.2d 1251, 1256 (1991)]

The court found that the Medical Center could be held liable for damages stemming from this invasion of privacy.

Similarly, in *Doe v. Borough of Barrington*, 729 F.Supp. 376 (D.N.J. 1990), after an HIV-positive male, given the pseudonym of John Doe in the litigation, warned police officers who were conducting a body search that he was HIV-positive, the police notified a neighbor of the Does that John Doe had AIDS.

Defendant Rita DiAngelo became upset upon hearing this information. Knowing that the four Doe children attended the Downing School in Runnemede, the school that her own daughter attended, DiAngelo contacted other parents with children in the school. She also contacted the media. The next day, eleven parents removed nineteen children from the Downing School due to a panic over the Doe children's attending the school. The media was present, and the story was covered in the local newspapers and on television. At least one of the reports mentioned the name of the Doe family. Plaintiffs allege that as a result of the disclosure, they have suffered harassment, discrimination, and humiliation. They allege they have been shunned by the community. [729 F.Supp. 376, 379 (1990)]

The court held the defendants could be liable for the invasion of privacy of John Doe.

A case where there was no liability for wrongful disclosure because there was no harm is *Doe v. Southeastern Pennsylvania Transit Authority (SEPTA)*, 72 F.3d 1133 (3rd Cir. 1995). There the appellate court set aside a $125,000 damage award for the plaintiff on the grounds that although his privacy might have been violated, there had been no demonstrable harm. In that case, a SEPTA administrator conducting a utilization review of the company's drug program received data from the provider on the cost of prescription drugs used by employees, including a list of those employees who had filled prescriptions for more than $100 in a month, by employee name and medications purchased. Among others, John Doe's name appeared on the list, and inquiries of a SEPTA physician revealed that the medications he was taking were only for the treatment of AIDS. When the physician informed the SEPTA general counsel of the audit he instructed the administrator to destroy her list and to request that all future documentation from the provider delete employee name identifiers. Doe learned of the audit from the physician and later brought suit for an invasion of privacy.

In its decision overturning Doe's lower court judgment, the court said: "In addition, we recognize the possible harm to Doe from disclosure. . . . Although AIDS hysteria may have subsided somewhat, there still exists a risk of much harm from non-consensual dissemination of the information that an individual is afflicted with AIDS. This potential for harm, however, should not blind us to the absence of harm in this case. Despite Pierce's disclosures to her subordinate, Aufschauer, and to Dr. Press that Doe had AIDS, SEPTA promoted him and still retains him in his responsible position [72 F.3d 1133, 1995 U.S.App. LEXIS 36983 at 23].

AIDS, PRIVACY LAW, AND SOCIAL WORK PRACTICE

As emphasized, confidentiality and privacy laws are particularly subject to change when dealing with persons with HIV/AIDS. These changes are in part a response to rapid developments in treatment and technology, to public fears of a growing and often fatal disease, at times to a legitimate need to know HIV/AIDS information, but are also within the context of valid fears of violations of privacy and discrimination. The resulting law has reflected and probably will continue to reflect great variation and inconsistency. HIV testing and disclosure of a person's HIV-positive condition may be allowed in some instances but not in others. Penalties for wrongful disclosure can be severe. And pre- and post-test counseling or disclosure may be mandated by law, ethics, or practice. Finally, whether HIV/AIDS falls within the broader duty to protect or warn remains unresolved in many states, and in conflict with broad AIDS confidentiality statutes in others. All of this argues that the social worker student and professional must keep abreast of changes in this rapidly evolving area.

CHAPTER TEN

SELECTED PROBLEM AREAS

The reader of the preceding chapters is aware that there is virtually no area of privacy and confidentiality that is not in some way problematic in law and social work practice. In this final chapter, various topics that social workers may find particularly difficult or that do not fit easily elsewhere are addressed. Included are discussions of confidentiality and privacy considerations for certain types of records and information and confidentiality when working with certain populations. First, specifically protected records—records in federally funded drug and alcohol programs as well as child abuse, adoption, and juvenile court records—will be discussed. Then confidentiality in family and group therapy and with self-help groups will be considered.

Confidentiality and Specially Protected Records

FEDERALLY FUNDED SUBSTANCE ABUSE PROGRAMS

The confidentiality of records in federally funded alcohol and drug treatment programs is protected by federal law, 42 U.S.C. §290dd-2, and regulations set forth in 42 C.F.R. 2-1 ff.[1] The statutory confidentiality protections are broad, inclusive, and stringent, comprising some of the most far-reaching legal protections of patient and client privacy in the health and human services. Penalties that can be assessed for a violation of the statute are not insignificant, with fines ranging from $500 to $5,000 for each offense.

The statute is designed both to protect the privacy of program participants and to encourage others to participate in those programs without carrying the public stigma of alcoholic or drug addict. The rationale for its statutory predecessor, the Drug Abuse Office and Treatment Act of 1972 [21 U.S.C. §1175], is applicable to the current legislation:

> If society is to make significant progress in the struggle against drug abuse, it is imperative that all unnecessary impediments to voluntary treatment be removed. There is clear agreement among drug abuse treatment program operators that their ability to assure patients and prospective patients of anonymity is essential to the success of their programs. The identification of a person as a patient of a general practitioner or hospital clinic is not ordinarily of great significance, but the identification of a person as an enrolee in a narcotic treatment program can, in and of itself, have profoundly adverse consequences. [Federal Register vol. 37, no. 223, Nov. 17, 1972: 24636]

In general, the act broadly protects the confidentiality of substance abuse program records: "Records of the identity, diagnosis, prognosis, or treatment of any patient which are maintained in connection with the performance of any program or activity relating to substance abuse education, prevention, training, treatment, rehabilitation, or research, which is conducted, regulated, or directly or indirectly assisted by any department or agency of the United States shall, except as provided in subsection (e), be confidential and be disclosed only for the purposes and under the circumstances expressly authorized under subsection (b)" [42 U.S.C. §290dd-2a].

Disclosures are permitted (1) when there is written informed consent of the patient; (2) in emergencies to medical personnel; (3) for research, evaluation, and audits; and (4) by court order for good cause [42 U.S.C. §290dd-2(b)(1)-(2)(A–C)]. Disclosure by court order for good cause is permitted "[i]f authorized by an appropriate order of a court of competent jurisdiction granted after application showing good cause therefor, including the need to avert a substantial risk of death or serious bodily harm. In assessing good cause the court shall weigh the public interest and the need for disclosure against the injury to the patient, to the physician-patient relationship, and to the treatment services. Upon the granting of such order, the court, in determining the extent to which any disclosure of all or any part of any record is necessary, shall impose appropriate safeguards against unauthorized disclosure" [42 U.S.C. §290dd-2(b)(2)(C)].

Excluded from the confidentiality requirements are transfers of records within the military and Veterans Administration and disclosures of child abuse. The child abuse exception states: "The prohibitions of this section do not apply to the reporting under State law of incidents of suspected child abuse and neglect to the appropriate State or local authorities" [42 U.S.C. §290dd-2(e)]. However, the accompanying regulations make it clear that this disclosure exception is only for reporting suspected child abuse and does not apply to subsequent proceedings: "the restrictions continue to apply to the original alcohol or drug abuse patient records maintained by the program including their disclosure and use for civil or criminal proceedings which may arise out of the report of suspected child abuse and neglect" [42 C.F.R. 2.12(c)(6)].

Violations of the act are penalized by criminal fines: not more than $500 for a first offense and not more than $5,000 for each subsequent offense [42 C.F.R. §2.4].

To illustrate the broad coverage of the statute, some of the accompanying definitions found in the federal regulations are discussed below. (See generally 42 C.F.R. 2.1 et seq.)

"Program" is defined broadly, to include a separate entity, a unit of a larger organization, a group of personnel, or an individual.[2]

"Federal assistance" is also broadly defined and includes federal programs, state and local programs receiving federal money that is or could be used for substance abuse programs, and other programs receiving any federal assistance including tax relief.[3]

A "patient" is "any individual who has applied for or been given diagnosis or treatment for alcohol or drug abuse at a federally assisted program and includes any individual who, after arrest on a criminal charge, is identified as an alcohol or drug abuser in order to determine that individual's eligibility to participate in a program."

"Diagnosis" means "any reference to an individual's alcohol or drug abuse or to a condition which is identified as having been caused by that abuse which is made for the purpose of treatment or referral for treatment."

"Treatment" means "the management and care of a patient suffering from alcohol or drug abuse."

Thus patients include those who are receiving treatment, those who have received treatment, those being diagnosed for treatment, and those who are applying for diagnosis or treatment, and diagnosis includes "any reference" to drug or alcohol abuse or a condition caused by abuse if made for treatment or referral purposes. Conceivably, then, any conversation between an individual and a person coming within the definition of a program with federal assistance discussing possible substance abuse, whether or not it is a problem or even exists, would fall within the strictures of the act. For example, a conversation between a high school student and a representative of a program covered by the act taking place at school in which substance abuse was referred to would be confidential and protected under the statute.

"Disclosure" is "a communication of patient identifying information, the affirmative verification of another person's communication of patient identifying information, or the communication of any information from the record of a patient who has been identified," where patient identifying information includes "the name, address, social security number, fingerprints, photograph, or similar information by which the identity of a patient can be determined with reasonable accuracy and speed either directly or by reference to other publicly available information." However, patient identifying information does not include nonidentifying case numbers.

"Records" consist of "any information whether recorded or not, relating to a patient received or acquired by a federally assisted alcohol or drug program." Thus the act includes both recorded and unrecorded information that would identify a patient—or any information relating to an identified patient—and covers any communication, written, oral, or electronic. However, it appears that direct observations by staff do not fall within the definition of a record. In *State v. Brown*, 376 N.W.2d 451 (Minn.App. 1985), in response to a police inquiry, an employee of a drug program informed the police that a description provided appeared to fit a former resident who was currently on interstate parole from Kentucky, but did not provide a name. This information was used to locate the defendant. The Minnesota court of appeals found that the identifying information did not come from Brown's confidential record and said: "A counselor's direct personal observations are not a 'record' even if reduced to writing or testified to in court" [376 N.W. 2d at 454].

Along with the court-ordered release and child abuse reporting exceptions discussed above, additional exceptions are listed in the accompanying regulations. Included here are exceptions relating to records in the Veterans Administration and the armed forces. Exceptions are also provided for communications within a program or between a program and the agency administering it.[4]

Among other exceptions are communications to a "qualified service organization" where that organization agrees to provide the same confidentiality, and limited communications to law enforcement personnel in regard to the commission of a crime on the program premises or against program personnel, or the threat of such a crime.

Social workers should pay particular attention to the provisions for a patient's informed consent for disclosure of information [42 C.F.R. §2.31] and the notice that must accompany any disclosure, limiting any redisclosure of the confidential information [42 C.F.R. §2.32]. Sample forms for informed consent and redisclosure are provided in the regulations. Consent must be written, time-limited, and specific as to what is to be disclosed to whom for what purposes. Redisclosure is not allowed without the written informed consent of the patient.

Violations of the law may result in fines; however, case law suggests that there is no private action for a violation of the statute. Information received in violation of the statute may still be used in court. For example, in some cases undercover agents were placed in substance abuse programs and provided information in violation of the statute which was used in subsequent prosecutions. The courts have held that while the violation may be penalized by a fine, the illegally obtained information may still be used in court.[5]

CONFIDENTIALITY OF CHILD ABUSE RECORDS

Traditionally states have protected child abuse reports and records from public disclosure. Those making reports are assured of confidentiality and anonymous reporting is permitted. This policy is designed both to promote the reporting of possible abuse and to protect the child, the subject of the report, from damaging publicity. As a consequence, state agencies covered by the confidentiality statutes argue they are statutorily prohibited from discussing pending, opened, or closed child abuse cases. For example, in many states, the individual reporting suspected child abuse cannot learn if the abuse was substantiated or not, if there was a case opened, or even if there was any investigation of the report. Charges that state agencies have used the confidentiality statutes to shield mismanagement from the public view have resulted in pressure to allow agencies to reveal minimal information about a reported case of abuse to selected individuals.

A second problematic area of child abuse reporting concerns unsubstantiated reports of abuse. In many states, once a protective services agency receives a report and makes an investigation, the case file remains within the agency's data system even though the abuse is unfounded or unsubstantiated. This may have future consequences since many programs, such as Head Start, foster care, and group homes, routinely search child protective services files for abuse reports as part of their procedures for hiring new employees. Thus it is possible for an individual not to be hired for a position in these areas and never learn the reason, since the confidentiality of the child abuse record is protected.

If the child abuse report is unsubstantiated, some states have procedures for expunction of the record from the child protective services database; however, other states retain the records. Several cases have addressed this issue.

In *Hodge v. Jones,* 31 F.3d 157 (4th Cir. 1994), the appellate court held the state child protective services agency not liable for damages for its refusal to expunge an unfounded report of abuse from its records. The court described the issue:

> On January 20, 1989, David and Marsha Hodge took their three-month-old son Joseph to the Carroll County General Hospital in Westminster, Maryland, for examination and treatment of the child's swollen right arm. The examining physician diag-

nosed a fractured ulna "'without adequate historical explanation'" and, pursuant to state law . . . contacted the Carroll County Department of Social Services (CCDSS) to report suspected child abuse. An investigation was initiated the next day . . . which ultimately yielded no evidence of abuse. The caseworker filed a report with the CCDSS classifying the case as "unsubstantiated" and "ruled out."

Within a week of the incident, the Hodges took Joseph to two medical specialists for further examination. The specialists diagnosed the swelling as osteomyelitis, a bacterial bone infection, and performed the necessary corrective surgery. Five days after the caseworker closed his investigation, Marsha Hodge called CCDSS with news of the corrected diagnosis. On February 16, 1989, David Hodge wrote CCDSS, again informing them of the misdiagnosis and requesting a copy of any CCDSS case file on the incident. In March 1989, Defendant Alan L. Katz, Assistant Director of CCDSS, replied by letter that "the Department's report reflects that suspected child abuse was ruled out and unsubstantiated," and attached a redacted copy of the case file.

Between February 1989 and May 1990, the Hodges . . . [requested] among other things, the full report and the destruction or expunction of any CCDSS file or document regarding the Hodge investigation. Each request was refused under Maryland's statutory bar against disclosure of confidential materials . . . and CCDSS's purported inability to expunge the file until 1994. CCDSS maintained the Hodge investigation report up to and beyond the filing date of the instant action. CCDSS also registered the names David, Marsha, and Joseph Hodge in MDHR's Automated Master File (AMF), a computerized database containing a record of every Maryland citizen who has received any services, ranging from food stamps to child protective services, from a local Department of Social Services office. The AMF information pertaining to the Hodges is alphanumerically coded and shielded by state and federal law from disclosure to the general public. Maryland is also required to ensure that "all records concerning . . . reports of child abuse and neglect are confidential and that their unauthorized disclosure is a criminal offense," but "may authorize by statute disclosure to [certain persons and agencies] under limitations and procedures the State determines. [31 F.3d 157, 160 (1994)]

One of the court's reasons for reversing the lower court was that it was not clear that family privacy had been invaded because the records remained confidential:

> Moreover, given the extensive confidentiality provisions protecting the Hodge investigation report, we see no avenue by which a stigma or defamation labeling the Hodges as child abusers could attach. . . . Data concerning a child abuse investigation and its disposition is entered into the AMF in alphanumeric code and is not accessible to the general public. Information from these records may be disclosed only to a limited number of persons specified by state statute, including social services or CPS officials investigating abuse or providing services to persons named in the reports or otherwise carrying out their official functions, licensed practitioners rendering medical care to an abused child, and under certain circumstances the parent or custodian and the alleged abuser. We agree with the district court that these safeguards "adequately limit access to the information [pertaining to the Hodges]." [31 F.3d 157, 165 (1994)]

A second factor was that plaintiffs had failed to show they had suffered harm by the retention of the records. Although they alleged the reports could affect their security clearances, the court cited another decision holding that clearances were not a property right and so there could be no harm.

Lastly, the court pointed to the advantages of retaining unsubstantiated records: "The retention of these investigation reports continues to serve legitimate state interests in the welfare of children. For instance, a series of 'unsubstantiated' or 'ruled out' entries for a given child may arouse suspicion of a pattern or practice of emotional and physical harm to a child, warranting further inquiry by the State. Retained records could, in fact, protect the individual whose record is kept by preventing repeated investigations when more than one person makes the same accusation. Finally, such records allow the state to defend itself in the event of a suit alleging inadequate investigation of a reported instance of child abuse" [31 F.3d 157, 166 (1994)].

A different result occurred in *Valmonte v. Bane,* 18 F.3d 992 (2nd Cir. 1994). There the plaintiff was the subject of an anonymous child abuse report that she had mistreated her eleven-year-old child. After an investigation, the protective services agency concluded she had engaged in "excessive corporal punishment" and opened a case. Subsequently, the family court dismissed the charges, but Valmonte's name remained on the state's central registry of child abuse cases. While the information in this registry was confidential, it was accessible to a range of interested parties, including some prospective employers:

> As noted earlier, the information in the Central Register is generally confidential. The names of individuals on the Central Register are not publicly available, although there are numerous exceptions for, among others, public agencies, law enforcement personnel, and judicial officers.
>
> More significant, for purposes of this case, are the statutory provisions requiring certain employers in the child care field to make inquiries to the Central Register to determine whether potential employees are among those listed. The purpose of these provisions is to ensure that individuals on the Central Register do not become or stay employed or licensed in positions that allow substantial contact with children, unless the licensing or hiring agency or business is aware of the applicant's status. Numerous state agencies, private businesses, and licensing agencies related to child care, adoption, and foster care are required by law to inquire whether potential employees or applicants are on the Central Register. SSL §424-a(1). For purposes of simplicity, this group will be referred to as "employers," even though licensing agencies are included within that designation.
>
> When such employers make an inquiry, the state DSS will inform the potential employer if the individual is the subject of an indicated report on the Central Register. SSL §424-a(1)(e). The state DSS will not inform the employer of the nature of the indicated report, but only that the report exists. If the potential employee is on the list, the employer can only hire the individual if

the employer "maintains a written record, as part of the application file or employment record, of the specific reasons why such person was determined to be appropriate" for working in the child or health care field. SSL §424-a(2)(a). [18 F.3d 992, 995 (1994)]

The Valmonte court held that the state statutory scheme violated Valmonte's due process rights:

> There is no dispute that Valmonte's inclusion on the list potentially damages her reputation by branding her as a child abuser, which certainly calls into question her "good name, reputation, honor, or integrity." The state contends, however, that there is no "stigma" attached to her inclusion because there is no disclosure of information on the Central Register except to authorized state agencies or potential employers in the child care field.
>
> Dissemination to potential employers, however, is the precise conduct that gives rise to stigmatization. . . . [A]lthough Valmonte's presence on the Central Register will not be disclosed to the public, it will be disclosed to any employer statutorily required to consult the Central Register. Since Valmonte states that she will be applying for child care positions, her status will automatically be disclosed to her potential employers. . . .
>
> We hold that the high risk of error produced by the procedural protections established by New York is unacceptable. . . . The crux of the problem with the procedures is that the "some credible evidence" standard results in many individuals being placed on the list who do not belong there. Those individuals must then be deprived of an employment opportunity solely because of their inclusion on the Central Register, and subject to the concurrent defamation by state officials, in order to have the opportunity to require the local to do more than merely present some credible evidence to support the allegations.[6] [18 F.3d 992, 1000 (1994)]

ACCESS TO CONFIDENTIAL CHILD PROTECTIVE SERVICE RECORDS

In *Pennsylvania v. Ritchie*, 480 U.S. 39 (1987), the Supreme Court upheld in part a Pennsylvania court decision allowing a defendant possible access to confidential child abuse records to discover the names of witnesses and evidence that could be used in his defense in a criminal child abuse prosecution. Balancing the Confrontation Cause of the Sixth Amendment with the state's desire to preserve confidentiality in child abuse records, the Court endorsed limited access: the trial court could review the records *in camera* and could disclose any "material" information to the defendant. The court noted that the child abuse record is not totally confidential in that the state statute provides for disclosure to the court, among others:

> Given that the Pennsylvania Legislature contemplated some use of CYS records in judicial proceedings, we cannot conclude that the statute prevents all disclosures in criminal prosecutions. In the absence of any apparent state policy to the contrary, we therefore have no reason to believe the relevant information would not be disclosed when a court of competent jurisdiction determines that the information is "material" to the defense of the accused. . . .
>
> We find that Ritchie's interest (as well as that of the Commonwealth) in ensuring a fair trial can be protected fully by requiring that the CYS files be submitted only to the trial court for in camera review. Although this rule denies Ritchie the benefits of an "advocate's eye," we note that the trial court's discretion is not unbounded. If a defendant is aware of specific information contained in the file (e.g., the medical report), he is free to request it directly from the court, and argue in favor of its materiality. Moreover, the duty to disclose is ongoing; information that may be deemed immaterial upon original examination may become important as the proceedings progress, and the court would be obligated to release information material to the fairness of the trial. [480 U.S. 39, 58 (1987)]

However, the court did impose restrictions on the defendant's access to the confidential files:

To allow full disclosure to defense counsel in this type of case would sacrifice unnecessarily the Commonwealth's compelling interest in protecting its child abuse information. If the CYS records were made available to defendants, even through counsel, it could have a seriously adverse effect on Pennsylvania's efforts to uncover and treat abuse. Child abuse is one of the most difficult crimes to detect and prosecute, in large part because there often are no witnesses except the victim. A child's feelings of vulnerability and guilt and his or her unwillingness to come forward are particularly acute when the abuser is a parent. It therefore is essential that the child have a state-designated person to whom he may turn, and to do so with the assurance of confidentiality. Relatives and neighbors who suspect abuse also will be more willing to come forward if they know that their identities will be protected. Recognizing this, the Commonwealth—like all other States—has made a commendable effort to assure victims and witnesses that they may speak to the CYS counselors without fear of general disclosure. The Commonwealth's purpose would be frustrated if this confidential material had to be disclosed upon demand to a defendant charged with criminal child abuse, simply because a trial court may not recognize exculpatory evidence. Neither precedent nor common sense requires such a result. [480 U.S. 39, 60 (1987)]

CONFIDENTIALITY OF JUVENILE COURT RECORDS

In 1967, in *In re Gault*, 387 U.S. 1—a Supreme Court decision that resulted in the procedural transformation of the juvenile court system—the Court noted:

Beyond this, it is frequently said that juveniles are protected by the process from disclosure of their deviational behavior. As the Supreme Court of Arizona phrased it in the present case, the summary procedures of Juvenile Courts are sometimes defended by a statement that it is the law's policy "to hide youthful errors from the full gaze of the public and bury them in the graveyard of the forgotten past." This claim of secrecy, however, is more rhetoric than reality. Disclosure of court records is discretionary with the judge in most jurisdictions. Statutory restrictions almost invariably apply only to the court records, and even as to those the evidence is that many courts routinely furnish information to the FBI and the military, and on request to government agencies and even to private employers. Of more importance are police records. In most States the police keep a complete file of juvenile "police contacts" and have complete discretion as to disclosure of juvenile records. Police departments receive requests for information from the FBI and other law-enforcement agencies, the Armed Forces, and social service agencies, and most of them generally comply. Private employers word their application forms to produce information concerning juvenile arrests and court proceedings, and in some jurisdictions information concerning juvenile police contacts is furnished private employers as well as government agencies. [387 U.S. 1, 24 (1967)]

Thirty years later, the confidentiality of juvenile court records and proceedings continues to be debated [Trasen, 1995:372]. Trasen notes that thirty-nine states, the District of Columbia, and Puerto Rico leave access to juvenile proceedings to the discretion of the court:

The vast majority of states have statutes within their juvenile codes that grant the juvenile court judge the discretion to admit or exclude the public from juvenile proceedings. These proceedings are typically closed unless a third party can show a "direct" or "proper" interest in the case. A crucial element in many states is whether opening the proceedings to the public is in the best interest of the child. In these states, if the court finds that publicity may have an adverse effect on the juvenile, the judge may grant a court closure order, although these orders are highly scrutinized. A few states determine access to juvenile proceedings based on the seriousness of the charge, under the theory that a juvenile charged with "adult crimes" such as murder and rape should be subject to any adult treatment the press and public wish to render. [Trasen, 1995:373]

While records are confidential, disclosure may be permitted for a number of reasons. For example in the *J.P. v DeSanti* decision, discussed in Chapter 3, the juvenile's confidential record was made available to fifty-five different health and human service agencies participating in the "social services clearinghouse." More recently, there is increasing public pressure to relax confidentiality requirements so that juvenile offenders are publicly identified and thus presumably deterred from delinquent activity.

Given the legitimate concerns about access to juvenile records, one approach is to allow that the record later be expunged, that is, that the juvenile's name be removed from the record. This is within the discretion of the court, and is more likely to occur where there has been a mistake or charges have been dropped.

In *Moore v. Tielsch,* 525 P.2d 250 (Wash. 1974), the Supreme Court of Washington denied an appeal from three juveniles requesting expungement of court records containing charges that were dismissed and charges for which they were found guilty. The court said:

> Complete expunction of petitioners' arrest records, juvenile court files and what they have categorized as social and legal files, however, would be contrary to the underlying philosophy of our juvenile law. The purpose of our juvenile court law has been protection, guidance and rehabilitation, not punishment. . . .
>
> In implementing that philosophy and purpose the statute provides for probation counselors to assist the juvenile court. The law directs the counselor to "inquire into the antecedents, character, family history, environments and cause of dependency or delinquency of every alleged dependent or delinquent child brought before the juvenile court . . ." In short, the judge, facing one of the most difficult tasks in the judicial system, needs all the help and information possible to reach a decision as to how to best correct and aid the juvenile before him. Obviously that decision may be a literal turning point in the young offender's life. [525 P.2d 250 (1974)][7]

Confidentiality
and Adoption Records

The confidentiality of adoption records is particularly difficult in that the privacy rights of three separate parties, biological parents, adoptive parents, and adoptees, may be involved, along with the interests of the state. There was no adoption at common law, since adoption was in conflict with the policy of inheritance through blood relations. The first adoption law in the United States was enacted in Massachusetts in 1851, but not until 1917 was a law enacted—in Minnesota—sealing adoption records. By the 1950s, such laws had been enacted in most states [Kuhns, 1994:260].

The law in most states is that adoption records, including the adoptee's original birth certificate, are sealed upon adoption and are not accessible without a court order. A new birth certificate is issued for the adopted child, listing the adopting parents as parents. Frequently, unless there is an adoption by relatives, adoption of an older child, or an "open adoption," the identity of the birth parents is unknown to the adopting parents of the adopted child. Similarly, once a child is placed for adoption, the identity of the adoptive parents and the new identity of the adopted child are often unknown to the birth parents.

This arrangement is often contractual. The birth mother or birth parents are promised confidentiality by the adoption agency when they consent to the adoption—that their identities will not be revealed at a later time. Similarly, adopting parents are promised that their identities and that of their adopted child will not become known to the biological parents.

A New Jersey decision summarizes the privacy interests of the three parties:

> The purpose of the confidentiality surrounding the birth records
> arises out of the circumstances that lead to the legal proceedings.
> The natural parents, having determined that it is in their own
> and the child's best interests, have placed the child up for adoption.
> For example, this decision may be precipitated by an illegitimate birth status of the child and the inability of the unwed
> mother or father to care properly for the child. The assurance of
> secrecy regarding the identity of the natural parents enables
> them to place the child for adoption with a reputable agency,

with the knowledge that their actions and motivations will not become public knowledge. Assured of this privacy by the State, the natural parents are free to move on and attempt to rebuild their lives after what must be a traumatic and emotionally tormenting episode in their lives.

The adopting parents also have an interest in having the birth records placed under seal. They have taken into their home a child whom they will regard as their own and whom they will love and raise as an integral part of their family unit. It is important to these adopting parents that they may raise this child without fear of interference from the natural parents and without fear that the birth status of an illegitimate child will be revealed or used as a means of harming the child or themselves. The State has an active interest in protecting and nurturing the growing family relationship it has statutorily created.

Sealing the birth records serves the interests of the child. It protects the child from any possible stigma of illegitimacy which, though fading, may still exist, and insures that the relationship with his or her new parents can develop into a loving and cohesive family unit uninvaded by a natural parent who later wishes to intrude into the relationship. The statute requiring that the records be sealed clearly serves the interests of all three parties in the adoptive triangle: adoptive parents, natural parents and the child. [*Mills v. Atlantic City Board of Vital Statistics,* 148 N.J. Super. 302, 307 (1977)]

RELEASE OF NONIDENTIFYING INFORMATION

At least forty-five states provide for some access to nonidentifying information from confidential adoption records, such as medical information [Bebensee, 1993:405 n. 65].

Non-identifying information generally consists of the date and place of the adoptee's birth; the age of the biological parents at the time of placement and a description of their general physical appearance; the race, ethnicity and religion of the biological parents; the medical history of the biological parents and adoptee;

whether the termination was voluntary or court-ordered; the facts and circumstances relating to the adoptive placement; the age and sex of any other children of the biological parents at the time of adoption; the educational levels of the birth parents, their occupations, interests, skills, etc.; and any supplemental information about the medical or social conditions of members of the biological family provided since the adoption was complete. [Kuhns, 1994: 263 n. 29]

For example, the Oregon statute provides:

(1) After January 1, 1980, before any final decree of adoption of a minor is entered, the court shall be provided a medical history of the child and of the biological parents as complete as possible under the circumstances. (2) When possible, the medical history shall include, but need not be limited to: (a) A medical history of the adoptee from birth up to the time of adoption, including disease, disability, congenital or birth defects, and records of medical examination of the child, if any; (b) Physical characteristics of the biological parents, including age at the time of the adoptee's birth, height, weight, and color of eyes, hair and skin; (c) A gynecologic and obstetric history of the biological mother; (d) A record of potentially inheritable genetic or physical traits or tendencies of the biological parents or their families; and (e) Any other useful or unusual biological information that the biological parents are willing to provide. (3) The names of the biological parents shall not be included in the medical history. (4) The court shall give the history to the adoptive parents at the time the decree is entered and shall give the history to the adoptee, upon request, after the adoptee attains the age of majority. [Ore. Rev. Stat. §109.342][8]

RELEASE OF IDENTIFYING INFORMATION

Good Cause. Release of confidential adoption information, including the original birth certificate,[9] which allows the adoptee to learn the identity of birth parents is often supported by adult adoptees who argue they have a psychological need to learn their identities and reunite with their biological parents.[10] It is often opposed by biological parents who argue that at the time of adoption they were promised confidentiality, they relied on these promises, and have started a new life in which reopening the past would be detrimental.[11]

Until recently, confidential adoption record information that identified birth parents was generally not available to adult adoptees. Most states allow access to this information only by court order upon a showing of good cause, with the determination of what constitutes "good cause" discretionary to the court. In a few decisions, such as *Mills,* the court has held that a psychological need to know does constitute good cause. However, generally courts have held that an adult adoptee's "psychological need to know" the identity of one's birth parents requires proof of a serious mental problem caused by not knowing one's biological parents. In *Alma Society v. Mellon,* 601 F.2d 1225 (2nd Cir. 1979), the federal court rejected the plaintiffs' argument that their psychological need to know the identity of their biological parents constituted a Fourteenth Amendment constitutional privacy issue. In *In re Janice Assalone,* 512 A.2d 1383 (1986), the Rhode Island Supreme Court rejected an appeal by adult adoptees arguing that their psychological need to know their birth parents' identities constituted good cause:

> However, unless consent of the birth parents is obtained, a thinly supported claim of "psychological need to know" will not support a finding of good cause. Proof must establish that deep psychological problems stem from the lack of information. In some states this implies that the adult adoptee must show that he/she is a burden to society due to psychological problems resulting from the lack of identifying information. Although good cause must be determined on a case-by-case basis, most courts require the adoptee who alleges psychological problems as a basis for the petition to prove a "concrete and compelling need" to learn the facts of one's ancestry, in order to outweigh the birth parents' rights to privacy.
>
> The petitioner testified that she had not sought or received professional counseling in relation to her quest to seek out her biological parents and admitted that her curiosity had led her to the courthouse. She stated her belief that knowing her parents'

identities would help her to improve herself as she is "a little un-settled not knowing [her] past or anything about herself. . . ." Although we sympathize with petitioner and the plight of other adoptees similarly situated, the record is devoid of any evidence to support the trial justice's conclusion that petitioner had a compelling need for the information she sought. She is not suf-fering from any mental or physical ailment due to her lack of knowledge that precipitated this action. [512 A.2d 1383 (1986)][12]

Adoption Registries. A number of states now permit the release of identifying information from confidential adoption records if both the adult adoptee and the birth parents consent. Often this takes place through an adoption registry. There are two general types, sometimes called passive and active. Under a passive registry, both the adult adoptee and the birth parent must register, indicating they would like to identify and contact the other. If this happens, a meeting is arranged. However, if only one party registers, there is no match, and the state may not contact the unregistered party seek-ing his or her consent.[13] At least twenty-six states have such statutes [Lum, 1993:505]. In an active registry, if either party registers and the other does not, the state may seek out the other party, attempting to obtain their con-sent. At least seventeen states have such search and consent statutes.[14]

Recent Statutes. Several states recently have enacted statutes in which adult adoptees may request and have access to confidential identifying in-formation from adoption records.[15] For example, in 1996, Tennessee en-acted legislation releasing adoption records to adoptees twenty-one years old or their legal representatives [Tenn. Code Ann. §36-1-126 *et seq.*]. The legislation provides for a "contact veto" whereby a parent or sibling, among others, can register and prevent contact by the adoptee [§36-1-128]. How-ever, the biological parent or sibling cannot prevent disclosure of the confi-dential record. Attempts by the adoptee to contact a person who has executed a contact veto are prohibited and, if there is provable harm, can be punished as a misdemeanor offense along with punitive and compensatory damages [§36-1-132].

In subsequent litigation, a federal district court refused to issue an in-junction and prevent the implementation of the law, finding that the legisla-tion violated no state or federal constitutional privacy rights; and although the state had promised confidentiality to birth parents when they placed their child for adoption, the state could enact retroactive legislation voiding these agreements [*Doe v. Sundquist,* 943 F.Supp. 886 (MD Tenn. 1996)]. This decision was upheld upon appeal. The appellate court observed: "The element of public interest also weighs against enjoining enforcement of the Tennessee statute. The statute appears to be a serious attempt to weigh and balance two frequently conflicting interests: the interest of a child adopted at an early age to know who that child's birth parents were, an interest entitled to a good deal of respect and sympathy, and the interest of birth parents in the protection of the integrity of a sound adoption system" [*Doe v. Sundquist,* 106 F.3d 702 (6th Cir. 1997), 1997 U.S. App. *LEXIS* 2178 at 10].

Confidentiality with Families and Groups

"Defining the boundaries of confidentiality in group therapy is even more difficult because communications are made to both the therapist and to other group members. In fact, multiperson therapies can be considered outside the coverage of any otherwise applicable privilege because communications are usually not considered confidential if made in the presence of third parties. The rationale is that a disclosure made in front of a third party is equivalent to making that information available to the world. . . . As a result, a group member may be divulging intimate information to 'a pool of legal witnesses'" [Roback, Ochoa, et al., 1992:82, quoting Foster, 1975].

Encouraging the free flow of communication and protecting the confidentiality of disclosures that may be necessary for diagnosis or treatment are certainly as important when working with couples, families, or groups as when working with a single individual. Yet at law, there may be significant differences in the confidentiality and privacy afforded communications in multiperson settings.

The common-law doctrine is that the presence of a third party to a confidential communication nullifies that confidentiality. (See generally Chapter 2.) Where the third party is a spouse, common law or statutory marital privilege might save the confidential nature of the communication. While some states have rejected the third party rule, others still adhere to that policy. Some states by statute protect confidentiality in family therapy, and a few specifically provide confidentiality protection in group therapy. Some statutes are quite specific, for example protecting couples and families only in respect to marital counseling or protecting confidentiality in group therapy only when the group leader is a psychologist. In several states there are court decisions upholding confidentiality in group settings.

Where these legal protections are in place, the participants in the family or group therapy can refuse to disclose communications in those settings—with the usual qualifications and legal limitations—and can instruct the social worker or therapist not to divulge the confidential communications. Generally, when only one of the participants wishes to divulge the confidential communication, the privilege would prevent this. Where the participants wish to disclose the communication and the therapist does not, the participants as holders of the privilege control disclosure. This situation might occur if there was litigation between the participants and the therapist.

Where statutory or judicial protections are not in place, however, there is no guarantee of confidentiality in group settings. Moreover, even where there are confidentiality provisions, these protect participants from being compelled to divulge the information in court but are less effective in preventing a participant from disclosing confidential information to others outside of court. As the number of participants grows, the likelihood of enforcing confidentiality diminishes. The current NASW Code of Ethics warns practitioners: "Social workers should inform participants in families, couples, or group counseling that social workers cannot guarantee that all participants will honor such agreements" [standard 1.07(f)]. (See Chapter 4.)

A survey of clinicians found that 54 percent of those responding knew of breaches of confidentiality occurring at least once during their practice: "The unauthorized identification of a group member to an outsider was the most frequently occurring type of violation, followed by disclosure of sexual indiscretions by a co-member. In contrast, work-related incidents and illegal activities were rarely discussed outside of group." "Reactions of the groups to the violations of confidence included anger, reduction of self-disclosure, and a decline in group cohesiveness, though these somewhat dissipated over time" [Roback, Ochoa, et al., 1992:86, 88].

Additionally, a group leader may be compelled to violate the confidence of the group and make a disclosure required by law—such as child abuse—as described elsewhere in the text. This again points to the importance of alerting patients and clients to the boundaries of confidentiality. In *State in the Interest of J.P.B.*, 143 N.J.Super, 96 (1976), J.P.B., a sixteen-year-old on commitment to a state institution, was required to participate in "guided group instruction," where residents were instructed to "bare their souls," and it was understood "What you say in the group will stay in the group." There were severe penalties for not entering wholeheartedly into this process, including transfer to a more restrictive institution. After being challenged by the group, which questioned his honesty, J.P.B. revealed that he was previously involved in an unsolved mugging and he later learned that the victim had died. Without telling J.P.B. or the group, the group leader notified the authorities, who interrogated the youth and obtained a confession. J.P.B. appealed his subsequent conviction on the basis of a violation of confidentiality. The New Jersey court held that J.P.B.'s statements were inadmissible both because they were the result of a custodial investigation without a Miranda warning and also because of confidentiality considerations: "When, as here, the State exacts information under a promise or assurance of confidentiality, it cannot, consistent with due process and fundamental fairness, violate that confidentiality and defeat the expectations raised by its promise by using the information in a criminal trial as incriminating evidence against the one who offered it" [143 N.J.Super. 96, 106 (1976)].

One state providing statutory privilege for group therapists is Colorado. The statute protects disclosures in certain group settings: where the individuals are participating in psychotherapy and where the group is conducted by a legally authorized professional. If these conditions are met, neither the leader of the group nor any of the participants can be examined in court about "any knowledge" they have gained during the group session without the consent of the individual making the disclosure.[16]

There are a few case decisions dealing with confidentiality in group therapy. In *Minnesota v. Andring*, 342 N.W.2d 128 (Minn. 1984), the defendant was charged with child sexual abuse and was participating in court-ordered group therapy prior to his trial. Members of the group were told that the sessions were confidential and only staff could have access to anything disclosed. Andring told the group about the child sexual abuse. The court reversed the trial court and held that the disclosures to the group were privileged, since the actual report of the abuse had already occurred:

> We then reach the question . . . as to whether confidential group therapy sessions which are an integral and necessary part of a patient's diagnosis and treatment are to be included within the scope of the medical privilege. The troublesome aspect of this question lies in the fact that third parties, other patients and participants in the therapy, are present at the time the information is disclosed. Does their presence destroy the privilege?
>
> McCormick, in discussing the issue of whether the presence of third parties renders a statement to a physician nonprivileged, argues that the court should analyze the problem in terms of whether the third persons are necessary and customary participants in the consultation or treatment and whether the communications were confidential for the purpose of aiding in diagnosis and treatment. McCormick's Handbook of the Law of Evidence, §101 (E. Cleary 2d ed. 1972). Under this approach, we conclude that the medical privilege must be construed to encompass statements made in group psychotherapy. The participants in group psychotherapy sessions are not casual third persons who are strangers to the psychiatrist/psychologist/nurse–patient relationship. Rather, every participant has such a relationship with the attending professional, and, in the group therapy setting, the participants actually become part of the diagnostic and therapeutic process for co-participants.
>
> The chief characteristic of group therapy that distinguishes it from individual analysis is that each patient becomes the therapeutic agent of the others. . . . Effective social interaction within the group is therefore a crucial prerequisite to group therapy. The type of interaction required can only be achieved, however, when group members respond to each other spontaneously, both in their speech and their actions. . . . No group participant would make himself vulnerable to community scorn and loss of spouse, job, or freedom by placing his most secret thoughts before the group, unless he could be assured of confidentiality. . . . Although there may be occasional losses [of relevant important

information] such sporadic occurrences are overshadowed by the potential destruction of the therapeutic relationship. [342 N.W.2d 128, 133 (1984)][17]

CONFIDENTIALITY AND SELF-HELP GROUPS[18]

On New Year's Eve of 1988, Paul Cox drank beer and kamikazes at a bar called Garry's Barleycorn in New Rochelle, New York. On the way home he was involved in a car accident and walked 2½ miles to the house where he used to live with his parents. He broke in, got a knife from the kitchen, went up to the bedroom where his mother and father once slept, and murdered Shanta and Lakshman Rao Chervu. Cox stole nothing— he just slashed the throats of the two innocent victims. Cox then went to his parents' house in Larchmont, New York, and went to sleep. When he woke up, he remembered nothing from the night before. The police found fingerprints at the scene, but since Cox had never before been arrested, there was nothing to match.

Four years later, Cox joined Alcoholics Anonymous ("A.A."). "It is part of the 12 steps of the A.A. [process] to search for somebody and start telling him your past, to admit guilt." [n1] At the time, Cox was rooming with a young man and woman, both A.A. members. He told them and other A.A. members that he dreamed he had committed a crime. Later, he said that "he believed he had done it, but he had no real recollection of the night. He remembered finding a bloody knife and throwing it in the water." One member of A.A. went to the police via an intermediary. That member gave the names of other A.A. members who had been privy to the information and informed the police that Cox had been having dreams or dream fragments of killing the Chervus.

Cox was charged with double homicide in 1993. In June 1994, seven A.A. members were compelled by subpoena to testify. Judge Cowhey, the presiding judge, refused to allow the A.A. members to claim a privilege as an extension of either the priest-penitent or the spousal privileges. Instead, he held that New York law does not extend a testimonial privilege to self-help groups. Although the A.A. members maintained that they were bound by A.A. principles to protect Cox's confidences, all seven were ordered to testify. They were not required to disclose their full names, and no press pictures of the seven witnesses were allowed. [Weiner, 1995:243]

Estimates are that there may be one-half million self-help groups currently in America, with as many as ten million members [Weiner, 1995:248]. Self-help groups range from the well-known Alcoholics Anonymous and Gamblers Anonymous to support groups for drug abusers, overeaters, victims of child abuse, victims of domestic violence, perpetrators of child abuse, and perpetrators of domestic violence, to name only a few.

A tenet of the self-help groups based on the AA model is the confidentiality of anything said in the group: "Meetings customarily begin with the Serenity Prayer, followed by a formal statement defining the group and its goals which usually includes a general statement that 'whatever is said in the room stays in the room' and a discussion of the importance of anonymity and confidentiality" {Weiner, 1995:254].

While a general agreement to keep matters confidential may be sufficient to encourage members not to reveal matters discussed in a self-help group, a legally enforceable confidentiality faces several challenges. First, in that self-help groups are usually run by lay people, not licensed professionals, there is no professional to whom a legal privilege could attach. Moreover, if there were, it would have to be shown that the material shared in confidence pertained to professional practice. Finally, as with group therapy, there is the problem of multiple membership, which often operates to nullify any privilege that might have existed.

The confidentiality of self-help group participants was addressed in a criminal case, *State v. Boobar*, 637 A.2d 1162 (Me. 1994). There, the defendant in a murder case spoke with an AA leader who was visiting him in jail.

Specifically, DesIsles testified that "[Boobar] started telling me, in the beginning, of how he went out with three—I think it was three girls and a guy and they were out partying and—and, then, he dropped off all but one girl and, then, they went out parking and, then, they got into an argument and he can't remember what happened after that." According to DesIsles, his reaction was to seek to discourage Boobar from discussing these events further, because they did not relate to the AA program. But, according to DesIsles, Boobar persisted: "Well, he was giving me telling me different stuff in between, you know, and I was trying to say about the Twelve Step program. And, at the end, he looked at me and he said, 'You and one other person know that I did it.' And, then, at the end when I was walking out, he said, 'I did it.'"

The defendant's attempt to extend the existing state privilege statute for licensed counselors and therapists to self-help groups because they performed a similar function was unavailing: "It is not reasonable to conclude, however, that by the language of section 13856(6), the legislature intended to sweep information disclosed to peer counselor or self-help groups like AA within the privilege set forth in section 13862 [therapists and counselors]" [637 A.2d 1162, 1169 (1994)].

SOCIAL WORK PRACTICE, CONFIDENTIALITY, AND PRIVACY WITH RECORDS AND GROUPS

The topics in Chapter 10 are varied and disparate, ranging from adoption records and records in federally funded drug programs to communications made in group therapy and self-help groups. Yet there are commonalities. In many of these areas, the existing laws are or have been undergoing change. The existing laws for federally funded substance abuse programs have been modified to allow for release of confidential information when child abuse is suspected or certain crimes committed. There is greater access to child protective services and juvenile court records than before, and in some states expungement procedures have been instituted or clarified. The confidentiality of adoption records has changed dramatically in recent years, as the text indicates. There is a growing recognition of the need for greater confidentiality protections in multiple-person therapies, and some courts and legislatures have responded by protecting communications and information in these settings. Legal confidentiality in self-help groups, however, remains problematic and has not really been addressed at law, despite rapid growth in numbers.

In many of these areas, a tension between legitimate demands for disclosure and equally legitimate demands for maintaining confidentiality runs strong, be it adult adoptees desiring to access confidential birth information and birth parents who do not wish to be located, confidential child abuse information and alleged perpetrators who wish to defend themselves, or juveniles and adults trying to expunge their records and law enforcement and judicial officials who wish to retain the information in case of later violations. Sometimes compromises have been achieved. Birth parents who wish to be located can be united with adult adoptees. Courts can review child abuse records in private and make a determination to release selective information, or none at all. Requests to expunge records can be reviewed and, if warranted, information can be changed or deleted. At other times, there is no easy resolution.

Finally, a theme running through these topics is that although confidentiality may be promised, this does not ensure that it is a legal reality. Perhaps most protected are records in federally funded drug programs, and least protected are any disclosures made within self-help groups, whatever confidentiality promises may have been made. Confidential adoption records can be accessed by adult adoptees for good cause in most states, and now in a few virtually on demand. Confidential child abuse records may be accessed, and it is safe to assume that portions will increasingly be made public. The same holds true for confidential juvenile records, which may have a broad, yet legal, dispersal to a wide range of agencies. For social workers, then, an awareness of these very different laws and, just as importantly, their limitations is crucial if workers are to serve effectively their patient and client populations—both in their own work and in alerting their patients and clients to the many meanings of confidentiality and privacy.

SOCIAL WORKER *and* PSYCHOTHERAPIST
PRIVILEGE: STATE STATUTES *and* RULES

State	Social Worker Privilege	Psychotherapist Privilege
ALABAMA	———	Ala. Code §34-26-2
ALASKA	———	Alaska Rule Evid. 504
ARIZONA	Ariz. Rev. Stat. Ann. §32-3283	Ariz. Rev. Stat. §32-2085
ARKANSAS	Ark. Code Ann. §17-46-107	Ark. Rule Evid. 503

Source: *Jaffee v. Redmond,* 135 L.Ed.2d 337, 349 n. 17; 135 L.Ed. 2d 337, 346 n. 11 (1996).

State	Social Worker Privilege	Psychotherapist Privilege
CALIFORNIA	Cal. Evid. Code Ann. §§ 1010, 1012, 1014	Same
COLORADO	Colo. Rev. Stat. §13-90-107	Colo. Rev. Stat. §13-90-107(g)(1)
CONNECTICUT	Conn. Gen. Stat. §52-146q	Conn. Gen. Stat. §52-146c
DELAWARE	Del. Code Ann., Tit. 24 §3913	Del. Uniform Rule Evid. 503
DISTRICT OF COLUMBIA	D.C. Code §14-307	Same
FLORIDA	Fla. Stat. §90-503	Same
GEORGIA	Ga. Code Ann. §24-9-21	Same
HAWAII	———	Haw. Rules Evid. 504, 504.1
IDAHO	Idaho Code §54-3213	Idaho Rule Evid. 503
ILLINOIS	Ill. Comp. Stat., ch. 225 §20/16	Ill. Comp. Stat., ch. 225 §15/5
INDIANA	Ind. Code §25-23.6-6-1	Ind. Code §25-33-1-17
IOWA	Iowa Code §622.10	Same
KANSAS	Kan. Stat. Ann. §65-6315	Kan. Stat. Ann. §74-5323

State	Social Worker Privilege	Psychotherapist Privilege
KENTUCKY	Ky. Rule Evid. 507	Same
LOUISIANA	La. Code Evid. Ann., Art. 510	Same
MAINE	Me. Rev. Stat. Ann., Tit. 32, §7005	Me. Rule Evid. 503
MARYLAND	Md. Cts. & Jud. Proc. §9-121	Md. Cts. & Jud. Proc. §9-109
MASSACHUSETTS	Mass. Gen. Laws §112:135A	Mass. Gen. Laws §233:20B
MICHIGAN	Mich. Comp. Stat. Ann. §339.1610	Mich. Comp. Laws Ann. §333.18237
MINNESOTA	Minn. Stat. Ann. §595.02	Same
MISSISSIPPI	Miss. Code Ann. §73-53-29	Miss. Rule Evid. 503
MISSOURI	Mo. Rev. Stat. §337.636	Mo. Rev. Stat. §491.060
MONTANA	Mont. Code Ann. §37-22-401	Mont. Code Ann. §26-1-807
NEBRASKA	Neb. Rev. Stat. Ann. §71-1,335	Neb. Rev. Stat. §27-504
NEVADA	Nev. Rev. Stat. Ann. §§49.215, 49.225, 49.235	Nev. Rev. Stat. Ann. §49.209

State	Social Worker Privilege	Psychotherapist Privilege
NEW HAMPSHIRE	N.H. Rev. Stat. Ann. §330-A:19	N.H. Rule Evid. 503
NEW JERSEY	N.J. Stat. Ann. §45:15BB-13	N.J. Stat. Ann. §45:14B-28
NEW MEXICO	N.M. Stat. Ann §61-31-24	N.M. Rule Evid. 11-504
NEW YORK	N.Y. Civ. Prac. Law §4508	N.Y. Civ. Prac. Law §4507
NORTH CAROLINA	N.C. Gen. Stat. §8-53.7	N.C. Gen. Stat. §8-53.3
NORTH DAKOTA	———	N.D. Rule Evid. §503
OHIO	Ohio Rev. Code Ann. §2317.02	Same
OKLAHOMA	Okla. Stat., Tit. 59 §1261.6	Okla. Stat., Tit. 12 §2503
OREGON	Ore. Rev. Stat. §40.250	Ore. Rules Evid. 504, 504.1
PENNSYLVANIA	———	42 Pa. Cons. Stat. §5944
RHODE ISLAND	R.I. Gen. Laws §§5-37.3-3, 5-37.3-4	Same
SOUTH CAROLINA	S.C. Code Ann. §19-11-95	Same

State	Social Worker Privilege	Psychotherapist Privilege
SOUTH DAKOTA	S.D. Codified Laws §§36-26-30	S.D. Codified Laws §§19-13-6 to 19-13-11
TENNESSEE	Tenn. Code Ann. §63-23-107	Tenn. Code Ann. §24-1-207
TEXAS	Tex. Rules Civ. Evid. 510	Tex. Rules Civ. Evid. 509, 510
UTAH	Utah Rule Evid. 506	Same
VERMONT	Vt. Rule Evid. 503	Same
VIRGINIA	Va. Code Ann. §8.01-400.2	Same
WASHINGTON	Wash. Rev. Code §18.19.180	Wash. Rev. Code §18.83.110
WEST VIRGINIA	W.Va. Code §30-30-12	W.Va. Code §27-3-1
WISCONSIN	Wis. Stat. §905.04	Same
WYOMING	Wyo. Stat. §33-38-109	Wyo. Stat. §33-27-123

CHAPTER 1. CONFIDENTIALITY AND PRIVACY IN SOCIAL WORK:
AN OVERVIEW

1. In this text a client is "an individual . . . that employs a professional to advise or assist it in the professional's line of work" and a patient is a "person under . . . treatment or care." *Black's Law Dictionary,* 1991.

2. See National Association of Social Workers, *Code of Ethics,* standards 1.07, 1.08 (1996).

3. See for example the Video Privacy and Protection Act of 1988, 18 U.S.C. §2710 (videotapes); N.J. Stat. Ann. 18A:73-43.1 (library records).

4. See California Constitution, Article I, section 1. The New Jersey Supreme Court has held that a right to privacy is implicit in the state constitution; see, for example, *Matter of Quinlan,* 70 N.J. 10, 355 A.2d 687 (1976).

5. Jurisdiction is a key legal concept, referring to a court's legal authority to hear a case. There are two main types, *subject matter jurisdiction* and *personal jurisdiction.* Subject matter jurisdiction is jurisdiction over the type of dispute;

personal jurisdiction is jurisdiction over persons or things residing or located within the court's geographic boundaries. Subject matter jurisdiction might include a family court's jurisdiction over divorce, custody, child abuse; a tax court's jurisdiction over tax issues; a probate court's jurisdiction over wills, incompetence, and guardianship; an appellate court's jurisdiction over appeals from lower courts, and so forth. In personal jurisdiction, a court must have jurisdiction over either at least one of the parties or the items in dispute.

6. Article III, section 2, of the constitution provides: "The judicial Power shall extend to all Cases, in Law and Equity, arising under this Constitution, the Laws of the United States, and Treaties made, or which shall be made, under their Authority; —to all cases affecting ambassadors, other public Ministers and Consuls; —to all Cases of admiralty and maritime Jurisdiction; —to Controversies to which the United States shall be a Party; —to Controversies between two or more States; —between a State and Citizens of another State; —between Citizens of different States; —between Citizens of the same State claiming Lands under Grants of different States, and between a State, or the Citizens thereof, and foreign States, Citizens or Subjects." For federal statutory law see 28 U.S.C. §1331 ff., federal district court jurisdiction; 28 U.S.C. §1291 ff., circuit court jurisdiction; and 28 U.S.C. §1251 ff., U.S. Supreme Court jurisdiction. Also note that under 28 U.S.C. §2284 a three-judge district court may be convened under special circumstances and under 28 U.S.C. §1253 decisions of this court may be appealed directly to the U.S. Supreme Court.

7. For further information, the reader should consult Harvard Law Review Staff, *The Blue Book*, 1996.

8. At present some useful Web sites include Washburn University School of Law at http://lawlib.wuacc.edu/washlaw; Cornell University Law School at http://www.cornell.edu; U.S. Government Services Agency at http://fedlaw.gsa.gov; and Findlaw at http://www.findlaw.com.

CHAPTER 2. CONFIDENTIAL AND PRIVILEGED COMMUNICATIONS

1. In its brief in support of a federal psychotherapist-patient privilege, the Menninger Clinic argued: "The success of psychotherapy depends on the patient's full disclosure; without it the therapy is ineffective. As the Group for the Advancement of Psychiatry found in 1960, the psychotherapist's 'capacity to help his patients is completely dependent upon their willingness to talk freely. This makes it difficult if not impossible for him to function without being able to assure his patient of confidentiality and, indeed, privileged communication.'

In short, 'A privilege for those receiving psychotherapy is necessary if the psychiatric profession is to fulfill its medical responsibility to its patients.'" Menninger Foundation, 1996:73.

2. "Unlike other rules of evidence, privileges are not fashioned primarily to exclude unreliable evidence or otherwise to aid in the truth-seeking function. Indeed, as deviations from the centuries-old common law principle that 'the public had a right to every man's evidence,' privileges expressly subordinate the goal of truth seeking to other societal interests." Note, Developments, 1985:1454.

3. The terms are confusing since some states distinguish between confidential and privileged communications, with the latter more protected; others treat confidential communications as the equivalent of privileged communications.

4. An exception is one's HIV-positive status, where a disclosure of this confidential information may be actionable. Wiley, 1992:236 ff.

5. One professional reported: "It's tricky because you are laying out confidentiality with people and that's important to establish, but there's also the dilemma about whether you emphasize that [reporting mandate] and not get disclosures that . . . need to be disclosed and discussed and treated. So I don't go crazy emphasizing that. . . . I don't know if I am violating people's rights in that. It's an ongoing question that's hard to answer, but I do make clear what confidentiality is, especially when you are working with kids." Levine, 1993:724.

6. See for example *Canterbury v. Spence*, 464 F.2d 772 (D.C. Cir. 1972); *Largey v. Rothman*, 540 A.2d 504 (N.J. 1988).

7. One exception is in the case of clergy-parishioner privilege, where the clergyperson may be the holder of the privilege and can make a decision whether to disclose information or not. See Wigmore, 1961:§2395.

8. The refusal to obey a court order to divulge confidential but nonprivileged communications could result in the professional being held in contempt of court, resulting in fines and even incarceration.

9. As used here, common law refers to "the body of those principles and rules of action . . . which derive their authority solely from usages and customs . . . or from the judgements and decrees of the courts recognizing, affirming, and enforcing such usages and customs; and, in this sense, particularly the ancient unwritten law of England." *Black's Law Dictionary*, 1991.

10. See *Berd v. Lovelace*, 21 Eng.Rep. 33 (1577). Spousal privilege occurred at almost the same time; see Wigmore, 1961:§2227, and Note, Developments, 1985:1456.

11. In *Jaffee v. Redmond,* the U.S. Supreme Court presented its rationale for privilege: "The common-law principles underlying the recognition of testimonial privileges can be stated simply 'for more than three centuries it has now been recognized as a fundamental maxim that the public . . . has a right to examine every man's evidence. When we come to examine the various claims of exemption, we start with the primary assumption that there is a general duty to give what testimony one is capable of giving, and that any exemptions which may exist are distinctly exceptional, being so many derogations from a positive general rule.' Exceptions from the general rule disfavoring testimonial privileges may be justified, however, by a 'public good transcending the normally predominant principle of utilizing all rational means for ascertaining the truth.'" 135 L.Ed. 2d 337, 344 (1996).

12. The Arizona statute includes certified baccalaureate social workers, certified master social workers, and certified independent social workers, including those involved in community service, social planning, research, and administration. Ariz. Rev. Code. §32-3291–§32-3293.

13. In Florida, a "mental health counselor" is a "person licensed or certified as a clinical social worker, marriage and family therapist, or mental health counselor . . . who is engaged primarily in the diagnosis or treatment of a mental or emotional condition, including alcoholism and other drug addiction" [Florida Rev. Stat. §90-503]. In Iowa, "mental health professional" means "a psychologist . . . , a registered nurse . . . , a social worker . . . , a marital and family therapist, a mental health counselor . . . , or an individual holding at least a master's degree in a related field as deemed appropriate by the board of behavioral science examiners" [Iowa Code §622.10]. In Rhode Island, "Health care provider" "means any person licensed by this state to provide or otherwise lawfully providing health care services, including, but not limited to, a physician, hospital, intermediate care facility or other health care facility, . . . psychiatric social worker, or psychologist, and any officer, employee or agent of that provider acting in the course and scope of his or her employment or agency related to or supportive of health services" [R.I. Gen. Laws §5-37.3-3]. In Vermont, a "mental health professional" includes "physician, psychologist, social worker, or nurse with professional training, experience and demonstrated competence in the treatment of mental illness, or a person reasonably believed by a patient to be a mental health professional" [Vermont Rule of Evidence §503].

14. In the Appendix, see for example Arkansas, Colorado, and Illinois.

15. In the Appendix, see for example Connecticut, New Jersey, New York, and North Carolina.

16. In the Appendix, see for example Indiana and South Dakota.

17. The dissent in *Jaffee v. Redmond* took issue with the breadth of social worker privilege statutes, citing as an example the Oklahoma statute where "the social worker's 'professional capacity' is expansive, for the 'practice of social work' in Oklahoma is defined as: 'The professional activity of helping individuals, groups, or communities enhance or restore their capacity for physical, social and economic functioning and the professional application of social work values, principles and techniques in areas such as clinical social work, social service administration, social planning, social work consultation and social work research to one or more of the following ends: Helping people obtain tangible services; counseling with individuals, families and groups; helping communities or groups provide or improve social and health services; and participating in relevant social action.'" 135 L.Ed. 2d 337, 357 (1996).

18. The Oregon statute specifically applies only to noninvestigatory communications. See Ore. Rev. Stat. §40.250(5).

19. See for example *Scull v. Superior Court*, 254 Cal.Rptr. 24 (Cal. App. 1988), where the court wrote: "It is well settled in California that the mere disclosure of the patient's identity violates the psychotherapist-patient privilege. The rationale for this rule is that the harm to the patient's interest of privacy is exacerbated by the stigma that society often attaches to mental illness. . . . In short, the disclosure that an individual is seeing a therapist may well serve to discourage any treatment and thereby interfere with the patient's freedom to seek and derive the benefits of psychotherapy. When a patient seeks out the counsel of a psychotherapist, he wants privacy and sanctuary from the world and its pressures. . . . The patient's purpose would be inhibited and frustrated if his psychotherapist could be compelled to give up his identity without his consent. Public knowledge of treatment by a psychotherapist reveals the existence and, in a general sense, the nature of the malady." 254 Cal.Rptr. 24, 26 (1988).

20. New York provides social worker privilege for "a communication made by his client to him, or his advice given thereon, in the course of his professional employment" [N.Y. Civ. Pract. Law §4508]. Minnesota includes "any information or advice based thereon" [Minn. Stat. §595.02]. See also Michigan Stat. Ann. §18.425(1610).

21. In *Allen v. Holyoke Hospital*, the court held that the worker could not disclose what she was told, but could describe what she observed. "Com-

munications to the department's social workers from the decedent's grandparents and foster parents while consulting with the social workers fall within the privilege. . . . Regarding the disclosure of information contained in the department's records acquired through the personal observations of social workers in the plaintiff's home, we reach a different result. The language of §135 clearly limits the privilege to communications 'from a person,' and the observations of the social worker are clearly not such." 496 N.E.2d 1368, 1372 (Mass. 1986).

22. In *State v. Curtis*, the court held that the purpose was investigation, not treatment, and therefore the disclosures could not be privileged: "The more difficult issue in this case lies in discerning when communications to an SRS caseworker are made for the purpose of diagnosis or treatment by a mental health professional. When an SRS caseworker is performing an investigative function, communications made to that caseworker are not for the purpose of diagnosis or treatment by a mental health professional within the meaning of the patient's privilege. Rather, those communications are made for the purpose of investigation, so as to enable the state to take appropriate protective measures. Such communications do not fall within the patient's privilege." 597 A.2d 770, 772 (Vt. 1991).

23. Me. Rev. Stat. Ann., Tit. 32, §7005; N.H. Rev. Stat. Ann. §330-A:19; N.C. Gen. Stat. §8-53.7; Va. Code Ann. §8.01-400.2; see also Wash. Rev. Code §18.83.110. The Virginia statute, for example, provides: "Except at the request of or with the consent of the client . . . no licensed clinical social worker, as defined in §54.1-3700, . . . shall be required in giving testimony as a witness in any civil action to disclose any information communicated to him in a confidential manner, properly entrusted to him in his professional capacity and necessary to enable him to discharge his professional or occupational services according to the usual course of his practice or discipline, wherein such a person so communicating such information about himself or another is seeking professional counseling or treatment and advice relative to and growing out of the information so imparted; provided, however, that . . . *when a court, in the exercise of sound discretion, deems such disclosure necessary to the proper administration of justice,* no fact communicated to, or otherwise learned by, such practitioner in connection with such counseling, treatment or advice shall be privileged, and disclosure may be required" (emphasis supplied). Similarly, the North Carolina statute provides: "No person engaged in delivery of private social work services, duly certified pursuant to Chapter 90B of the General Statutes shall be required to disclose any information which he or she may have

acquired in rendering professional social services, and which information was necessary to enable him or her to render professional social services: *provided, that the presiding judge of a superior or district court may compel such disclosure, if in the court's opinion the same is necessary to a proper administration of justice and such disclosure is not prohibited by other statute or regulation"* (emphasis supplied).

24. See also *Commonwealth v. Mandeville*, 436 N.E.2d 912 (Mass. 1982), where a staff psychologist who was not licensed to practice psychiatry or psychology was held not to be a psychotherapist under Massachusetts privilege statute; and *Commonwealth v. Clemons*, 427 N.E.2d 761 (Mass. App. 1981), where the court held communications with a therapist could not be made confidential when the therapist was supervised by a psychotherapist whom the defendant had never met.

25. In Maryland, the courts have held that a minor's privilege cannot necessarily be waived by a parent, but that in custody determinations an independent guardian must be appointed to make this decision: "the chancellor erred in refusing to appoint a guardian to act for the child regarding the assertion or waiver privilege of nondisclosure pursuant to section 9-109. Although arguably the parent who pursuant to court order has custody of a child could qualify . . . it is patent that such custodial parent has a conflict of interest in acting on behalf of the child in asserting or waiving the privilege of nondisclosure. We believe that it is inappropriate in a continuing custody 'battle' for the custodial parent to control the assertion or waiver of the privilege of nondisclosure. . . . Keeping in mind 'the best interest of the child,' we believe the appointment of an attorney to act as the guardian of the child in the instant matter is required. Furthermore, the appointment of a neutral third party would eliminate the very real possibility, as may exist in this case, of one of two warring parents exercising the power of veto for reasons unconnected to the polestar rule of 'the best interests of the child.'" *Nagle v. Hooks*, 460 A.2d 49, 52 (Md. 1983); See also *Kovacs v. Kovacs*, 633 A.2d 425 (Md. App. 1993).

26. Utah is an exception: privilege ends with the death of the individual. See Utah Rules of Evidence Rule 506.

27. For example, in Wisconsin, "'Social worker' means an individual who is certified as a social worker . . . or an individual reasonably believed by the patient to be a social worker." Wis. Rev. Stat. §905.04 1(g).

28. In *In the Matter of John Doe v. Levario*, the court said: "Communications between psychotherapists and patients are not ipso facto confidential. To be

confidential, two conditions must be present: (1) the patient 'intended' the communications to be undisclosed; and (2) that non-disclosure would further the interest of the patient. . . . 'Intention' is a state of mind seldom capable of direct proof and is determinable only through logical deduction from proven facts. . . . In the absence of words, there must be conduct. . . . It is not sufficient for a patient to say that in the patient's mind the communications were confidential. . . . It must be manifested in some fashion with words or words and conduct which lead a psychotherapist to understand or believe that the information obtained was intended to be confidential. . . . During consultation, examination or interview, a psychotherapist may inquire about confidentiality but is under no duty to do so. The psychotherapist is ordinarily neutral on this issue until nondisclosure is conveyed. The patient is not neutral because disclosure or nondisclosure may further the patient's interest in the consultation, examination or interview." 649 P.2d 510, 514 (N.M. 1985).

29. Federal Rule of Evidence 501 provides: "Except as otherwise required by the Constitution of the United States or provided by Act of Congress, or in rules prescribed by the Supreme Court pursuant to statutory authority, the privilege of a witness, person, government, State, or political subdivision thereof shall be governed by the principles of the common law as they may be interpreted by the courts of the United States in the light of reason and experience. However, in civil actions and proceedings, with respect to an element of a claim or defense as to which State law supplies the rule of decision, the privilege of a witness, person, government, State or political subdivision thereof shall be determined in accordance with State law." *Jaffee v. Redmond,* L.Ed. 2d 337, 342 (1996).

30. The *Jaffee* decision, 135 L.Ed.2d 337, 359 n. 5 (1996), lists statutes and rules excluding suspected child abuse: Ariz. Rev. Stat. Ann. §32-3283; Ark. Code Ann. §17-46-107(3); Cal. Evid. Code Ann. §1027; Colo. Rev. Stat. §19-3-304; Del. Rule Evid. 503(d)(4); Ga. Code Ann. §19-7-5(c)(1)(G); Idaho Code §54-3213(3); La. Code Evid. Ann., Art. 510(B)(2)(k); Md. Cts. & Jud. Proc. Code Ann. §9-121(e)(4); Mass. Gen. Laws, §119:51A; Mich. Comp. Laws Ann. §722.623; Minn. Stat. §595.02.2(a); Miss. Code Ann §73-53-29(e); Mont. Code Ann. §37-22-401(3); Neb. Rev. Stat. §28-711; N.M. Stat. Ann. §61-31-24(C); N.Y. Civ. Prac. §4508(a)(3); Ohio Rev. Code Ann. §2317.02(G)(1)(a); Ore. Rev. Stat. §40.250(4); R.I. Gen. Laws §5-37.3-4(b)(4); S.D. Codified Laws §36-26-30(3); Tenn. Code Ann. §63-23-107(b); Vt. Rule Evid. 503(d)(5); W.Va. Code §30-30-12(a)(4); Wyo. Stat. §14-3-205.

31. For example, in *People v. Bass,* the court held that confidential statements

made to a certified social worker with privilege could not be divulged in a criminal trial, even though they had been reported to the state child welfare agency under the mandatory reporting law. The court held: "1) The statements were made by the defendant to a certified social worker acting in his professional capacity; 2) The statements were made to enable the social worker to assess the defendant's mental health problems and to thereby act in his professional capacity; 3) The statements were intended by the defendant to be confidential . . . ; 4) The information in the defendant's statements was necessary for treatment by the clinic. In determining this, it is immaterial that as here, treatment was never actually given by the clinic." 529 N.Y.S.2d 961, 964 (N.Y. Sup. Ct. 1988).

32. Disclosures of confidential communications based on the welfare of a child may depend on showing a specific need. In *Perry v. Fiumano,* the plaintiff attempting to gain custody of the child alleged that the defendant's ex-husband was mentally and emotionally unstable and therefore unfit. She requested disclosure of social work counseling records, privileged in New York state. The court rejected the request, observing: "It is not our purpose, however, to discourage troubled parents from seeking professional assistance from the many public and private counseling agencies which are available to aid in relaxing matrimonial tensions and preserving family entities. Nor would we want a custodial parent to forgo needed psychiatric or other help out of fear that confidences will later be unfairly and unnecessarily revealed through the animus act of a present or former spouse. To avoid such potentially chilling effects, it is apparent that these privileges may not cavalierly be ignored or lightly cast aside. There first must be a showing beyond 'mere conclusory statements' that resolution of the custody issue requires revelation of the protected material. . . . [W]e are not unmindful that the petitioner's moving papers are drawn in vague, generalized terms and may not readily be interpreted as alleging that respondent's capacity to care for his son has diminished in the brief period since the petitioner agreed to give custody to respondent and later reaffirmed that agreement by causing its incorporation into a divorce decree. . . . Petitioner offers purely conclusory and largely inadmissible opinions as to respondent's condition. . . . Petitioner's unfounded speculation that the privileged matter 'could be of utmost importance' to the psychiatrist is not at all helpful." 403 N.Y.S.2d 382, 386 (N.Y. 1978).

33. There are significant differences among the states in respect to disclosure of illegal activity. The *Jaffee* dissent noted: "But turning to those States that do have an appreciable privilege of some sort, the diversity is vast. In Illinois and

Wisconsin, the social-worker privilege does not apply when the confidential information pertains to homicide, see Ill. Comp. Stat., ch. 740, §110/10(a)(9); Wis. Stat. §905.04(4)(d); and in the District of Columbia when it pertains to any crime 'inflicting injuries' upon persons, see D.C. Code §14-307(a)(1). In Missouri, the privilege is suspended as to information that pertains to a criminal act, see Mo. Rev. Stat. §337.636(2), and in Texas when the information is sought in any criminal prosecution, compare Tex. Rule Civ. Evid. 510(d) with Tex. Rule Crim. Evid. 501 et seq. In Kansas and Oklahoma, the privilege yields when the information pertains to 'violations of any law,' see Kan. Stat. Ann. §65-6315(a)(2); Okla. Stat., Tit. 59, §1261.6(2); in Indiana, when it reveals a 'serious harmful act,' see Ind. Code Ann. §25-23.6-6-1(2); and in Delaware and Idaho, when it pertains to any 'harmful act,' see Del. Code Ann., Tit. 24, §3913(2); Idaho Code §54-3213(2)." 135 L.Ed.2d 337, 358 (1996).

CHAPTER 3. PRIVACY AND THE LAW

1. Among other state constitutional privacy provisions are: Alaska Const. art. I, 22; Ariz. Const. art. II, 8; Cal. Const. art. I, 1; Fla. Const. art. I, 12, 23; Haw. Const. art. I, 6, 7; Ill. Const. art. I, 6, 12; La. Const. art. I, 5; Mont. Const. art. II, 10; S.C. Const. art. I, 10; Wash. Const. art. I, 7.

2. In *Meyer v. Nebraska*, the Court struck down a state statute designed to promote "civic development" by forbidding teaching foreign languages to children before completion of eighth grade. Holding that this was a violation of a due process liberty interest, the court said: "While this court has not attempted to define with exactness the liberty thus guaranteed, the term has received much consideration and some of the included things have been definitely stated. Without doubt, it denotes not merely freedom from bodily restraint but also the right of the individual to contract, to engage in any of the common occupations of life, to acquire useful knowledge, to marry, establish a home and bring up children, to worship God according to the dictates of his own conscience, and generally to enjoy those privileges long recognized at common law as essential to the orderly pursuit of happiness by free men" [262 U.S. 390, 399 (1923)]. See also *Pierce v. Society of Sisters,* 268 U.S. 510 (1925) (statute forbidding children to attend parochial school unconstitutional); *Skinner v. Oklahoma,* 316 U.S. 535 (1942) (statute requiring sterilization of those convicted of two or more felonies that involved "moral turpitude" unconstitutional); *Loving v. Virginia,* 388 U.S. 1 (1967) (statute criminalizing interracial marriage unconstitutional).

3. See for example *Matter of Conroy,* 98 N.J. 321 (1985). See also *Matter of Jobes,* 108 N.J. 394 (1987), *Matter of Peters by Johanning,* N.J. 365 (1987), and *Matter of Farrell,* 108 N.J. 335 (1987).

4. Beyond its implications for privacy, the *Bowers v. Hardwick* decision is significant in that it has been cited in a number of lower court cases upholding differential treatment of homosexuals both in the military and in governmental employment. See, for example, *Ben-Shalom v. March,* 881 F.2d 454 (7th Cir. 1989) (military); and *High Tech Gays v. Defense Industry Security Clearance Office,* 895 F.2d 563 (9th Cir. 1990) (restrictions on government employment). However, in a recent decision, *Roemer v. Evans,* 116 S.Ct. 1620, 1996 LEXIS 3295 (1996), the Supreme Court held that a Colorado constitutional amendment prohibiting the state from extending any protections to homosexuals was unconstitutional. In *Roemer,* the Court never acknowledged its previous *Bowers* decision, which suggests it may have less impact in the future.

5. This area, the "exclusionary rule" doctrine, is beyond the scope of this text. See generally *Weeks v. U.S.,* 232 U.S. 383 (1914), barring the use in federal prosecutions of evidence from an illegal search or seizure conducted by federal agents; *Elkins v. U.S.,* 364 U.S. 206 (1960), barring the use in federal prosecutions of evidence from an illegal search or seizure conducted by state law enforcement agents; and *Mapp v. Ohio,* 367 U.S. 643 (1961), barring the use in state prosecutions of evidence from illegal search or seizure conducted by state agents.

6. In *California v. Ciraolo,* 476 U.S. 207 (1986), the Court upheld a warrantless visual search for marijuana by helicopter, including photographing a backyard surrounded by a ten-foot fence, on the grounds that the helicopter was in public airspace and the individual homeowner had no reasonable expectation of privacy from such a search. Similarly, in *Florida v. Riley,* 488 U.S. 445 (1989), the Court in a plurality opinion upheld a visual search and photographing of marijuana grown in a greenhouse by a low-flying helicopter, where part of the roof and several sides of the greenhouse were open although shielded from normal view by trees and shrubs. In *U.S. v. Penny-Feeney,* 773 F.Supp. 220 (1991), the police, after several anonymous tips, took readings with a heat-sensing forward-looking infrared device (FLIR) in a helicopter flyover of the Penny-Feeney home. The readings indicated that artificial lighting was being used in their garage and corroborated reports that marijuana was being illegally grown indoors. The district court held that this did not constitute an illegal search because there was no expectation of privacy of heat emissions. Several other

circuits have come to the same conclusion. See *United States v. Myers,* 46 F.3d 668 (7th Cir. 1995); *United States v. Ford,* 34 F.3d 992 (11th Cir. 1994); *United States v. Pinson,* 24 F.3d 1056 (8th Cir. 1994). In a recent case in the 10th Circuit, however, the court held that the measuring of heat emissions did constitute a search protected by the Fourth Amendment. See *United States v. Cusumano,* 67 F.3d 1497 (10th Cir. 1995).

7. See *California v. Greenwood,* 486 U.S. 35 (1988) (no expectation of privacy for garbage cans left by the street); *U.S. v. Scott,* 975 F.2d 927 (1991) (no expectation of privacy for shredded paper left in plastic bags); and *U.S. v. Hendrick,* 922 F.2d 396 (7th Cir. 1991) (no expectation of privacy for garbage cans on one's property).

8. "Conversely, individuals have a categorically different and lesser expectation of privacy in their fingerprints, visual images, or voice prints—even when their production is compelled—because they are personal attributes that are routinely exposed to the public at large in daily life" [*Katz v. United States,* 389 U.S. 347, 351 (1967)]. Decisions in this area include voiceprints, *U.S. v. Dionisio,* 410 U.S. 1 (1973); handwriting, *U.S. v. Mara,* 410 U.S. 19 (1973); fingerprints and fingernail scrapings, *Cupp v. Murphy,* 412 U.S. 291 (1973).

9. *Dicta* are "opinions of a judge which do not embody the resolution or determination of the specific case before the court. Expressions in court's opinion which go beyond the facts before the court and therefore are individual views of author of the opinion and not binding in subsequent cases as legal precedent." *Black's Law Dictionary,* 1991.

10. Two other privacy decisions by the Court are *Nixon v. Administrator of General Services,* 433 U.S. 425 (1979), and *Detroit Edison Co. v. National Labor Relations Board,* 440 U.S. 301 (1979).

11. "Social histories contain information from a number of sources, including the complaining parties, the juveniles themselves, their parents, school records, and their past records in the juvenile court. They also include any information on record pertaining to other members of the family, and any other information that the probation officer thinks is relevant to the disposition of a case before the juvenile court. Receipt of written consent from juveniles or their families is not a prerequisite to compilation of social histories, and although access to social histories is available to juveniles' lawyers, access is not available to juveniles or their families." *J.P. v. DeSanti,* 653 F.2d 1080 (6th Cir. 1981).

CHAPTER 4. PRIVACY, CONFIDENTIALITY, AND THE SOCIAL WORKER'S ETHICAL RESPONSIBILITIES

1. "Psychologists do not engage in sexual harassment. Sexual harassment . . . (1) is unwelcome, is offensive, or creates a hostile workplace environment . . . or (2) is sufficiently severe or intense to be abusive to a reasonable person in the context. Sexual harassment can consist of a single intense or severe act or of multiple persistent or pervasive acts." APA, 1992: standard 1.1.

2. However, the line between enforceable standards and desirable conduct is not clear. The NASW code states: "Some of the standards that follow are enforceable guidelines for professional conduct, and some are aspirational. The extent to which each standard is enforceable is a matter of professional judgement to be exercised by those responsible for reviewing alleged violations of ethical standards." NASW, 1996:7.

3. Recent revisions in the American Medical Association support this position. See Council on Ethical and Judicial Affairs, "Ethical Issues Involved in the Growing AIDS Crises," 259 J. Amer. Med. Assoc. 1360 (1988).

CHAPTER 5. WORKPLACE PRIVACY: SELECTED ISSUES

1. See *Wilkinson v. Times Mirror,* 264 Cal.Rptr. 194 (Cal.App. 1989), and cases cited therein.

2. "Employees who are stopped and searched may assert several claims against employers. Among these are invasions of privacy; defamations; false imprisonment; false arrest; malicious prosecution; intentional infliction of emotional distress; and constitutional right infringement." Decker, 1987:311.

3. The decisions were *Camara v. Municipal Court,* 387 U.S. 523 (1967), *New Jersey v. T.L.O.,* 469 U.S. 325 (1985), and *Marshall v. Barlow's, Inc.,* 436 U.S. 307 (1978).

4. However, the Court cautioned: "The operational realities of the workplace, however, may make some employees' expectations of privacy unreasonable when an intrusion is by a supervisor rather than a law enforcement official. Public employees' expectations of privacy in their offices, desks, and file cabinets, like similar expectations of employees in the private sector, may be reduced by virtue of actual office practices and procedures, or by legitimate regulation. . . . An office is seldom a private enclave free from entry by supervisors, other employees, and business and personal invitees. Instead, in many cases offices are continually entered by fellow employees and other visitors during the workday for conferences, consultations, and other work-related visits. Given

the great variety of work environments in the public sector, the question whether an employee has a reasonable expectation of privacy must be addressed on a case-by-case basis." *O'Connor v. Ortega*, 480 U.S. 709, 718 (1987).

5. In a public sector locker search case, *American Postal Workers Union v. U.S. Postal Service*, 671 F.Supp. 497 (S.D.Ohio 1987), the court did uphold a search of postal employee lockers, finding that the postal employees had no reasonable expectation of privacy because all postal workers had signed an agreement when their lockers were assigned which stated that the lockers were government property and subject to inspection at any time, and the union collective bargaining agreement specifically stated that locker searches were permissible in the presence of a union shop steward, who was present at the search.

6. Even legitimate surveillance devices may be used for illegitimate purposes, thereby subjecting the employer to liability. In *Doe v. B.P.S. Guard Services*, 945 F.2d 1422 (8th Cir. 1991), video surveillance cameras were in use throughout a convention center during a "Working Women's Survival Show." However, they were used by security guards to videotape models in a dressing area while they dressed and undressed for the fashion segment of the show. Parts of the tape later appeared on local television. The court found that the employer could be held liable for over $400,000 in actual and punitive damages under agency principles for the actions of the guards, its employees.

7. In *Watkins v. L. M. Berry & Co.*, the employer had a policy of monitoring telephone solicitation calls to which all employees consented. Personal calls were permitted, and employers were told that these would not be listened to once it was established they were of a personal nature. Watkins received a personal call at lunchtime during which she discussed a job interview with another employer. She later learned from her supervisor that he had listened to the call. In response to her suit for violation of the ECPA, the company argued that there had been implied consent. The court rejected this contention: "It is clear, to start with, that Watkins did not actually consent to interception of this particular call. Furthermore, she did not consent to a policy of general monitoring. She consented to a policy of monitoring sales calls but not personal calls. . . . We therefore hold that consent within the meaning of section 2511(2)(d) is not necessarily an all or nothing proposition; it can be limited" [704 F.2d 577, 581 (11th Cir. 1983)]. The court also rejected the company's assertion that the call came within the "ordinary course of business" exception: "The phrase 'in the ordinary course of business' cannot be expanded to mean anything that interests a company. . . . Berry Co. might have been curious about Watkins' plans, but it

had no legal interest in them. Watkins was at liberty to resign at will and so at liberty to interview with other companies. Her interview was thus a personal matter, neither in pursuit nor to the legal detriment of Berry Co.'s business. . . . In other words, a personal call may be intercepted in the ordinary course of business to determine its nature but never its contents" [704 F.2d 577, 583 (11th Cir. 1983)]. For a different result, see *Briggs v. American Air Filter Co.*, 630 F.2d 414, 419 (5th Cir. 1980).

8. In *Epps v. St. Mary's Hospital*, 802 F.2d 412 (11th Cir. 1986), two workers, both within the hospital, had a telephone conversation in which they made disparaging remarks about their supervisors. The call was overheard and taped. The employees sued, and the hospital argued that the ECPA did not apply because the call was on an internal hospital telephone system. The court disagreed, holding that the call came within the ECPA since the hospital system was connected to an outside provider and therefore was capable of use in interstate commerce.

9. Several unpublished decisions from California have been discussed in the literature. See *Flanagan v. Epson America, Inc.* and *Shoars v. Epson America, Inc.*, discussed in Natt Gantt, 1995:398, and Hash & Ibrahim, 1996:906. In these, a private employer was upheld in actions by employees whose e-mail was routinely read by supervisors without their specific knowledge. While the actions were brought under California law, the court also discussed the federal wiretapping statutes suggesting that e-mail would be excluded under both the prior consent and business use exceptions.

10. In 1971, Congress directed the Secretary of Defense to "prescribe and implement procedures . . . [to] identify, treat, and rehabilitate members of the Armed Forces who are drug or alcohol dependent persons" [85 Stat. 348, 361]. Pursuant to this command, the army initiated mandatory toxicological testing of its military forces, a program that by 1982 resulted in comprehensive military testing [*National Federation of Federal Employees v. Cheney*, 884 F.2d 603, 605 (D.C. Cir. 1989)].

11. "Eating poppy seed cakes, which naturally contain some morphine, can cause an individual to have a positive urine test for opiates. The tests cannot distinguish between an ingestion of morphine from poppy seeds and an injection of heroin, since the result for either is a true positive for morphine. [n58] Similarly, a drug analysis cannot differentiate between a person who is taking legally prescribed medication such as phenobarbital for epilepsy and a person who is abusing the drug without a prescription. Both will show positive results because the drug is present. Drinking certain brands of herbal tea can also cause a person to

have a positive urine test for cocaine metabolite. These teas actually contain enough cocaine to cause intoxication. The results from eating poppy seeds or drinking herbal tea are not correctly classified as false positives because the compounds are actually present in the urine. They are instead true positives, even though the results may not be caused by drug abuse." Neal, 1987:881.

12. See for example *Bettie v. City of St. Petersburg Beach,* 733 F.Supp. (M.D.Fla. 1990) (testing firefighters unconstitutional); *Penny v. Kennedy,* 915 F.2d 1065 (6th Cir. 1990) (testing firefighters upheld). In *Capau v. City of Plainfield,* 643 F.Supp. 1507 (D.N.J. 1986), city officials conducted a surprise mass drug test of its firemen at a fire station, locking doors and requiring all personnel to submit urine samples while under surveillance. The district court found the testing unconstitutional.

13. In *O'Keefe v. Passaic Valley Water Commission,* 624 A.2d 578 (N.J. 1993), the court did not reach the constitutional question of mandatory drug testing for water meter readers. Applicants for the position had to sign the following: "I hereby agree that the taking of this drug test is voluntary on my part and that the results will remain confidential between the doctor, the Commission and myself. I further understand and agree that should the results of said test prove positive, my application for employment with the Commission may be rejected. Notwithstanding the above, I hereby agree to submit to said drug test voluntarily and of my own free will." The Court found there were adequate reasons, in addition to the refusal to take the test, for the company not to hire the applicant.

14. Similarly, in *Georgia Association of Educators v. Harris,* 749 F.Supp. 1110 (N.D.Ga. 1990), the district court upheld an injunction preventing testing of all applicants for state employment, including teachers: "[D]efendants have failed to specifically identify any governmental interest that is sufficiently compelling to justify testing all job applicants. Moreover, defendants remain oblivious to Von Raab's (and indeed, the fourth amendment's) requirement that it connect its interest in testing to the particular job duties of the applicants it wished to test. Instead, defendants attempt to justify their comprehensive drug testing program based on a generalized governmental interest in maintaining a drug-free workplace. Defendants' position is untenable because neither Von Raab nor its progeny recognize such a generalized interest as sufficiently compelling to outweigh an individual's fourth amendment rights" [749 F.Supp. 1110, 1114 (1990)]. Among the state's arguments in favor of the legislation was that since drug testing was widespread among private employers in Georgia, the state would become a "dumping-ground" for drug addicts [749 F.Supp. 1110, 1115 (1990)].

Recently, in *Chandler v. Miller,* 137 L.Ed.2d 513 (1997), the Supreme Court held that a Georgia statute requiring drug tests for candidates for state offices was unconstitutional under the Fourth Amendment.

15. The Rhode Island statute provides: "(a) No employer or agent of any employer shall, either orally or in writing, request, require, or subject any employee to submit a sample of his or her urine, blood, or other bodily fluid or tissue for testing as a condition of continued employment. Nothing herein shall prohibit an employer from requiring a specific employee to submit to testing if: (1) The employer has reasonable grounds to believe based on specific objective facts, that the employee's use of controlled substances is impairing his or her ability to perform his or her job; and (2) The employee provides the test sample in private, outside the presence of any person; (3) The testing is conducted in conjunction with a bona fide rehabilitation program; (4) Positive tests are confirmed by means of gas chromatography/mass spectrometry or technology recognized as being at least as scientifically accurate; (5) The employer provides the employee, at the employer's expense, the opportunity to have the sample tested or evaluated by an independent testing facility and so advises the employee; and (6) The employer provides the employee with a reasonable opportunity to rebut or explain the results.

"(b) Any employer who subjects any person employed by him or her to such a test, or causes, directly or indirectly, any employee to take such a test, except as provided for by this chapter, shall be guilty of a misdemeanor punishable by a fine of not more than one thousand dollars ($1,000) or not more than one year in jail, or both" [RI. Gen. Laws §28-6.5-1]. An employee can bring a suit for violation of the statute, and may be awarded punitive damages, attorney's fees, and injunctive relief. The law exempts mass transport and public utility industries as well as positions where federal law requires testing. Testing is permitted for job applicants who have been offered employment conditioned on a negative drug test result.

16. "(2) If an employer implements a drug-free workplace program in accordance with §440.102 which includes notice, education, and procedural requirements for testing for drugs and alcohol pursuant to law or to rules developed by the Agency for Health Care Administration, the employer may require the employee to submit to a test for the presence of drugs or alcohol and, if a drug or alcohol is found to be present in the employee's system at a level proscribed by rule adopted pursuant to this act, the employee may be terminated and forfeits his eligibility for medical and indemnity benefits. However, a drug-free workplace program must require the employer to notify all employees that it is a con-

dition of employment for an employee to refrain from reporting to work or working with the presence of drugs or alcohol in his or her body, and, if an injured employee refuses to submit to a test for drugs or alcohol, the employee forfeits eligibility for medical and indemnity benefits." Fla. Stat. §440.101.

17. *Luedtke v. Nabors Alaska Drilling*, 708 P.2d 1123 (Alaska 1989); *Folmsbee v. Tech Tool Grinding and Supply, Inc.*, 630 N.E.2d 586 (Mass. 1994); *Hennessey v. Coastal Eagle Point Oil Company*, 609 A.2d 11 (N.J. 1992). In *Hennessey*, the court stated: "In ascertaining whether an employee's individual rights constitute a 'clear mandate of public policy,' we must balance the public interest against the employee's right. If the employee's duties are so fraught with hazard that his or her attempts to perform them while in a state of drug impairment would pose a threat to co-workers, to the workplace, or to the public at large, then the employer must prevail." 609 A.2d 11, 36 (1992).

18. The Employee Polygraph Protection Act of 1988, 29 U.S.C. §§2001–2009, prohibits most private sector employers from testing job applicants. However, where there is a reasonable suspicion of theft or other illegal activity, present employees may be tested under some circumstances.

19. Nye notes: "Essentially, the confidentiality of employee-clients should be equally protected whether the EAP is internal or external. However, the rules for internal EAP's will be determined by the employer-sponsor's written policies and procedures, and by the representations the company has made to employees about program confidentiality, on the basis of which the client has been induced to accept EAP services. The rules for an external EAP, on the other hand, will be determined by the contract between the EAP and the sponsor. In both internal and external EAP models, state law may regulate disclosure to the sponsor." Nye, 1990:55.

20. "The employer may disclose any information about an employee to the EAP, but the EAP provider may disclose client information to the employer only in accordance with the client's informed express consent and the policies, procedures, and representations that have been made part of the client's contract. Policies and procedures must therefore provide a mechanism for feedback to the employer referral sources, including a clear statement about exactly what is to be shared under what circumstances and with whom. Typically, unless the client agrees to additional sharing, only the fact that the employee has sought assistance at the EAP, and if applicable, the fact of a referral for treatment, will be shared." Nye, 1990:55.

21. "Of course, neither the courts nor the E.E.O.C. have suggested that every

instance of sexual harassment gives rise to a Title VII claim against an employer for a hostile work environment. Rather, the plaintiff must allege and prove a number of elements in order to establish her claim. These elements include the following:

"(1) the employee belongs to a protected group. As in other cases of sexual discrimination, this requires a simple stipulation that the employee is a man or a woman.

"(2) the employee was subject to unwelcome sexual harassment: The E.E.O.C. regulations helpfully define the type of conduct that may constitute sexual harassment: 'sexual advances, requests for sexual favors, and other verbal or physical conduct of a sexual nature. . . . ' In order to constitute harassment, this conduct must be unwelcome in the sense that the employee did not solicit or incite it, and in the sense that the employee regarded the conduct as undesirable or offensive.

"(3) the harassment complained of was based upon sex. The essence of a disparate treatment claim under Title VII is that an employee or applicant is intentionally singled out for adverse treatment on the basis of a prohibited criterion. In proving a claim for a hostile work environment due to sexual harassment, therefore, the plaintiff must show that but for the fact of her sex, she would not have been the object of harassment. . . .

"(4) the harassment complained of affected a 'term, condition, or privilege' of employment. The former fifth circuit has held that the state of psychological well being is a term, condition, or privilege of employment within the meaning of Title VII. The court in Rogers made it clear, however, that the "mere utterance of an ethnic or racial epithet which engenders offensive feelings in an employee" does not affect the terms, conditions, or privileges of employment to a sufficiently significant degree to violate Title VII. For sexual harassment to state a claim under Title VII, it must be sufficiently pervasive so as to alter the conditions of employment and create an abusive working environment. Whether sexual harassment at the workplace is sufficiently severe and persistent to affect seriously the psychological well being of employees is a question to be determined with regard to the totality of the circumstances." 682 F.2d 897, 904 (1982).

22. The court explained: "We note that the reasonable victim standard we adopt today classifies conduct as unlawful sexual harassment even when harassers do not realize that their conduct creates a hostile working environment. Well-intentioned compliments by co-workers or supervisors can form the basis

of a sexual harassment cause of action if a reasonable victim of the same sex as the plaintiff would consider the comments sufficiently severe or pervasive to alter a condition of employment and create an abusive working environment. That is because Title VII is not a fault-based tort scheme. 'Title VII is aimed at the consequences or effects of an employment practice and not at the . . . motivation' of co-workers or employers. To avoid liability under Title VII, employers may have to educate and sensitize their workforce to eliminate conduct which a reasonable victim would consider unlawful sexual harassment. See 29 C.F.R. 1604.11(f) ('Prevention is the best tool for the elimination of sexual harassment.')" 924 F.2d 872, 880 (1991).

CHAPTER 6. PRIVACY AND CONFIDENTIALITY IN FILES AND RECORDS

1. In *Commonwealth v. Bishop,* 617 N.E.2d 990 (Mass. 1993), the court outlined five stages in determining whether the confidential material could be used in court: "Stage 1—privilege determination. A criminal defendant in a case of rape or sexual abuse moves to compel production of the various records pertaining to the complainant. If the complainant or the keeper of the target records refuses to produce the records because of a statutory privilege against disclosure, the fact is brought before the judge. The judge shall then decide whether the records are privileged. . . .

"Stage 2—relevancy determination. On notice of the judge's written finding that the target documents are privileged, defense counsel shall submit to the judge, in writing, the theory or theories under which the particular records sought are likely to be relevant to an issue in the case. If the judge decides that the records are not likely to be relevant or that the defendant's request is supported only by a desire to embark on 'an unrestrained foray into confidential records in the hope that the unearthing of some unspecified information would enable [the defendant] to impeach the witness,' the judge shall deny the request. If, on the other hand, the judge decides that the defendant's proffer shows that the records are likely to be relevant to an issue in the case, the judge shall review the records in camera, out of the presence of all other persons, to determine whether the communications, or any portion thereof, are relevant. . . .

"Stage 3—access to relevant material. The judge shall allow defense counsel and the prosecutor access to the relevant portions of the privileged records for the sole purpose of determining whether disclosure of the relevant communications to the trier of fact is required to provide the defendant a fair trial. . . .

"Stage 4—disclosure of relevant communications. The burden is on the defendant to demonstrate that disclosure of the relevant portions of the records to the trier of fact is required to provide the defendant a fair trial. If the defendant meets this burden, the judge shall permit the disclosure of those portions of the records which are shown to be needed for the purpose of preparing and mounting a defense. The judge may condition disclosure on appropriate terms and conditions. In arriving at this determination the judge shall resolve any doubt he or she may have in the defendant's favor. . . .

Stage 5—trial. At trial, the judge shall determine the admissibility of the records that counsel may wish to introduce in a voir dire examination. In considering the admissibility of the records the judge shall be mindful of the requirements of the rape shield statute" [617 N.E.2d 990, 997 (1993)]. Along with *Commonwealth v. Bishop,* see *Commonwealth v. Two Juveniles,* 491 N.E.2d 234 (1985), and *Commonwealth v. Stockhammer,* 570 N.E.2d 992 (1991).

2. For a complete listing of all state subpoena statutes and rules, as well as a comprehensive discussion of the issues, see Polowy and Gilbertson, 1997.

3. A subpoena duces tecum is "a court process, initiated by party in litigation, compelling production of certain specific documents and other items, material and relevant facts in issue in a pending judicial proceeding, which documents are in custody and control of person or body served with process." *Black's Law Dictionary,* 1991.

4. For example, the Federal Rules provide: "Every subpoena shall (A) state the name of the court from which it is issued; and (B) state the title of the action, the name of the court in which it is pending, and its civil action number; and (C) command each person to whom it is directed to attend and give testimony or to produce and permit inspection and copying of designated books, documents or tangible things in the possession, custody or control of that person, or to permit inspection of premises, at a time and place therein specified." Federal Rule 45 §(a)(1).

5. Federal Rule 45(e) specifies: "Contempt. Failure by any person without adequate excuse to obey a subpoena served upon that person may be deemed a contempt of the court from which the subpoena issued."

6. "The clerk shall issue a subpoena, signed but otherwise in blank, to a party requesting it, who shall complete it before service. An attorney as officer of the court may also issue and sign a subpoena on behalf of (A) a court in which the attorney is authorized to practice; or (B) a court for a district in which a depo-

sition or production is compelled by the subpoena, if the deposition or production pertains to an action pending in a court in which the attorney is authorized to practice." Federal Rule 45(a)(3).

7. "Subject to paragraph (d)(2) of this rule, a person commanded to produce and permit inspection and copying may, within 14 days after service of the subpoena or before the time specified for compliance if such time is less than 14 days after service, serve upon the party or attorney designated in the subpoena written objection to inspection or copying of any or all of the designated materials or of the premises. If objection is made, the party serving the subpoena shall not be entitled to inspect and copy the materials or inspect the premises except pursuant to an order of the court by which the subpoena was issued. . . .

"(3) (A) On a timely motion, the court by which a subpoena was issued shall quash or modify the subpoena if it (i) fails to allow reasonable time for compliance; (ii) requires a person who is not a party or an officer of a party to travel to a place more than 100 miles from the place where that person resides, is employed or regularly transacts business in person, except that, subject to the provisions of clause (c)(3)(B)(iii) of this rule, such a person may in order to attend trial be commanded from any such place within the state in which the trial is held, or (iii) requires disclosure of privileged or other protected matter and no exception or waiver applies, or (iv) subjects a person to undue burden.

"(B) If a subpoena (i) requires disclosure of a trade secret or other confidential research, development, or commercial information, or (ii) requires disclosure of an unretained expert's opinion or information not describing specific events or occurrences in dispute and resulting from the expert's study made not at the request of any party, or (iii) requires a person who is not a party or an officer of a party to incur substantial expense to travel more than 100 miles to attend trial, the court may, to protect a person subject to or affected by the subpoena, quash or modify the subpoena or, if the party in whose behalf the subpoena is issued shows a substantial need for the testimony or material that cannot be otherwise met without undue hardship and assures that the person to whom the subpoena is addressed will be reasonably compensated, the court may order appearance or production only upon specified conditions." Rule 45(c)(2)(B).

8. Some states have extended the statute of limitations by statute. See for example Washington Rev. Stat. §4.16.340(2), New Jersey Stat. Ann. §2A:61B-1. In *Evans v. Eckelman*, 265 Cal.Rptr. 605 (1990), the plaintiffs, who were between twenty-eight and thirty-one years old, were suing for abuse during foster

care twenty-one years previously. The court held the lawsuit was not barred by the statute of limitations and could go forward.

9. As required under the Freedom of Information Act unless it is covered by the exemptions of that act, including national security, personal privacy, and privileged information.

10. Gostin notes: "To many civil libertarians, however, the SSN presents the gravest potential for privacy invasion that is possible with a unique health care identifier. They are disturbed by the proliferation of the SSN for purposes unrelated to the administration of the Social Security system and the use of the number to uncover and link databases on many aspects of a person's life. Since the SSN originated in 1936, it has been used extensively for a large variety of purposes that are not related to Social Security. Although the Privacy Act of 1974 makes it unlawful for a government agency to deny a right, benefit or privilege because of a refusal to disclose a SSN, several federal departments do use these numbers, including the Internal Revenue Service, Department of Defense, Parent Locator Service, Food Stamp Program, and Selective Service system. The SSN is also widely used in other government agencies and in the private sector, including debt collectors, department stores, utilities, check validation services, supermarkets, cable television, credit card issuers, banks, major oil companies, mailing list companies, credit bureaus, insurance companies, the Medical Information Bureau, motor vehicle departments, law enforcement agencies, employers, schools, and universities. The extensive use of the SSN in the public and private sectors leads to the concern that it has become a de facto national identifier." Gostin, 1995:460.

11. The Veterans Health Administration is an example: "The Veterans Health Administration (VHA) operates the Decentralized Hospital Computer Program (DHCP), the country's largest health information system. . . . The VHA's tool for delivering health care is in place at 167 hospitals, 229 outpatient clinics, 122 nursing homes, and 27 veterans homes. . . . These facilities support 1.1 million inpatients, 23.9 million outpatients and over 6 million records." Gostin, 1995:466 n. 74.

CHAPTER 7. THE DUTY TO BREACH CONFIDENTIALITY
TO WARN OR PROTECT A POTENTIAL VICTIM

1. See among many others Bongar, 1991; Perlin, 1989; Reamer, 1994; Simon, 1992; and Swenson, 1993; and the references cited therein.

2. This rule derives from the common law's distinction between misfeasance

and nonfeaseance, and its reluctance to impose liability for the latter. Morally questionable, the rule owes its survival to "the difficulties of setting any standards of unselfish service to fellow men, and of making any workable rule to cover possible situations where fifty people might fail to rescue." *Tarasoff*, 17 Cal. 3d 425, 435 N. 5 (1976).

3. For a comprehensive analysis of duty to warn or protect cases and statutes, see Perlin, 1989.

4. The *Brady* court wrote: "Nowhere in the complaint are there allegations that Hinckley made any threats regarding President Reagan, or indeed that he ever threatened anyone. At most, the complaint states that if Dr. Hopper had interviewed Hinckley more carefully, he would have discovered that Hinckley was obsessed with Jody Foster and the movie 'Taxi Driver,' that he collected books on Ronald Reagan and political assassination, and that he practiced with guns. According to plaintiffs, if Dr. Hopper had properly performed his professional duties, he would have learned that Hinckley suffered from delusions and severe mental illness, as opposed to being merely maladjusted. Even assuming all of these facts and many of plaintiffs' conclusions to be true, the allegations are still insufficient to create a legal duty on the part of Dr. Hopper to protect these plaintiffs from the specific harm." 570 F.Supp. 1333, 1339 (1983).

5. See for example *Hedlund v. Superior Court of Orange County*, 669 P.2d 41 (Cal. 1983); and *Hamman v. County of Maricopa*, 775 P.2d 1122 (Ariz. 1989).

6. "No attempt was made to locate Jablonski's prior medical records. . . . [The] expert witness . . . testified that . . . given the potential danger and the patient's reluctance to reveal his past medical treatment, Kopiloff should have obtained Jablonski's prior medical history at the veterans facilities in the Los Angeles and Long Beach area. He stated that these records could have been obtained by telephone without Jablonski's consent. The hospital records of Jablonski's prior treatment revealed that in 1968 he had received extensive care at an Army hospital in El Paso. The El Paso records reported that Jablonski had a 'homicidal ideation toward his wife,' that on numerous occasions he had tried to kill her, that he 'had probably suffered a psychotic break and the possibility of future violent behavior was a distinct probability,' and that he was 'demonstrating some masculine identification in beating his wife as his father did frequently to his mother.' The final diagnosis concluded in part that Jablonski had a 'schizophrenic reaction, undifferentiated type, chronic, moderate; manifested by homicidal behavior toward his wife.'" 712 F.2d 391, 393 (1983).

7. Some agencies now require that certain high-risk patients or clients sign a

contract promising not to harm themselves or others. Perhaps effective as a treatment technique, it has no legal consequence, and as in the *Peck* case, reliance on such a promise would be misplaced.

8. See also *White v. U.S.*, 780 F.2d 97 (D.C. Cir. 1986). In *White*, the therapist decided not to warn a patient's wife of the patient's fantasy of harming her because the patient could differentiate between the fantasy and acting on it, had not been violent for over a year, and had never harmed a woman. The wife sued the therapist and hospital for damages from injuries inflicted by the patient. The court upheld the therapist's decision as reasonable. "In defining the duty to warn, the courts have made it clear that the duty is not triggered by the mere existence of a threatening statement by a patient to his psychotherapist. 'Such statements are commonly expressed to psychiatrists and merely pose but do not answer the difficult question of whether or not danger is actually present.' Before a hospital or psychotherapist incurs an obligation to warn, the patient must present a 'serious danger of violence' to a 'foreseeable victim of that danger.' Furthermore, in determining whether the Hospital should have warned appellant, this court must focus on whether Dr. Brown's handling of the fantasy was consistent with the standards of her profession." 780 F.2d 97, 101 (1986).

9. See California, Cal. Evid. Code. §1010, §43.92; Colorado, Col. Rev. Stat. §13-21-117; Indiana, Ind. Rev. Stat. §34-4-12.4-1–4.4; Kentucky, Ken. Rev. Stat. Ann. §202A.400, §202A.011; Minnesota, Minn. Rev. Stat. §§148.975, 148.976; Montana, Mont. Code Ann. §27-1-1101–1103; New Jersey, N.J. Stat. Ann. §2A:62A-16; Utah, Utah Code Ann. §78-14a-101(4).

10. "Where a patient or client is under the control of an institution, such as through an involuntary commitment, the institution and its staff have a responsibility to protect the individual from self harm where they reasonably believe that harm may occur. Outpatient situations differ in that there is less control, and so some courts have held that professionals do not have the same degree of responsibility." Bongar, 1991:42.

11. "We disagree with plaintiffs in their contention that Tarasoff v. Regents of University of California created a duty on the part of the defendant in this instance to breach the confidence of a doctor-patient relationship by revealing to them disclosures made by their daughter about which conditions might cause her to commit suicide. . . .

"The imposition of a duty upon a psychiatrist to disclose to others vague or even specific manifestations of suicidal tendencies on the part of the patient who is being treated in an out-patient setting could well inhibit psychiatric treatment.

In his amici brief, counsel points out that the dynamics of interaction between the psychotherapist and the patient seen in office visits are highly complex and subtle. Intimate privacy is a virtual necessity for successful treatment. Were it not for the assurance of confidentiality in the psychotherapist-patient relationship, many in need of treatment would be reluctant to seek help. Even those who do seek help under such circumstances may be deterred from fully disclosing their problems. An element usually assumed essential is the patient's trust that matters disclosed in therapy will be held in strict confidence." 146 Cal.Rptr. 535, 539 (1978).

In a later California decision, *Gross v. Allen*, 27 Cal.Rptr.2d 429 (Cal. App. 1994), the court rejected a psychiatrist's argument based on *Tarasoff* and *Bellah* that he had no duty to breach confidentiality and inform a fellow psychiatrist that a common patient was suicidal.

CHAPTER 8. MINORS AND PRIVACY

1. See generally Clark, 1992; Areen, 1992.

2. See also *In re Gault*, where the Court said: "[W]hatever may be their precise impact, neither the Fourteenth Amendment nor the Bill of Rights is for adults alone." 387 U.S. 1, 13 (1967).

3. Included here are the requirement of proof beyond a reasonable doubt, *In re Winship*, 397 U.S. 358 (1970); the prohibition of double jeopardy, *Breed v. Jones*, 421 U.S. 519 (1975); the rights to notice, counsel, confrontation, and cross-examination, and not to incriminate oneself, *In re Gault*, 387 U.S. 1 (1967); and the protection against coerced confessions, *Gallegos v. Colorado*, 370 U.S. 49 (1962); *Haley v. Ohio*, 332 U.S. 596 (1948).

4. See *McKeiver v. Pennsylvania*, 403 U.S. 528 (1971).

5. See *Prince v. Massachusetts*, 321 U.S. 158 (1944); *Ginsberg v. New York*, 390 U.S. 629 (1968).

6. See *Ingraham v. Wright*, 430 U.S. 651 (1976).

7. See *Stanford v. Kentucky*, 492 U.S. 361 (1989), upholding capital punishment for juveniles.

8. See, for example, *Pierce v. Society of Sisters*, 268 U.S. 510 (1925) (parental selection of private schools); *Meyer v. Nebraska*, 262 U.S. 390 (parental upbringing and education of children); *Wisconsin v. Yoder*, 406 U.S. 205 (1972) (Amish parents' choice not to educate children past eighth grade). In *Bellotti v. Baird*, 443 U.S. 622 (1979), the Supreme Court noted: "The nature of both the State's interest in fostering parental authority and the problem of determining

'maturity' makes clear why the State generally may resort to objective, though inevitably arbitrary, criteria such as age limits, marital status, or membership in the Armed Forces for lifting some or all of the legal disabilities of minority. Not only is it difficult to define, let alone determine, maturity, but also the fact that a minor may be very much an adult in some respects does not mean that his or her need and opportunity for growth under parental guidance and discipline have ended" [443 U.S. at 640, 643 n.23 (1979)]. See also *Kingsley v. Kingsley*, 623 So.2d 780 (1993), where the Florida appellate court refused to allow Gregory Kingsley, a minor, to petition for termination of his parents' rights so that he could be adopted by another party. However, the court did permit the termination of the parental rights based on the application of Gregory's attorney, as his representative.

9. The court held: "We therefore conclude that if the State decides to require a pregnant minor to obtain one or both parents' consent to an abortion, it also must provide an alternative procedure whereby authorization for the abortion can be obtained. A pregnant minor is entitled in such a proceeding to show either: (1) that she is mature enough and well enough informed to make her abortion decision, in consultation with her physician, independently of her parents' wishes; or (2) that even if she is not able to make this decision independently, the desired abortion would be in her best interests." 443 U.S. 622, 642 (1979).

10. "If the pregnant minor can convince 'any judge of a court of competent jurisdiction' that she is 'mature and capable of giving informed consent to the proposed abortion,' or that an abortion without notice to both parents would be in her best interest, the court can authorize the physician to proceed without notice. The statute provides that the bypass procedure shall be confidential, that it shall be expedited, that the minor has a right to court-appointed counsel, and that she shall be afforded free access to the court '24 hours a day, seven days a week.' An order denying an abortion can be appealed on an expedited basis, but an order authorizing an abortion without notification is not subject to appeal." 497 U.S. 417, 427 (1990).

11. "Notwithstanding any other provision of the law, any minor sixteen (16) years of age or over, where no parent or guardian is immediately available, may give consent to the performance and furnishing of hospital, medical or surgical treatment or procedures and such consent shall not be subject to disaffirmance because of minority. The consent of a parent or guardian of such a minor shall not be necessary in order to authorize the proposed hospital, medical or surgical treatment or procedures." Kan. Stat. Ann. §38-123b.

12. "Any physician may provide birth control information and services to any person without regard to the age of such person and a minor 15 years of age or older, may give consent to hospital care, medical or surgical diagnosis or treatment by a physician licensed by the Board of Medical Examiners for the State of Oregon, and dental or surgical diagnosis or treatment by a dentist licensed by the Oregon Board of Dentistry, without the consent of a parent or guardian, except as may be provided by ORS 109.660." Ore. Rev. Stat. §109.640.

13. "A hospital or any physician or dentist as described in ORS 109.640 may advise the parent or parents or legal guardian of any such minor of such care, diagnosis or treatment or the need for any treatment, without the consent of the patient, and any such hospital, physician or dentist shall not be liable for advising such parent, parents or legal guardian without the consent of the patient." Ore. Rev. Stat. §109.650.

14. "The professional may inform the parent or legal guardian of the minor patient of any treatment given or needed where, in the judgment of the professional, failure to inform the parent or guardian would seriously jeopardize the health of the minor patient." Minn. Rev. Stat. §144.346.

15. "The physician shall not notify a parent, legal guardian, person standing in loco parentis, or a legal custodian other than a parent when granted specific authority in a custody order to consent to medical or psychiatric treatment, without the permission of the minor, concerning the medical health services set out in G.S. 90-21.5(a), unless the situation in the opinion of the attending physician indicates that notification is essential to the life or health of the minor. If a parent, legal guardian[,] person standing in loco parentis, or a legal custodian other than a parent when granted specific authority in a custody order to consent to medical or psychiatric treatment contacts the physician concerning the treatment or medical services provided to the minor, the physician may give information." N.C. Rev. Stat. §90-21.4(b).

16. Note that in two cases discussed below, locking children in the schools while drugs were searched for (including a strip search of some girls), and testing student athletes' urine (including having a monitor watch grade school students as they urinated), parents joined the schools in supporting the actions.

17. One of the U.S. circuit court judges described the results of the search: "The raid lasted about three hours. After the sniffing and examination of 2,780 students, the searchers found fifteen high school students—and no junior high students—in possession of illicit materials. School and police authorities removed five high school students—three girls and two boys—from their classrooms and

subjected them to personal interrogations and thorough, but not nude, searches. None was found to be in possession of any contraband. Three or four junior high students were similarly treated and cleared. Four junior high students—all girls—were removed from their classes, stripped nude, and interrogated. Not one of them was found to possess any illicit material." *Doe v. Renfrow,* 631 F.2d 91, 93 (1980).

18. The court said: "It does not require a constitutional scholar to conclude that a nude search of a thirteen-year-old child is an invasion of constitutional rights of some magnitude. More than that: it is a violation of any known principle of human decency. Apart from any constitutional readings and rulings, simple common sense would indicate that the conduct of the school officials in permitting such a nude search was not only unlawful but outrageous under 'settled indisputable principles of law.' . . . It is not enough for us to declare that the little girl involved was indeed deprived of her constitutional and basic human rights. We must also permit her to seek damages from those who caused this humiliation and did indeed act as though students 'shed at the schoolhouse door rights guaranteed by * * * any * * * constitutional provision.' " 631 F.2d 91 (7th Cir. 1980).

19. In *Zamora v. Pomeroy,* 639 F.2d 662, 670 (10th Cir. 1981), the court said: "Inasmuch as the school had assumed joint control of the locker it cannot be successfully maintained that the school did not have a right to inspect it. Therefore, the search was legal once the probability existed that there was contraband inside of the locker. We fail to see that there was any violation of Vidal Zamora's rights under the Fourth Amendment. As a result of this, it cannot be seriously challenged that the school had reasonable cause to search the locker. Whether the fruits of such a search should be used in a criminal action we need not decide." The dissent in the companion case to *New Jersey v. T.L.O.* has been cited favorably in other decisions: "The majority emphasizes a student's expectation of privacy in a locker by characterizing it as a 'home away from home.' Needless to say, the record in this case does not support that assertion. It would be well for school authorities to dispel any such notion of privacy by notifying students that their lockers are subject to inspections by the school principal or vice-principal when he has a reasonable suspicion that a search is justifiable to insure compliance with school regulations." *State v. Engerud,* 94 N.J. 331, 356 n.2 (1983).

20. Wayne Acton, the father of the student, explained his opposition to the drug testing policy: [Suspicionless testing] "sends a message to children that are

trying to be responsible citizens . . . that they have to prove that they're innocent . . . , and I think that kind of sets a bad tone for citizenship." The seventh
grade student, James Acton, explained his opposition to the testing: "Because I
feel that they have no reason to think I was taking drugs." In her dissent, Justice
O'Connor said of these statements: "It is hard to think of a manner of explanation that resonates more intensely in our Fourth Amendment tradition than
this." 132 L.Ed.2d 564, 593–594 (1995).

21. Directory information includes "the student's name, address, telephone listing, date and place of birth, major field of study, participation in officially recognized activities and sports, weight and height of members of athletic teams,
dates of attendance, degrees and awards received, and the most recent previous educational agency or institution attended by the student." 20 U.S.C.
§1232g(a)(5)(A).

22. "Students or parents who have obtained access to the students' educational
records . . . and found information therein which they consider inaccurate, misleading, or a violation of privacy, should consider initiating and pressing a request to amend those records. If the educational agency or institution involved
declines to make the requested amendments, the agency or institution must afford the students or parents, on request, an opportunity for a hearing to challenge the content of the records" [34 C.F.R. 99.21(a)]. Such a hearing must be
conducted within a reasonable time after receipt of the request therefor [34
C.F.R. 99.22(a)] and on reasonable advance notice to the students or parents
[34 C.F.R. 99.22(b)]; may be presided over by an official who does not have a
direct interest in the outcome [34 CFR 99.22(c)]; and must afford the students
or parents, who may be assisted or represented by counsel at their own expense,
a full and fair opportunity to present relevant evidence [34 CFR 99.22(d)]. The
decision of the agency or institution must be based solely on the evidence presented at the hearing [34 CFR 99.22(f)]; and even if the agency or institution
still does not find the records to be inaccurate, misleading, or in violation of the
student's rights, the students or parents have the right to place a statement in the
records, to be maintained as long as the records are maintained and disclosed
whenever pertinent portions of the records are disclosed, commenting on the
contesting information or stating why they disagree with the decision of the
agency or institution, or both [34 CFR 99.21(b)(2), (c)].

23. In *Krebs v. Rutgers, The State University of New Jersey*, 797 F.Supp. 1246
(D.C.N.J. 1992), the court described the process and, finding it inadequate, held
that a plaintiff need not exhaust administrative remedies before bringing suit.

24. In *Krebs v. Rutgers, The State University of New Jersey,* 797 F.Supp. 1246 (D.C.N.J. 1992), the court enjoined the university from distributing or posting class rosters containing student names and social security numbers as a violation of FERPA.

25. See *Doe v. Knox County Board of Education,* 918 F.Supp. 181 (E.D.Ky. 1996), where the court held that although they were barred by sovereign immunity from a state tort action, the parents of a thirteen-year-old hermaphrodite could proceed with a §1983 claim for the school's violation of FERPA by disclosing her condition to a local newspaper.

26. The Minnesota statute provides: "A parent or the parent's minor child may not be examined as to any communication made in confidence by the minor to the minor's parent. A communication is confidential if made out of the presence of persons not members of the child's immediate family living in the same household. This exception may be waived by express consent to disclosure by a parent entitled to claim the privilege or by the child who made the communication or by failure of the child or parent to object when the contents of a communication are demanded." Minn. Rev. Stat. §595.02(j).

27. "A certificated school counselor regularly employed and designated in such capacity by a public school shall not, without the consent of the student, be examined as to any communication made by the student to the counselor in the official capacity of the counselor in any civil action or proceeding or a criminal action or proceeding in which such student is a party concerning the past use, abuse or sale of drugs, controlled substances or alcoholic liquor. Any violation of the privilege provided by this subsection may result in the suspension of certification of the professional school counselor as provided in ORS 342.175, 342.177 and 342.180. However, in the event that the student's condition presents a clear and imminent danger to the student or to others, the counselor shall report this fact to an appropriate responsible authority or take such other emergency measures as the situation demands." Ore. Rev. Stat. §40.245(2).

28. In *Pesce v. J. Sterling Morton High School District 201,* 830 F.2d 789 (7th Cir. 1987), a student showed the school psychologist a note from another student which suggested that "something sexual" had occurred with a teacher. The psychologist met with the student and assured him confidentiality. The student denied that any sexual acts had occurred between the male teacher and him, but stated that the teacher had once shown him "pictures" when he visited the teacher's home. "Pesce reached a professional judgment that it was in J.D.'s best interest for Pesce to honor their confidential relationship and not to inform

school authorities about J.D.'s communications without his consent. Pesce considered the legal and psychological implications before choosing this course of action; he consulted with his attorney and a psychologist and considered relevant state laws, school regulations and guidelines of the American Psychological Association. After due consideration and in good faith Pesce chose not to notify any school officials of the rumored sexual activity" [830 F.2d 789, 790 (1987)]. During the following week, J.D. revealed that there had been sexual contact with the teacher, and Pesce notified the authorities. The court upheld the school district's suspension and demotion for Pesce's failure to notify the school administration sooner. Citing the Illinois mandatory child abuse reporting law and the immunity for good faith reporting statute, the court found no violation in the suspension and demotion.

CHAPTER 9. CONFIDENTIALITY, PRIVACY, AND PERSONS WITH AIDS

1. "The term HIV refers to the human immunodeficiency virus, while the term AIDS refers to the acquired immune deficiency syndrome. HIV is a retrovirus which infects several types of cells, and is transmitted by an exchange of bodily fluids, such as semen, blood, saliva, or transfused blood products, and causes AIDS." Thomas L. Stedman, *Stedman's Medical Dictionary,* 37–38 (25th ed. 1990).

2. All data are from the Centers for Disease Control's "HIV/AIDS Semi-annual Surveillance Report, June 1996," available at the CDC statistical Web site, http://cdc.gov/scientific.htm.

3. "In January 1993, the CDC revised its definition of AIDS, expanding the list of conditions that qualify as AIDS-defining and thereby adding tens of thousands of people to the list of people with AIDS.[1] Since 1987, the CDC has defined AIDS as the presence of HIV antibodies and the manifestation of at least two of twenty-three specific opportunistic infections associated with immune system suppression due to HIV. In response to criticism that this definition failed to include a number of AIDS-related disorders, especially ones affecting women, the CDC implemented a revised definition for AIDS that became effective in January 1993. In addition to including three new opportunistic infections, the revised definition allows an AIDS diagnosis when a person tests positive for HIV antibodies and has a CD4 lymphocyte blood count of 200 or less." Doughty, 1994:136. Doughty's note 1 reads: "The CDC estimates that the new definition could cause the number of AIDS cases reported in 1993 to jump by 75% over the level expected under the old definition. If all HIV-positive persons in the

United States were tested, and their immune status were known, the new definition would theoretically add between 120,000 and 190,000 people to AIDS registries."

4. See generally Burris et al., 1993; Dalton et al., 1987; and Dickson, 1995.

5. "There is a popular misperception that voluntarist policies represent a departure from a tradition of coercive measures, a departure attributable to the self-interested efforts of a powerful gay, civil-rights lobby. In fact, systematic coercion to promote public health has a dubious history. The harsh forms of quarantine and ostracism in pre-modern times had as little impact on disease as prayer and alchemy. Modern medical knowledge has reduced, rather than increased the need for quarantine and isolation, and has, with most diseases, succeeded in offering the best possible inducement to voluntary treatment, a cure. In the United States, public health efforts to force large numbers of people into treatment—notably the World War I–era campaign against venereal disease—failed to reduce prevalence, even as public education and voluntary testing were working well. Programs to induce *voluntary* behavior change—in smoking, eating, drinking—have moved to the forefront of public health work, with important success, while the nation's experience with Prohibition to prevent alcohol abuse was a total failure, and the war on drugs repeats the mistake" [Burris et al., 1993:120]. See also Gostin in Burris et al., 1993:59–62.

6. In a footnote in the *Arline* decision, the Court noted: "This case does not present, and we therefore do not reach, the question of whether a carrier of a contagious disease such as AIDS could be considered to have a physical impairment, or whether such a person could be considered, solely on the basis of contagiousness, a handicapped person as defined by this act." A number of other courts have held that AIDS is a disability under the act. See for example *Chalk v. U.S. District Court*, 849 F.2d. 701 (9th Cir. 1988), holding that a person with AIDS qualifies as a person with a disability under Section 504 and does not solely on the basis of that infection constitute a significant risk to others.

7. A third possibility, testing that is not voluntary or mandatory, exists in some health care facilities, where patients are routinely tested for HIV but are not aware of the test or the results. Gostin, 1989:13.

8. See for example the New Jersey statute N.J.S.A. §26H:5C-6.

9. For example, the N.J. Department of Public health may designate up to six sites for anonymous testing. N.J.S.A. §26:5C-6.

10. Ill. Ann. Stat. Ann. ch. 410, 325/5.5. "The Illinois law brings to life many of the deepest concerns surrounding the fragility of confidentiality protections.

First, it was passed despite overwhelming evidence that the program would identify few, if any, HIV-positive persons. Second, its enactment suddenly made intensely personal medical records of health care workers and patients alike open to scrutiny, to which the affected persons had given no consent whatsoever, much less informed consent. Third, such a program would almost certainly deter health care workers from voluntarily seeking HIV testing. Thus, at enormous cost, the program would achieve little while profoundly injuring privacy interests and deterring voluntary testing." Doughty, 1994:134.

11. See for example California Health and Safety Code §199.27(a)(1), requiring that a minor must be at least twelve to give consent. Wisconsin statutes provide for testing of a minor under fourteen with parental consent and without the consent of the minor. See Wis. Stat. Ann. §146.025(2).

12. At least eleven states have statutes explicitly authorizing minors to consent to an HIV test. See Ariz. Rev. Stat. Ann. §§36-661(2)-663; Cal. Health & Safety Code §§199.22, 199.27(a)(1); Colo. Rev. Stat. Ann. §25-4-1405(6); Del. Code Ann. tit. 16, §1202(f); Iowa Code Ann. §141.22; Mich. Comp. Laws Ann. §333.5127(1); Mont. Code Ann. §50-16-1007; N.M. Stat. Ann. §24-2B-3; N.Y. Pub. Health Law §2780(5); Ohio Rev. Code Ann. §3701.242(B); Wis. Stat. Ann. §146.025(2)(a)(4).

13. N.Y. Pub. Health Law §§2780(5), 2781(1) require written informed consent regardless of age as long as there is capacity to consent.

14. "In summary, the DOD policy provides that appointment or enlistment is denied to individuals with HIV infection, regardless of their health status, whether asymptomatic or symptomatic. Active duty service members testing positive are permitted to serve the remainder of their enlistment or commission; their HIV positive status does not bar application for reenlistment. For persons already serving on active duty in the armed forces, periodic HIV testing is mandatory. Service members with HIV infection are referred for medical evaluation of fitness for continued service, as would other personnel with progressive illness. HIV-infected personnel are not retired or separated from service only on the basis of their HIV status, although they can obtain discharge from the military for the convenience of the government." Wiley, 1992:78.

15. In *Local 1812, American Fed'n Gov't Employees v. State Dep't*, 662 F.Supp. 50 (D.D.C. 1987), the court found that AIDS testing was reasonable in light of the government's stated concern that appropriate medical care might not be available for AIDS-infected foreign service officers in remote postings. The court noted: "However, the testing program challenged in this case is not pri-

marily directed at stopping the spread of HIV infection. Rather, its focus is on fitness for duty in a specialized government agency. The testing involves only additional examination of a blood sample that the person undergoing an examination must provide as a matter of course under procedures already established for a number of years. On the evidence presently before the Court, inclusion of the test for HIV infection appears rational and closely related to fitness for duty. The Department of State has acted to ensure tests are conducted in a reasonable manner to protect privacy. While obviously psychological concerns of a deep personal nature may arise when a person is informed of HIV infection following a test, these concerns do not themselves raise constitutional privacy issues, especially as other serious diseases—notably cancer—that may be revealed by blood tests undoubtedly present similar concerns" [662 F.Supp 50, 53 (1987)]. For immigration policies and HIV see 101 stat. 475, 42 CFR 34.2(b), 34.4(a).

As of 1991, the Federal Bureau of Prisons and Alabama, Alaska, Arkansas, Colorado, Georgia, Idaho, Iowa, Michigan, Mississippi, Missouri, Nebraska, Nevada, New Hampshire, North Dakota, Oklahoma, Rhode Island, Utah, and Wyoming had laws providing for mandatory screening of prisoners. Burris et al., 1993:289 n. 25.

16. "Illinois' unhappy experience with premarital HIV screening indicates what happens when the social consensus breaks down: during the first six months of the program, marriage license applications dropped by nearly one-fourth as people married out of state or not at all. When the program was abandoned, one year after its inception, the state had located 8 HIV-positive people, from a pool of 70,846 applicants, at a cost of $312,000 each." Burris et al., 1993:121.

17. The California statute provides: "Sex crimes—Any defendant charged in any criminal complaint filed with a magistrate or court with any violation of Penal Code Sections 261, 261.5, 262, 266b, 266c, 286, 288, or 288a and any minor with respect to whom a petition has been filed in a juvenile court alleging violation of any of the foregoing laws, shall be subject to an order of a court having jurisdiction of the complaint or petition requiring testing as provided in this chapter. If an alleged victim listed in the complaint or petition makes a written request for testing under this section, the prosecuting attorney, or the alleged victim may petition the court for an order authorized under this section. . . . If the court finds that probable cause exists to believe that a possible transfer of blood, saliva, semen, or other bodily fluid took place between the defendant or

minor and the alleged victim in an act specified in this section, the court shall order that the defendant or minor provide two specimens of blood for testing as provided in this chapter. Copies of the test results shall be sent to the defendant or minor, each requesting victim and, if the defendant or minor is incarcerated or detained, to the officer in charge and the chief medical officer of the facility where the person is incarcerated or detained." Cal. Health & Safety Code §121055.

18. See Curnin, 1994, for a detailed discussion of the statute, then Assembly Bill No. 6747-B.

19. "Although all children who are born to HIV-positive women will test positive for the virus immediately after birth, only 25% will in fact turn out to be actually HIV-infected, the remaining three-fourths will 'seroconvert' by shirking off their mothers' antibodies while presenting none of their own. What occurs in utero is the transfer to the child, through the placenta, of the mother's antibodies and possibly the virus itself. Thus, the only certain indication of a positive newborn test is that the mother is infected. There is a window period of approximately twelve months when it is impossible to tell which infants are truly infected and which are presenting maternal antibodies which will later disappear in an otherwise healthy baby. During this window period, perhaps the most accurate description of these babies is 'antibody-positive'" (Curnin, 1994:885).

20. Among them are Cal. Health & Safety Code §199.27(b); Ill. Ann. Stat. ch. 111 1/2, para. 7309(j); and R.I. Gen. Laws §23-6-14.

21. See *Woods v. White*, 689 F.Supp. 874 (W.D.Wis. 1988). See also *Doe v. Coughlin*, 697 F.Supp. 1234, 1238 (N.D.N.Y. 1988), where the court enjoined transferring inmates to a unit solely for those who were HIV-positive.

22. See for example *Harris v. Thigpen*, 941 F.2d 1495 (11th Cir. 1991).

23. The Centers for Disease Control report a total of fifty-one documented HIV seroconversions in health care workers in the U.S. after occupational exposure to HIV. Twenty of these were nurses. C.D.C., "HIV/AIDS Surveillance Report," June 1996.

24. See also Penn. Stats., title 35 §7607.

25. For example, Washington provides as an exception to the general nondisclosure rule: "(c) The state public health officer, a local public health officer, or the centers for disease control of the United States public health service in accordance with reporting requirements for a diagnosed case of a sexually trans-

mitted disease" [Wash. Stat. §70.24.105]. Similar statutes are to be found in Penn. Stats. title 35 §7607(a), Fla. §381-609(3), and N.Y. Public Health §2782(1)(g).

26. For example, the California statute provides: "(e) Any person who willfully or maliciously discloses the content of any confidential public health record, as described in subdivision (a), to any third party, except pursuant to a written authorization, as described in subdivision (a), or as otherwise authorized by law, shall be subject to a civil penalty in an amount not less than one thousand dollars ($1,000) and not more than five thousand dollars ($5,000) plus court costs, as determined by the court, which penalty and costs shall be paid to the person whose record was disclosed." Cal. Health & Safety Code §121025.

CHAPTER 10. SELECTED PROBLEM AREAS

1. Prior to 1992, there were parallel statutory provisions for confidentiality in federally funded drug abuse programs (42 U.S.C. §290dd-3) and alcohol abuse programs (42 U.S.C. §290ee-3). These were combined by Congress into a single statute referring to substance abuse programs at 42 U.S.C. §290dd-2. The applicable federal regulations were unchanged.

2. "(a) An individual or entity (other than a general medical care facility) who holds itself out as providing, and provides, alcohol or drug abuse diagnosis, treatment or referral for treatment; or (b) An identified unit within a general medical facility which holds itself out as providing, and provides, alcohol or drug abuse diagnosis, treatment or referral for treatment; or (c) Medical personnel or other staff in a general medical care facility whose primary function is the provision of alcohol or drug abuse diagnosis, treatment or referral for treatment and who are identified as such providers." 42 C.F.R. 2.1.

3. "An alcohol abuse or drug abuse program is considered to be federally assisted if:

"(1) It is conducted in whole or in part, whether directly or by contract or otherwise by any department or agency of the United States. . . .

"(2) It is being carried out under a license, certification, registration, or other authorization granted by any department or agency of the United States. . . .

"(3) It is supported by funds provided by any department or agency of the United States by being: (i) A recipient of Federal financial assistance in any form, including financial assistance which does not directly pay for the alcohol or drug abuse diagnosis, treatment, or referral activities; or (ii) Conducted by a State or local government unit which, through general or special revenue sharing or other forms of assistance, receives Federal funds which could be (but are not necessarily) spent for the alcohol or drug abuse program; or

"(4) It is assisted by the Internal Revenue Service of the Department of the Treasury through the allowance of income tax deductions for contributions to the program or through the granting of tax exempt status to the program." 42 C.F.R. §2.12.

4. "The restrictions on disclosure in these regulations do not apply to communications of information between or among personnel having a need for the information in connection with their duties that arise out of the provision of diagnosis, treatment, or referral for treatment of alcohol or drug abuse if the communications are (i) Within a program or (ii) Between a program and an entity that has direct administrative control over the program." 42 C.F.R. §2.12(c)(iii).

5. See for example *Armenta v. Superior Court of Santa Barbara County,* 132 Cal.Rptr. 586 (Cal. App. 1976); *United States v. Coffman,* 567 F.2d 960 (10th Cir. 1977).

6. For a similar result, see *Achterhof v. Selvaggio,* 886 F.2d 826 (6th Cir. 1989).

7. The dissenting judge in the case was particularly concerned about the use of court records by prospective employers: "It appears that an arrest record in the world of commerce, as a practical matter, transmutes the legal presumption of innocence into one of guilt. The stigmatization as an arrestee, petitioners contend, automatically closes the door to many job opportunities otherwise available to the nonarrested applicant. There is abundant evidence that the nonconvicted arrestee is subjected to substantial discriminatory sanctions in the job marketplace. . . . Many employers have a flat policy against hiring an arrestee applicant. . . . Hiring sanctions against the arrested individual do not exist solely in the private sector, but are also in evidence in some governmental agencies, despite policies to the contrary. Furthermore, there is evidence that a similar stigmatization may take place within the education system. Thus, the arrested juvenile, in many instances, may be barred from educational or occupational opportunities irrespective of his guilt or innocence of any misdeed." 525 P.2d 250 (1974).

8. The Alaska statute goes beyond the release of medical information and includes a social history, information about siblings, and detailed information about biological parents. Alaska Stat. §18.50.510.

9. In Hawaii, a birth certificate contains: (1) child's name; (2) hospital or facility name; (3) date of birth; (4) city, town, or location of birth; (5) time of birth;

(6) sex of child; (7) attendant's name; (8) mother's name; (9) mother's age at this birth; (10) mother's state of birth; (11) whether mother was active in the U.S. military; (12) mother's residence; (13) mother's mailing address; (14) father's name; (15) father's age at this birth; (16) father's state of birth; (17) whether father was active in the U.S. military; (18) race of mother and father. Lum, 1993: 505.

10. "An adoptee who is moved to a court proceeding such as the one here is impelled by a need to know which is far deeper than 'mere curiosity.' The testimony before me is convincing that the need has its origins in the psychological makeup of the adoptee's identity, self-image and perceptions of reality. One adult adoptee who searched and found her natural mother testified that in addition to the desire to be able to relate hereditary and ethnic background information to her children, she was driven to search by a deep-seated feeling of unreality—that her origin was not from a human being but an adoption agency. Other adoptees testifying described similar feelings of not belonging anywhere or to anyone. From the testimony it appears that these feelings may manifest themselves in physical symptoms such as nervousness or insomnia, or in a psychological inability of the adoptees to devote themselves fully and wholeheartedly to their efforts. There was a general feeling among the adoptees that the search is one for mental contentment" [148 N.J.Super. 302, 318 (1977)]. However, another New Jersey court questioned the results in *Mills*. See *Backes v. Catholic Family and Community Services*, 509 A. 2d 283 (N.J. Super. 1985).

11. These views were summarized in the *Mills* decision. As to the rights of the biological parent, the court said: "As has been noted previously, the natural parent surrenders a child for adoption with not merely an expectation of confidentiality but with actual statutory assurance that his or her identity as the child's parent will be shielded from public disclosure. In reliance on these assurances the natural parent of an adult adoptee has now established new life relationships and perhaps a new family unit. It is highly likely that he or she has chosen not to reveal to his or her spouse, children or other relations, friends or associates the facts of an emotionally upsetting and potentially socially unacceptable occurrence 18 or more years ago. This natural parent has a right to privacy, a right to be let alone." 148 N.J.Super. 302, 310 (1977).

12. See also *In re Maples*, 563 S.W.2d 760 (Mo. 1978); *In re Roger B.*, 418 N.E.2d 751 (Ill. 1981); *Matter of Dixon*, 323 N.W.2d 549 (Mich. App. 1992); *Bradey v. Children's Bureau of South Carolina*, 274 S.E.2d 418 (S.C. 1981).

13. See N.Y. Pub. Health Law §4138-d for an example of a passive registry for-

bidding contact of non-registrants: "4(b) If the department determines that there is no corresponding registration for the adoptee and for the parents whose consent to the adoption was required or whose signature was required on an instrument of surrender to an authorized agency, it shall notify the agency which shall notify the registering person that no corresponding match has been made. The agency shall not solicit or request the consent of the non-registered person or persons."

14. Alabama, Ala. Code 26-10A-31; Arizona, Ariz. Rev. Stat. Ann. 8-134; Colorado, Colo. Rev. Stat. 19-5-304; Connecticut, Conn. Gen. Stat. 45a-751; Georgia, Ga. Code Ann. 19-8-23; Hawaii, Haw. Rev. Stat. 578-15; Illinois, Ill. Ann. Stat. ch. 40, 1522.3a; Kentucky, Ky. Rev. Stat. Ann. 199.572; Minnesota, Minn. Stat. Ann. 259.49; Missouri, Mo. Ann. Stat. 453.121; Nebraska, Neb. Rev. Stat. 43-119 to -146.13; North Dakota, N.D. Cent. Code 14-15-16; Pennsylvania, 23 Pa. Cons. Stat. Ann. 2905; Tennessee, Tenn. Code Ann. 36-1-141; Washington, Wash. Rev. Code Ann. 26.33.343; Wisconsin, Wis. Stat. Ann. 48.433; Wyoming, Wyo. Stat. 1-22-201–203. Lum, 1993:507.

15. Along with the Tennessee statutes discussed in the text, see Alaska Stat. §18.50.500; Hawaii Rev. Stat. §578-15; Kansas Stat. Ann. §65-2423.

16. The Colorado statute provides: "(1)(g) A licensed psychologist, professional counselor, marriage and family therapist, or social worker shall not be examined without the consent of such licensee's client as to any communication made by the client to such licensee or such licensee's advice given thereon in the course of professional employment . . . nor shall any person who has participated in any psychotherapy, conducted under the supervision of a person authorized by law to conduct such therapy, *including but not limited to group therapy sessions,* be examined concerning any knowledge gained during the course of such therapy without the consent of the person to whom the testimony sought relates" (emphasis supplied). Col. Rev. Stat. §13-90-107.

17. In *Sims v. State,* 251 Ga. 877 (1984), the issue was whether privilege applied to joint counseling. The court said: "[W]e join the weight of authority from other jurisdictions in holding that there is a strong public policy in favor of preserving the confidentiality of psychiatric-patient confidences where a third party is present as a necessary or customary participant in the consultation and treatment. The public policy in favor of protecting these confidences is strengthened when the third party is the communicant's spouse, in which case the communicant may also invoke the marital privilege under OCGA §24-9-21(1)" [251 Ga. 877, 881 (1984)]. Similarly, in an Indiana decision, *Daymude v. State,*

the court said: "There is no question that the family therapy sessions are an integral and necessary part of the patient's diagnosis and treatment. If the physician-patient privilege is denied to those family members involved in CHINS counseling, then the alleged child abusers will be discouraged from openly and honestly communicating with their counselors." 540 N.E.2d 1263, 1266 (Ind. App. 1989).

18. "Self-help groups are voluntary, small group structures for mutual aid and the accomplishment of a special purpose. They are usually formed by peers who have come together for mutual assistance in satisfying a common need, over-coming a common handicap or life disrupting problem, and bringing about de-sired social and/or personal change. The initiators and members of such groups perceive that their needs are not, or cannot be, met by or through existing social institutions. Self-help groups emphasize face-to-face social interactions and the assumption of personal responsibility by members. They often provide material assistance, as well as emotional support; they are frequently 'cause' oriented, and promulgate an ideology or values through which members may attain an enhanced sense of personal identity." Weiner, 1995:248.

Selected Bibliography

BOOKS

Albert, Raymond. 1986. *Law and Social Work Practice.* Springer.

American Psychological Association. 1992. *Ethical Principles of Psychologists and Code of Conduct.* American Psychological Association.

Areen, Judith. 1992. *Family Law: Cases and Materials.* 3rd ed. Foundation.

Black, Henry C. 1991. *Black's Law Dictionary.* 6th ed. West.

Bongar, Bruce. 1991. *The Suicidal Patient—Clinical and Legal Standards of Care.* American Psychological Association.

Burris, Scott, et al. 1993. *AIDS Law Today: A New Guide for the Public.* Yale.

Dalton, Harlon, Scott Burris, et al., 1987. *AIDS and the Law.* Yale.

Decker, Kurt. 1987. *Employee Privacy Law and Practice.* Wiley.

———. 1994. *Privacy in the Workplace: Rights, Procedures, and Policies.* LRP Publications.

Dickson, Donald T. 1995. *Law in the Health and Human Services: A Guide for Social Workers, Psychiatrists, Psychologists, and Related Professionals.* Free Press.

Harvard Law Review Staff. 1996. *The Blue Book: A Uniform System of Citation.* 16th ed. Harvard.

Kagle, Jill Doner. 1991. *Social Work Records.* 2nd ed. Wadsworth.

Knapp, Samuel, and Leon VandeCreek. 1987. *Privileged Communications in the Mental Health Professions.* Van Nostrand Reinhold.

Levi, Edward. 1949. *An Introduction to Legal Reasoning.* University of Chicago Press.

National Association of Social Workers. 1996. *Code of Ethics.* NASW Press.

Nye, Sandra. 1990. *Employee Assistance Law Answer Book.* Panel Publishers.

——. 1992. *Employee Assistance Law Answer Book, 1992 Supp.* Panel Publishers.

Perlin, Michael L. 1989. *Mental Disability Law: Civil and Criminal.* 3rd ed. Butterworth.

Reamer, Frederic G. 1994. *Social Work Malpractice and Liability.* NASW.

Rozovsky, Fay A. 1990. *Consent to Treatment: A Practical Guide.* 2nd ed. Little, Brown.

Simon, Robert I. 1992. *Clinical Psychiatry and the Law.* 2nd ed. American Psychiatric Press.

Stedman, Thomas L. 1990. *Stedman's Medical Dictionary.* 25th ed.

Strong, John W. (ed). 1992. *McCormick on Evidence.* 4th ed. West.

Swenson, Leland C. 1993. *Psychology and Law for the Helping Professions.* Brooks/Cole.

Van Hoose, William H., and Jeffrey Kottler. 1985. *Ethical and Legal Issues in Counseling and Psychotherapy.* 2nd ed. Jossey-Bass.

Wigmore, John Henry. 1961. *Evidence in Trials at Common Law.* West, McNaughten rev.

Wiley Law Publications Editorial Staff, eds. 1992. *AIDS and the Law.* 2nd ed. John Wiley.

Wilson, Suanna J. 1978. *Confidentiality in Social Work.* The Free Press.

ARTICLES AND PAPERS

Applebaum, Paul S., Howard Zonana, Richard Bonnie, and Loren Roth. 1989. "Statutory approaches to limiting psychiatrists' liability for their patients' violent acts." 146 *Am. J. Psychiatry* 821.

Bebensee, Paula K. 1993. "In the best interests of children and adoptive parents: The need for disclosure." 78 *Iowa L. Rev.* 397.

Burk, Dan L. 1992. "DNA identification testing: Assessing the threat to privacy." 24 *Toledo L. Rev.* 87.

Cavico, Frank J. 1993. "Invasion of privacy in the private employment sector: Tortious and ethical aspects." 30 *Houston L. Rev.* 1263.

Clark, Homer H. Jr. 1992. "Children and the constitution." 1992. *University of Illinois L. Rev.* 1.

Corcoran, Kevin, and William J. Winslade. 1994. "Eavesdropping on the 50-minute hour: Managed mental health care and confidentiality." 12 *Behavioral Sciences and Law* 351.

Cornish, Craig M., and Donald B. Louria. 1991. "Drug testing in the workplace: Employment drug testing, preventive searches, and the future of privacy." 33 *William and Mary L. Rev.* 95.

Crowley, Ellen M. 1995. "In camera inspections of privileged records in sexual assault trials: Balancing defendants' rights and state interests under Massachusetts's Bishop test." 21 *American J. L. and Medicine* 131.

Curnin, Kevin J. 1994. "Newborn HIV screening and New York Assembly Bill no. 6747-b: Privacy and equal protection of pregnant women." 21 *Fordham Urban L. J.* 857.

De Gorgey, Andrea. 1990. "The advent of DNA databanks: Implications for information privacy." 16 *American J. L. and Medicine* 381.

DeKraai, Mark B., and Bruce D. Sales. 1991. "Liability in child therapy and research." 59 *J. of Counseling and Clinical Psychology* 853.

Doughty, Roger. 1994. "The confidentiality of HIV-related information: Responding to the resurgence of aggressive public health interventions in the AIDS epidemic." 82 *California L. Rev.* 113.

English, Abigail. 1992. "The HIV-AIDS epidemic and the child welfare system: Protecting the rights of infants, young children, and adolescents." 77 *Iowa L. Rev.* 1509.

Felthous, Alan R. 1989. "The ever confusing jurisprudence of the psychotherapist's duty to protect." *J. Psychiatry and Law* 575.

Gerhart, Paul F. 1995. "Employee privacy rights in the United States." 17 *Comparative Labor L. J.* 175.

Goldstein, Bruce D. 1992. "Confidentiality and dissemination of personal information: An examination of state laws governing data protection." 41 *Emory L. J.* 1185.

Gostin, Lawrence O. 1989. "Hospitals, health care professionals, and AIDS: The 'right to know' the health status of professionals and patients." 48 *Maryland L. Rev.* 12.

Gostin, Lawrence O. 1995. "Health information privacy." 80 *Cornell L. Rev.* 451.

Gottfredson, Michael R., and Carolyn Uihlein. 1991. "Drug testing in the workplace: A view from the data." 33 *William and Mary L. Rev.* 127.

Hash, Paul E., and Christina M. Ibrahim. 1996. "E-mail, electronic monitoring, and employee privacy." 37 *South Texas L. Rev.* 893.

Hermann, Donald H. J., and Rosalind D. Gagliano. 1989. "AIDS, therapeutic confidentiality, and warning third parties." 48 *Maryland L. Rev.* 55.

Jenero, Kenneth A., and Lynne D. Mapes-Riordan. 1992. "Electronic monitoring of employees and the elusive 'right to privacy.'" 18 *Employee Relations L. J.* 71.

Johnson, Mark D. 1993. "HIV testing of health care workers: Conflict between the common law and the Centers for Disease Control." 42 *American University L. Rev.* 479.

Jones, Joni. 1995. "Note: Maintaining unsubstantiated records of 'suspected' child abuse: Much ado about nothing or a violation of the right to privacy?" 1995 *Utah L. Rev.* 887.

Joo, Anna Y. 1995. "Broadening counselor-patient privilege to protect the privacy of the sexual assault survivor." 32 *Harvard J. Legislation* 255.

Katner, David R. 1996. "The ethical dilemma awaiting counsel who represent adolescents with HIV/AIDS: Criminal law and tort suits pressure counsel to breach the confidentiality of the clients' medical status." 70 *Tulane L. Rev.* 2311.

Kermani, Ebrahim J., and Stanford L. Drob. 1987. "The Tarasoff decision: A decade later dilemma still faces psychotherapists." 41 *Am. J. Psychotherapy* 271.

Krent, Harold J. 1995. "Of diaries and data banks: Use restrictions under the Fourth Amendment." 74 *Texas L. Rev.* 49.

Kuhns, Jason. 1994. "The sealed adoption records controversy: Breaking down the walls of secrecy." 24 *Golden Gate University L. Rev.* 259.

Levine, Murray. 1993. "A therapeutic jurisprudence analysis of mandated reporting of child maltreatment by psychotherapists." 10 *New York Law School J. of Human Rights* 711.

Lum, Bobbi W. Y. 1993. "Privacy v. secrecy: The open adoption records movement and its impact on Hawaii." 15 *Hawaii L. Rev.* 483.

MacDonald, Paul H. 1990. "AIDS, rape, and the Fourth Amendment: Schemes for mandatory AIDS testing of sex offenders." 43 *Vanderbuilt L. Rev.* 1607.

McCarthy, Martha M., and Gail P. Sorenson. 1993. "School counselors and consultants: Legal duties and liabilities." 72 *J. of Counseling and Development* 159.

Menninger Foundation. 1996. "Brief of the Menninger Foundation as amicus curiae supporting respondents, *Jaffee v. Redmond,* 1996 *LEXIS.* 3879.

Miller, Janice L., David B. Balkin, and Robert Allen. 1993. "Employer restrictions on employees' legal off-duty conduct." 44 *Labor L. J.* 208.

Mills, Mark J., Greer Sullivan, and Spencer Eth. 1987. "Protecting third parties: A decade after Tarasoff." 144 *Am. J. Psychiatry* 68.

Minor, William H. 1995. "Identity cards and data bases in health care: The need for federal privacy protections." 28 *Columbia J. L. and Social Problems* 253.

Natt Gantt, Larry O. 1995. "An affront to human dignity: Electronic mail monitoring in the private sector workplace." 8 *Harvard J. L. and Technology* 345.

Neal, Marianne. 1987. "Drug testing in the workplace: The need for quality assurance legislation." 48 *Ohio State L. J.* 877.

Norwood, John M. 1994. "Drug testing in the private sector and its impact on employees' right to privacy." 45 *Labor L. J.* 731.

Note, "A psychotherapist's duty to protect." 1992. 25 *Creighton L. Rev.* 1461.

Note, "Developments in the law: Privileged communications." 1985. 98 *Harvard L. Rev.* 1450.

Note, "Multidisciplinary representation of children." 1994. 27 *John Marshall L. Rev.* 617.

Note, "Statutes limiting mental health professionals: Liability for the violent acts of their patients." 1989. 64 *Indiana L. J.* 391.

Note, "The psychiatric duty to warn: Walking a tightrope of uncertainty." 1987. 56 *Cincinnati L. Rev.* 269.

Oddi, A. Samuel. 1993. "Reverse informed consent: The unreasonably dangerous patient." 46 *Vanderbilt L. Rev.* 1417.

O'Donnell, Michael R. 1988. "Employee drug testing—balancing the interests in the workplace: A reasonable suspicion standard." 74 *University of Virginia L. Rev.* 969.

Olson, J. J. 1991. "A comprehensive review of private sector drug testing law." 8 *Hofstra Labor L. J.* 223.

Paquin, Gary W. 1992. "Confidentiality and privilege: The status of social workers in Ohio." 19 *Ohio Northern University L. Review.* 199.

Paul, Ellen Franker. 1990. "Sexual harassment as sex discrimination: A defective paradigm." 8 *Yale L. and Policy Rev.* 333.

Perlin, Michael L. 1992. "Tarasoff and the dilemma of the dangerous patient: New directions for the 1990's." 16 *Law and Psychology Rev.* 29.

Piller, Charles. 1993. "Bosses with x-ray eyes." *MacWorld,* July, p. 118.

Plass, Stephen A. 1991. "Testing hair follicles for drugs: In search of privacy, accuracy, and reliability." 42 *Labor L. J.* 111.

Pollack, Stewart G. 1996. "Brennan lecture: The art of judging." 71 *New York University L. Rev.* 591.

Polowy, Carolyn I., and Joel Gilbertson. 1997. "Social workers and subpoenas." Office of General Counsel Law Notes, *NASW* (Jan.).

Roback, Howard B., Elizabeth Ochoa, Frank Bloch, and Scot E. Purdon. 1992. "Guarding confidentiality in clinical groups: The therapist's dilemma." 42 *International J. of Group Psychotherapy* 81.

Roback, Howard B., Scot E. Purdon, Elizabeth Ochoa, and Frank Bloch. 1992. "Confidentiality dilemmas in group psychotherapy: Management strategies and utility of guidelines." 23 *Small Group Research* 169.

Seaquist, Gwen, and Eileen Kelley. 1996. "Employer rights and liability in regulating provocative dress in the workplace." 47 *Labor L. J.* 668.

Trasen, Jan L. 1995. "Privacy v. public access to juvenile court proceedings: Do closed hearings protect the child or the system?" 15 *Boston College Third World L. J.* 359.

VandeCreek, Leon, Samuel Knapp, and Cindy Herzog. 1988. "Privileged communications for social workers." 69 *Social Casework* 28.

Waller, Adele A. 1995. "Health care information issues in health care reform." 16 *Whittier L. Rev.* 15.

Warren, Samuel, and Louis Brandeis. 1890. "The right to privacy." 4 *Harvard L. Rev.* 193.

Weiner, Jessica G. 1995. "Comment: 'And the wisdom to know the difference': Confidentiality vs. privilege in the self-help setting." 144 *University of Pennsylvania L. Rev.* 243.

Winick, Raphael. 1995. "Searches and seizures of computers and computer data." 8 *Harvard J. L. and Technology* 75.

Winters, Steven. 1993. "Comment—the new privacy interest: Electronic mail in the workplace." 8 *High Technology L. J.* 197.

Wydra, Heather, A. 1994. "Keeping secrets within the team: Maintaining client confidentiality while offering interdisciplinary services to the elderly client." 62 *Fordham L. Rev.* 1517.

INDEX OF CASES

GENERAL INDEX